MOBILITY AND ARMENIAN BELONGING
IN CONTEMPORARY TURKEY

MOBILITY AND ARMENIAN BELONGING IN CONTEMPORARY TURKEY

Migratory Routes and the Meaning of the Local

Salim Aykut Öztürk

I.B.TAURIS
LONDON • NEW YORK • OXFORD • NEW DELHI • SYDNEY

I.B. TAURIS
Bloomsbury Publishing Plc
50 Bedford Square, London, WC1B 3DP, UK
1385 Broadway, New York, NY 10018, USA
29 Earlsfort Terrace, Dublin 2, Ireland

BLOOMSBURY, I.B. TAURIS and the I.B. Tauris logo are
trademarks of Bloomsbury Publishing Plc

First published in Great Britain 2023
This paperback edition published 2024

Copyright © Salim Aykut Öztürk, 2023

Salim Aykut Öztürk has asserted his right under the Copyright,
Designs and Patents Act, 1988, to be identified as Author of this work.

For legal purposes the Acknowledgements on p. ix constitute
an extension of this copyright page.

Series design by Adriana Brioso
Cover image © Salim Aykut Öztürk

All rights reserved. No part of this publication may be reproduced or
transmitted in any form or by any means, electronic or mechanical,
including photocopying, recording, or any information storage or retrieval system,
without prior permission in writing from the publishers.

Bloomsbury Publishing Plc does not have any control over, or responsibility for,
any third-party websites referred to or in this book. All internet addresses
given in this book were correct at the time of going to press. The author
and publisher regret any inconvenience caused if addresses have changed or
sites have ceased to exist, but can accept no responsibility for any such changes.

A catalogue record for this book is available from the British Library.

A catalog record for this book is available from the Library of Congress.

ISBN:	HB:	978-0-7556-4507-7
	PB:	978-0-7556-4511-4
	ePDF:	978-0-7556-4508-4
	eBook:	978-0-7556-4509-1

Series: Contemporary Turkey

Typeset by Integra Software Services Pvt. Ltd.

To find out more about our authors and books visit www.bloomsbury.com
and sign up for our newsletters.

To Aikaterini, Janine and Zoë

CONTENTS

List of figures	viii
Acknowledgements	ix
Notes on language	x
INTRODUCTION	1
A PRELUDE: LOST IN GEORGIA	27
Chapter 1 TAKING THE BUS ON THE WAY FROM HOMES	31
Chapter 2 EXPANDING OUTSIDES IN ARMENIA	55
Chapter 3 MAKING CENTRES AT THE MARGINS IN TURKEY	73
Chapter 4 FOLLOWING NEW ROADS IN OLD HOMELANDS	93
Chapter 5 BUILDING HOMES OF UNITY	109
Chapter 6 TAKING THE SLOW BOAT TO ISTANBUL	139
Chapter 7 AN ISLAND THAT IS NO MORE	151
CONCLUSION	167
EPILOGUE: CROSSING BACK TO GEORGIA IN A CHANGING WORLD	175
Notes	180
Bibliography	186
Index	204

FIGURES

1	Places of Significance to the Fieldwork	xi
2	A Building in Istanbul	1
3	A Map of Conflicted Zones in the South Caucasus	32
4	A Map of Istanbul's 'Old City Peninsula'	75
5	*Akşam* Newspaper (24 March 1929)	116
6	Aerial Photo of Kurtuluş (1970)	118
7	A Pirate Street Sign Commemorating Hrant Dink	120
8	Spraying the Street Signs in Kurtuluş	121
9	Commemorating Krikor Zohrab in Kurtuluş	122
10	Commemorating Zabel Yesayan in Kurtuluş	123
11	A Collage of Birlik Apartments in and around Kurtuluş	130
12	Spray Painting on a Kurtuluş Wall	135
13	Satellite Image of the Istanbul Seas	142
14	A Collage by Aikaterini Gegisian	167

ACKNOWLEDGEMENTS

I wrote parts of this book, and the PhD thesis behind it, in London, Yerevan and Istanbul, with significant detours through Adana, Thessaloniki and Copenhagen. This is why I must acknowledge a large number of people and institutions dispersed across five countries. The Bonnart Trust made it possible for me to pursue a PhD in the first place, and the Gulbenkian Foundation funded my research in various stages. The Koç University Research Center for Anatolian Civilizations (ANAMED) and SALT Research in Istanbul supported me both financially and intellectually, while the Armenian National Academy of Sciences, Institute of Archaeology and Ethnography, opened its arms to my work by providing a Hrant Dink Foundation fellowship in Yerevan. Finally, I would like to thank the Şişli Municipality for opening up its archives and allowing me to do research on the master plan and the tax database.

I cannot express my gratitude enough to my former advisors in the UCL Anthropology Department, Ruth Mandel and Susan Pattie. In addition to my advisors, I also owe special thanks to Sarah Green, who guided me with her comments in the later stages. All the other people listed here in alphabetical order have contributed immensely to the making of this book: Bekir Ağırdır, Armine Avetisyan, Erman Bakırcı, Suzanna Barseghyan, Lorans Tanatar Baruh, Gözde Benzet, Kristen Biehl, Maja Sbahi Biehl, Sibel Bozdoğan, Eray Çaylı, Sibil Çekmen, Haydar Darıcı, Leslie Demir, Selen Erdoğan, Beste Eriş, Sofia Manukyan Gagiki, Aikaterini Gegisian, Zoë Goodman, Nişan Güreh, Zeynep Güzel, Vazken Khatchig Hadjitavitian, Karen Hakobian, Nefise Kahraman, Alex George Kalayji, Ruben Karapetyan, Avetis Keshishyan, Nane Khachatryan, Hranush Kharatyan, Lusine Kharatyan, Mary Kuhn, Meghana Kumar, Fatih Mehmet Kurşun, Ümit Kurt, Anders Larsen, Tamar Nalcı, Sona Nersisyan, Armenuhi Nikoghosyan, Hrag Papazian, Banu Pekol, Eren Pultar, Caterina Scaramelli, Meltem Şendağ, Duygu Şendağ-Dickson, David Singerman, Janine Su, Lusine Tanajyan, Avantika Taneja, Sayat Tekir, Somnur Vardar, Duygu Yarımbaş, Anton Yavorsky, Fatma Yavuz, Hilal Yavuz and Besim Can Zırh. I owe special thanks to Ebru Şener who shared the aerial photo presented on page 118, Banu Pekol who shared the images of the collage on page 130 and Ruzanna Baghdasaryan who prepared the maps in this book. Finally, without Ced Öner and all other members of my family, especially my mother and sister, this book surely would not have been possible to conceive.

NOTES ON LANGUAGE

Armenian names, words and expressions cited in the text follow two different sets of rules on transliteration as Eastern Armenian as the official language of Armenia and Western Armenian as spoken and written in Istanbul (and in many other diasporic centres in the Middle East and elsewhere) follow different orthographies and are consequently transliterated differently. The translations of Western and Eastern Armenian used within the text are based on the Library of Congress system of transliteration, with exceptions. Armenians in both Istanbul and Armenia have formulated their own ways of transliteration in everyday life. On social media and in text messaging, or in situations where, for example, road directions, food recipes or song lyrics are being shared with non-Armenians, Armenians in both countries transliterate in a multiplicity of ways that are not recognized by rules of academic writing. In Istanbul, most Armenians are more comfortable writing Armenian in Latin script following Turkish orthography than in Armenian script. In the Republic of Armenia, one is fascinated by how a regular citizen is able to write in Armenian in three different scripts: Armenian, Cyrillic (as an ongoing legacy of the Russian influence) and Latin (from English or French language education).

As for the Turkish names, words and expressions used within the text, these are presented in their contemporary (i.e., post-Ottoman Latinized) orthography. A guideline to some unique Turkish vowels and consonants should help readers through the text:

(i) Ç/ç sounds like the 'Ch' in *Chechnya* or the 'Cz' in *Czech Republic*.
(ii) Ş/ş sounds like the 'Sh' in *Shanghai* or the 'Ch' in *Chicago*.
(iii) Ö/ö sounds like *Österreich* in German or the 'eux' in French *Montreux*.
(iv) Ü/ü sounds like *über* in German or the vowel in French *sur*.
(v) I/ı and İ/i should not be confused, as the lowercase of the former does not take a dot and the uppercase of the latter is dotted. The latter sounds like the 'I' in *Israel* or *India*, while the former is pronounced as the sound between consonants in any – tion or – sion ending in English, as in *dissertation, inspiration* or *dimension*. The dotted İ has not been used in some place names that appear most commonly in English-language texts without it, such as İstanbul.
(vi) Ğ/ğ is a glottal stop and always appears after a vowel. It can be omitted in pronunciation.
(vii) It should also be noted that the letter 'C' is pronounced differently than in any other language that uses the Latin script. It sounds like the 'J' in *Jamaica*.

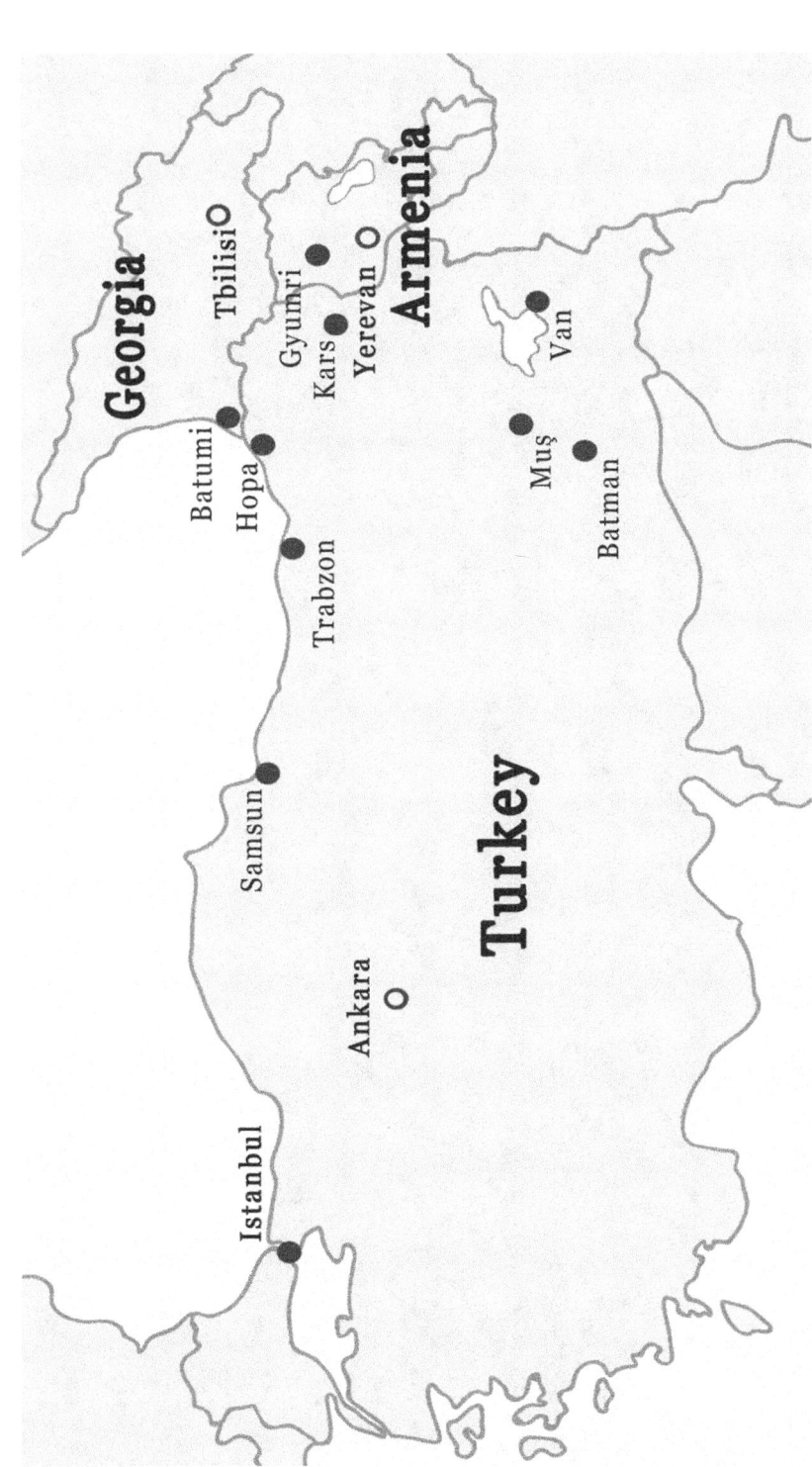

Figure 1 Places of Significance to the Fieldwork.

INTRODUCTION

Figure 2 A Building in Istanbul.

What can a building's name reveal?

In late 2014, I took a walk in the borough of Şişli in Istanbul and I noticed an old apartment building that I had not seen before. I was very surprised, as I had walked on that street probably hundreds of times over the course of the two years I spent in that particular part of Istanbul. The building was located only a couple of minutes in walking distance from the Osmanbey metro station on the M2 metro line that connected the northern financial districts to the southern historical and cultural centres of the city. This was a major shopping street connecting the wealthy neighbourhood of Nişantaşı and the relatively less prosperous Kurtuluş, where a great majority of my *Istanbullu* Armenian friends and informants lived. There were large international brand stores for teenagers next to minuscule old shops that served ageing customers. Many of the display windows that faced the street were full of stickers that read SALE (in English), İNDİRİM (in Turkish) and تخفيضات (in Arabic). Behind the façade of this major street, side streets were full of wholesale stores that sold fabrics produced in Turkey, often with textile workshops in their basements. The shop windows were full of other stickers that read оптов (lit. in bulk or wholesale) in Russian.

The building is located a few minutes away from one of Istanbul's most important and prestigious Armenian institutions, the Mkhitaryan School, which has been in operation since 1866. It is also not far from where the famous Armenian newspaper *Agos* was located until 2015, and where its editor-in-chief, Hrant Dink, was murdered by a young Turkish nationalist in 2007. Today a memorial plaque embedded in the pavement commemorates this violent event of recent Turkish history. The location of Dink's assassination has since become a major site for political protest. As I strive to contextualize here, the building is located *centrally* in relation to various places in the city and to recent and historical processes in which politics, society and economy took shape in Turkey, but I missed it during my lengthy research. How could this have happened?

I understand my former misrecognition of the building within wider processes of nation-building and the Turkification of various human and non-human components of post-Ottoman Turkey. As shown in Figure 2, the building is inscribed with two names. An Armenian family name was engraved in stone in capital letters: TAHTABURUNYAN APARTIMAN. Above the Armenian name, a plastic plate provided a different building name in Turkish, again in capital letters: BİRLİK AP. (lit. unity or union). The building numbers were also different, revealing a temporal gap in the installation of the name plates.

Over the course of my research in Istanbul, a crucial part of which combined strolling in the streets, comparing old and new street maps at libraries, and identifying building construction years in the municipal archives, I came to realize that there was a clear relationship between how the post-Ottoman nation-state 'imagined' its citizens and how it simultaneously 'crafted' the urban landscape (see Navaro-Yashin 2012). In other words, the particular spatial organization of the city of Istanbul reflected the histories of relationships between the state and its diverse citizens: stigmatization of particular populations as 'different' or 'foreign' triggered stigmatization of particular places, and vice versa. With this in mind as I walked past the apartment, I sought explanations for why an old building had two names and two street numbers. Why did the people who named the building for a second time not replace the former nameplate, and what did the newer name mean for the people who had opted for the name change? Another question that occupied my mind was about the passers-by, including myself, and the ways in which the building did or did not acquire visibility for us.

In *The Sacred Remains*, Richard Parmentier (1987) suggests that the investigation of the coding of historicity should involve a taxonomy of signs that physically manifest culturally (and historically) endowed meaning. This is not an easy task for researchers of history and space, as these signs have the capacity to seize, or more specifically deface and reinscribe, one another. Moreover, while similarly referring to Parmentier, Marcy Brink-Danan in *Jewish Life in Twenty-First-Century Turkey* (2012) draws our attention to the ways in which such acts of defacement or reinscription constantly create new meaning about the past that is usable towards present claims (73) – making it further difficult for researchers to detect, identify and decipher the everyday meanings of things. Following that, I find that it is the coexistence and simultaneous visibility of the two nameplates, rather than their defacement of each other, at the Birlik/Tahtaburunyan apartment building that create a new meaning for the past. Such physical signs that depend on a duality of images, names and narratives are scattered across Turkey, and I suggest here and throughout this book that these dualities create a particular epistemological regime in which the official and the personal not only oppose but also unexpectedly *complete* each other in many ways.

In terms of naming, I observed instances of having two or more names more than once in Istanbul and elsewhere in Turkey: in place and street names of the city, in the names of my neighbours and informants, and even in the names of particular daily practices, personal and more collective routines, and rituals. This has been a common practice, especially in the case of non-Muslims in the Republic of Turkey; however, the nation-building process has also left its mark on various Muslim populations such as Kurds or Arabs and migrants from former Ottoman territories in the Balkans, the Caucasus and the Middle East. As Amy Mills (2010) notes in *Streets of Memory*, different conceptualizations of the past among the residents of contemporary Istanbul provide them with different understandings of the city landscape, and vice versa: not only are there differences between older and more recent inhabitants of the city in terms of generation and migration, but there are also differences that stem from one's particular relationship to the Turkish nation-state.

Within a post-Ottoman hierarchy of citizenship, 'distances' to Turkishness have set the tone of the relationship between citizens and the state. In *Islam, Secularism and Nationalism in Modern Turkey*, Soner Cagaptay (2005) demonstrated that these distances were not only imagined by Turkish citizens alone but also carefully articulated by the state. Particular definitions of race, culture and citizenship by the state resulted in three different conceptualizations of Turkishness that simultaneously referred to Turkish (or in some contexts Turkic-language) speakers, Muslims and people born within the borders of Turkey in general (ibid.). In this articulation of Turkishness, there were many people who did not fit neatly within the matrix. There were people born within the boundaries of Turkey whose mother tongue was not Turkish (such as Kurds) or who were not Muslim (such as Armenians). There were also those who were Muslim but did not speak Turkish and were not born in Turkey (such as Bosnians). In this scheme of Turkishness, if one spoke Turkish, had a Muslim family heritage and was born in the territory of Turkey, she was a Turk. If one had Muslim heritage and was born in the territory of Turkey but did not speak Turkish, she was expected to be a Turk one day. If one was only born in the territory of Turkey and neither spoke Turkish nor had

Muslim heritage, she was only a Turkish citizen. This is why, as suggested in the scholarship of orientalist Bernard Lewis (1968), 'a non-Muslim in Turkey may be called a Turkish citizen, but never a Turk' (15; also quoted in İçduygu and Soner 2006: 454).

However, what if those who were denied Turkishness at times regard themselves as Turks?

Who is (not) a Turk? (And why does it matter?)

The three definitions of Turkishness imply different relationships and distances between citizens and the nation-state. However, I suggest that we not jump to the conclusion that the distances between the state and its citizens directly index ontological differences among Turkish citizens themselves. As Cagaptay (2005) reveals, state-imposed racial, cultural and territorial definitions of Turkishness also leave room for more complex understandings of the term among contemporary citizens of Turkey in everyday life (cf. Brink-Danan 2012). As Sam Kaplan suggests in *The Pedagogical State* (2006), the premises of citizenship and thus state-citizen relationships must be treated as objects of study and not as objective methods to study a particular society (16). This is because neither the two sides of these relationships nor the distances in between are fixed or inform monolithic entities of power, interest and identity (see Gupta 1995). In the context of Turkey, Kaplan (2006) notes that contemporary Turkish citizens 'articulate an ensemble of contingent subject positions as they come to understand and describe citizenship not only in ethnocultural terms, for example, but also in biological, sexual, moral, economic, and linguistic ones – all of which are closely interconnected' (18).

If we look back in history, Lerna Ekmekçioğlu, in *Recovering Armenia* (2016), wrote that in the period of transformation from empire to republic in the 1920s, Armenians who were committed to staying put in their homes had to adopt to the new circumstances quickly by fashioning personal and communal strategies in order to survive the hostile environment without giving up their understandings of the constitutive elements of Armenian identity (8). Some ninety years later, in line with Kaplan's (2006) suggestion, I was struck during my fieldwork by how the category of 'Turk' had different implications, although it had very particular political and historical baggage for a spectrum of people ranging from those who denied to those who were denied Turkishness as a hegemonic ethnic term and as a citizenship category, respectively. As Ekmekçioğlu noted (2016), at the beginning, Kemalism, the official ideology of the new post-Ottoman Turkey – and its Westernization project, which also necessarily included nation-building in the post-empire state – held out a promise for Armenians, and this was an important reason why at least some of them could have liked the new Turkey (117). She also noted that an 'intentional vagueness' in the definition of Turkishness in this early Republican period made it possible for Armenians to find avenues for inclusion although the state in practice differentiated between

Turks-by-lineage and Turks-by-citizenship (105). As a Turkish man from Turkey, I was surprised to find that the term 'Turkish' was not always understood as discriminatory by citizens who did not ethnically or culturally consider themselves Turks: at times the term informed a mode of affiliation with locality (as in 'local-ness' or a place of origin) and 'cultural intimacy' (Herzfeld 1997) among people who were positioned in different compartments of Turkishness (*a la* Cagaptay 2005). However, such a situation did not mean that the term's political and historical baggage did not matter. As I will clarify below, although this is not a study about people who consider themselves ethnic Turks per se, it inevitably situates Turkishness at its centre. Following Kaplan (2006), this is because it is those interconnections between different understandings of Turkishness (and non-Turkishness) that account for the emergence of a particular epistemological regime of dualities in Turkey.

The epistemological regime, as I construe it in this book, primarily concerns the production of truths and facts as direct consequences of mutual power relations between the state and its citizens, 'a system of ordered procedures for the production, regulation, distribution, circulation and operations of statements' (Foucault 1980: 133). By no means do I attempt here to identify who has power (and who does not) and put them in a hierarchy, as that is well beyond my task in this book. Nevertheless, I should comment on how I consider power as a creative field, a source of human organization and sociality in a Foucauldian sense. In this sense, power is not limited to 'authority'; rather, it refers to a larger field of interaction that produces, tabulates and imposes, and subsequently manipulates and diverts spaces of action (de Certeau 1984: 30). There should be two interrelated implications of such creativity of power for the production of knowledge (and truths and facts). On the one hand, as Foucault (1977) himself wrote, 'there is no power relation without the correlative constitution of a field of knowledge, nor any knowledge that does not presuppose and constitute at the same time power relations' (22). This is how power reaches and inserts itself into individuals' learning processes in general (Foucault 1980: 30). On the other hand, concerning specifically the anthropological production of knowledge, the power relations between the researcher and the informants, which are widely believed to reflect the wider power relationships between the colonizing and the colonized worlds, also imply the constitution of a particular epistemological regime in which knowledge has been produced and circulated. This is the epistemology of anthropology itself, and as Paul Rabinow (1986) argued, it is based on a very particular and historically contingent way of looking at the world as a discipline heavily invested in providing certainty of subjects' representations (241). In this view, we need to reject epistemology in anthropology as we do not need a new epistemology of the other. Instead, 'we should be attentive to our historical practice of projecting our cultural practices onto the other' (ibid.).

The epistemological regime has a very particular implication in the case of Turkey. It specifically refers to a 'post-genocide habitus' (Suciyan 2015) in which images, narratives and discourses conflict, coexist and constitute each other. As in the case of the apartment building I saw in Istanbul, physical signs seize each other

(Parmentier 1987, 2007) in Turkey where both the urban palimpsest and the rural landscape have particular material qualities in which all the repressed components of the past return and make the country an *unhomely* home in a Freudian sense (1955 [1919]), a situation that I will demonstrate in the core chapters of this book. This is because the country is haunted by the people and their things that are purposefully chosen to be both written-off history and ignored in our perception or forgotten in our memory (Saybaşılı 2008: 34), a situation that is also epitomized by my own lack of recognition of the Birlik/Tahtaburunyan apartment building during my research. As this book reveals, such a situation in contemporary Turkey is related to the century-long history of the Turkification of peoples and things led by the state.

In *Faces of the State*, Yael Navaro-Yashin (2002) writes that the state endures both as an idea and as reality as a direct result of what she calls 'the everyday life of statecraft', which involves a vast array of bureaucratic practices, routines and rituals and cultural and material production in the name of the state (178–9). In the context of Turkey, she notes that the practice of statecraft was historically reserved for the Muslim subjects of the Ottoman Empire and the subsequent Turkish nation-state (201), thus implying an inherent link between the people who are considered 'Turks' (people who are simultaneously from Turkey, Turkish-speaking and Muslim) in the eyes of the state and the people who rule. As she writes, 'more than any other symbol of identity, the state has been central to the constitution of Turkish identity' (ibid.). It is in this historical context of statecraft that we should also understand Turkishness as a unit of 'distance' between citizens and the state. However, it should be noted that the operation of Turkishness as a marker of identity in the country is not confined to citizens imagining those distances themselves. Perhaps more than anything else, the practical implementation of Turkishness as a distance marker has direct consequence for the political and spatial organization of the state. The peculiarities of the history of nation-building and structural discrimination in Turkey show that 'unity' (in Turkish: *birlik*) for Armenians has been simultaneously constructed inside and imposed from outside. As the core chapters of this book suggest, for Armenians the term often emerges as a rearticulation of state-imposed differences, while for the state its wide circulation in media and discourse is purposefully linked to a vital urge to hide and deny the unmistakable diversity of contemporary Turkey. This book approaches these issues of Armenian community-making with both an ethnographic lens on travelling and mobility and a particular metaphor of place-making that I unpack below.

The book

This book studies the ways in which regimes and everyday practices of short- and long-distance mobility produce physical and cultural distances among Armenians in and en route to Turkey. It is a description of place-making intended to demonstrate how people, cultures and things are remade as they travel (Tsing

2000: 347). It investigates how people dwell in mobility and its various forms (Urry 2000: 157). However, during my research in a multiplicity of localities, I observed how mobility is constituted through immobility and stasis, and vice versa (Clifford 1997), in the sense that the circulation of particular people and things was made possible at the expense of others who did not and could not move (Glick-Schiller and Salazar 2013). I also focused on how formalized systems of regulations, sanctions and laws were constantly attacked, critiqued and transformed by informal tactics of mobility by those subject to state power (see Morris and Polese 2014 on 'informality' and de Certeau 1984 on 'tactics').

This book is based on two and a half years of uninterrupted ethnographic research between 2011 and 2013 and various phases of follow-up in 2015, 2018 and 2020 in Turkey and Armenia, specifically in the Istanbul neighbourhoods of Kumkapı, Kınalıada and Kurtuluş; various urban and rural locations with significant Armenian heritage in predominantly Kurdish eastern provinces; the town of Hopa on the Turkish-Georgian border; the Armenian capital of Yerevan and the de-industrializing cities of Gyumri, Hrazdan and Vanadzor; and the passenger buses that connect the two countries via Georgia. Based on multi-sited research, this book is a narrative of Armenian place-making in a terrain formed by the routes, roads and networks through which people and things move, stay or have been left behind in a post-genocide context – a *terra infirma* (Rogoff 2000) that cannot be defined by the current national borders of Turkey and Armenia. Here, I do not directly borrow any particular terminology of place-making. The core chapters of the book attempt to explore this issue without concern for reaching a universal definition of the term. At most, my multiple understandings of the term share a concern to reflect the co-constitution of stasis and mobility in the way suggested by Clifford (1997).

In identifying the human and non-human components of long-distance travel between Armenia and Turkey and short-distance travel in and between neighbourhoods of Istanbul, my book challenges notions of Armenian population(s) in Turkey as a 'community' (in Turkish: *cemaat*) and 'minority' (in Turkish: *azınlık*), and of Armenians as 'foreigners' (in Turkish: *yabancı*). Armenians in contemporary Turkey can be best defined in relation to a 'multitude' (Hardt and Negri 2000) or 'singularities' (Agamben 2001 [1993]), referring to various smaller groupings of people produced by brutal nation-building processes (see Saybaşılı 2011). My intellectual enquiry aims to unpack various monolithic approaches to identifying Armenians in contemporary Turkey, whether defined from the 'inside' or 'outside'. As Hakem al-Rustom (2015) suggests in relation to the wider discipline of Armenian studies, scholars in the field 'have examined the ways in which a "majority" suppresses and confines "minority" groups, but what needs to be accounted for are the ways in which majorities have forged and achieved hegemonic status by inventing minorities' (413). While I recognize the importance of demonstrating how ethnic communities and minorities are 'crafted' and 'imagined' by the state and its citizens (as defined by Navaro-Yashin 2012), I strive to introduce a novel level of analysis by considering how minorities and communities imagine and help constitute majorities. It is in this sense that my analyses of (im)mobilities address how defining communities through a minority-majority comparison reproduces 'hegemonic centres' (Wolff 1993), those notions, embodiments and discourses that we take as given. As Sarah Green (2005) suggests, marginalization is always related to the 'heart of things'; hence, marginality is indicative of the power dynamics behind the invention, representation and materialization of things and people. Such 'hegemonic centres' have been reproduced in contemporary social sciences, which, in the case of Turkey, imagine Armenians in particular ways. At one level, they are imagined as 'foreigners' (Çetin 2002; Cagaptay 2005). At another level, Turks and non-Turks are imagined as ontologically different without paying attention to how the category of 'Turk' itself was invented (see Brink-Danan 2012 for a prime example of such categorization of Turks vs. non-Turks; see also Brubaker 2004: 8 on how such a 'scientific approach' comes to define groups as internally homogeneous and externally bounded).

It has been half a century since Barth (1959) called upon social scientists to divert our attention towards the 'borders' of ethnic communities instead of the 'cultural stuff' enclosed by those borders. However, as Ruth Mandel in *Cosmopolitan Anxieties* (2008) aptly asked, why did those borders as formulated by Barth need to be ethnic borders? Over the course of my research, I observed how these borders were constantly in the making. Moreover, as this book explores in detail, there are historically constituted structures of social order that do not rely on ethnicity – or culture. It is for this purpose that in this book, following Deleuze (2004), I have also made use of the metaphor of islands. However, the core constituting elements of these islands are not their distinct cultures and histories as understood by Marshall Sahlins in his *Islands of History* (1985), but rather imaginations about them as such entities in isolation. Thus, there are traces of the social-constructivist school in this book, although the most penetrating contribution comes from Yael Navaro-Yashin's attempt (2012) to weave its premises with those of the neo-materialist school, implying dialectics between how these islands are simultaneously 'imagined' in thinking and 'crafted' into materiality.

I see the post-genocide nation-state of Turkey as a Deleuzian island that has been deserted – and not willingly – by people who did not fit the state's definition of the category of the Turk and repopulated by particular others who have been made into Turks. As Deleuze asserted, human beings could only live on an island if they forgot its history and what it represented as an autonomous physical domain cut off from the direct intervention of the mainland or the nation-state; otherwise, the island would stay deserted (cited in Saybaşılı 2011: 178). In this sense, the island is simultaneously a physical landscape of depopulation and repopulation and a representation of a power domain that comes into existence through its relationship with the state. However, the metaphor of an island also arose frequently during my fieldwork. People in Armenia referred to their country as a landlocked island without any sea access. For them, it was an island surrounded by hard borders and enemies. Some 2,000 kilometres away, undocumented Armenian migrants in Istanbul referred to their small enclave of post-socialist peoples in the Kumkapı neighbourhood as an island within the city. They also believed

Armenian migrants from the Republic of Armenia constituted an island within an island – that is, within the island of Armenians from Istanbul (see also Muradyan 2015 for a similar observation). In the central Istanbul neighbourhood of Kurtuluş (also historically known as Tatavla, where the name change from Greek to Turkish came as part of the wider Turkification processes in the country), people spoke of 'islands' of blocks of apartment buildings in a grid-like neighbourhood with parallel and perpendicular streets. People constantly talked about those built islands specifically in relation to where they themselves and others lived. For instance, a first question of encounter among strangers in the neighbourhood would be 'which island do you live on?' (in Turkish: *hangi adada yaşıyorsunuz?*). Finally, also in Istanbul, there is the famous Prince Islands Archipelago (also widely referred to as the Princes' Islands Archipelago), where each island has a different majority population, including the island of Kınalıada, predominantly populated by Armenians in the summer (Belge 1994; Duru 2013; Erdenen 2014; Kaymak 2016).

All these islands index ambiguous, but not necessarily conflictual, relationships between Armenians and non-Armenians in contemporary Turkey. On a spectrum of tangible to intangible, built to natural and imagined to crafted borders, what is *enclosed* by the various Armenian islands I encountered during my research is defined through the very possibility of their transgression, and of the passages between them. Nermin Saybaşılı, in her PhD thesis entitled *Borders and 'Ghosts'* (2008), demonstrates that in a city like Istanbul the border between public and private spheres, the places where people tend to hide and reveal their differences from the nation-state's imagery of 'the Turk', respectively, is a zone rather than a one-dimensional line. This is also why, at a fundamental level, this book refrains from reinstating public and private spheres as distinct domains of 'power' and 'resistance'. It borrows and applies the notion of 'public life' to stress the participation of both the state and the people in the making of the 'political' in everyday life (Navaro-Yashin 2002: 2). Consequently, this book construes the border between Armenians and non-Armenians in contemporary Turkey as a very porous one – something that has to be defined not only in relation to the diversity of Armenians but also the diversity of Turkishness. Hence, with a focus on borders as zones, this book aims to account equally for the making of Armenians and non-Armenians in Turkey. I argue that the aforementioned islands are materializations of the making of Armenians into monolithic categories of community, minority or foreigners in contemporary Turkey. This is why the passages between these islands and their surrounding cultural and social universes are the central loci of this book.

In his seminal work *Routes* (1997), James Clifford referred to the circulation of representations of culture in academia and popular media (including literature), and the ways these are negotiated, adapted, co-produced or rejected as particular contexts of travelling and dwelling – or, more specifically, as junctures of travelling-in-dwelling and dwelling-in-travelling. In its broadest sense the latter comes to define making a life in constant mobility, epitomized in the ways bus or taxi drivers, shuttle-traders, smugglers, refugees and flight crews alter the ideas of a fixed home.

Meanwhile, the former term, travelling-in-dwelling, challenges the idea of a fixed home rather differently. It elaborates on the contacts between human populations made possible through various forms of migration and diasporization, and the simultaneous constitutions of 'here' and 'there', 'local' and 'foreign', and 'native cultures' and 'cultures of translation'. As I study the ways in which short- and long-distance mobility between various physical and imagined islands produce physical and cultural distances among Armenians (as well as between Armenians and others), thinking about travelling (i.e., travelling-through-stasis) and dwelling (i.e., dwelling-through-mobility) offers us a particular framework to critically engage with the main protagonists of my book: Armenians in and en route to Turkey.

Each chapter of this book deals with at least one instance of dwelling-in-travelling and/or travelling-in-dwelling, which refer to people on the move and people with various transnational links, respectively. Each chapter is ethnographically centred around travelling en route to an island – whether referring metaphorically to people, landscapes or neighbourhoods or referring literally to physical formations in the middle of the sea – and border transgressions along the way. While the chapters are ordered in such a way as to make sure that the reader shares a sense of movement with the author and his travel companions and friends, they are separated by their ethnographic focuses and theoretical interventions in discussing the current tropes of Armenian place-making in and around contemporary Turkey. The first chapter, entitled 'Taking the Bus on the Way from Homes', focuses on the 2,000-km-long road between Armenia and Turkey that stretches through contested post-imperial, post-socialist and post-genocide geographies. Based on my ethnography of the 40-hour bus journey that connects Istanbul and Yerevan via Georgia, this chapter introduces the narratives of two specific groups of people who maintain a living in dwelling-in-travelling between Armenia and Turkey: shuttle-traders and bus crews. Their particular 'mode of living' and the extent of their personal and business networks in both countries demonstrate their expertise in dealing with the multiple tangible and imagined borders between Armenia and Turkey.

The second chapter, entitled 'Expanding Outsides in Armenia', is based on my research among 'travellers' such as shuttle-traders and people who have been deported from Turkey and now reside in the depopulating post-industrial cities of Hrazdan and Gyumri in Armenia. It provides an ethnography of urban decay and marginalization in relation to earlier and more recent waves of migration and exile. At one level, it accounts for increasing Armenian insularity within the current political map of the post-socialist Caucasus in light of dramatic changes in the material conditions of infrastructure catalysed by an earthquake, war and closed borders. However, at a more specific level, the chapter locates post-independence Armenian insularity in relation to articulations of the bond with the 'remaining Armenians' in Turkey. It is in this sense that articulations of Turkishness in post-genocide Turkey challenge Armenians from Armenia to imagine cultural and historical proximities between people in Turkey and their own country.

The third chapter, entitled 'Making Centres at the Margins in Turkey', is based on my research on the everyday lives of undocumented migrants in Istanbul. With a specific focus on the migrant neighbourhood of Kumkapı, the chapter provides a narrative of marginalization manifested through multiple and overlapping histories of migration, population engineering and exile in the country. By accounting for the different phases of Armenian movement to and from the neighbourhood, at one level, the chapter aims to account for the contemporary histories of places through the eyes of their marginalized dwellers and travellers. However, at another level, it also locates the very physical, ideological and economic centres that simultaneously produce and are produced by these margins. The most important contribution of the chapter lies in its critical approach in discussing the 'ethnic' component behind the formation of migrant communities and enclaves, triggering a discussion that is very much relevant in both Turkish and Armenian studies.

The fourth chapter, entitled 'Following New Roads in Old Homelands', is based on research among Armenian travellers in the most general sense of the term and 'homeland tourists' as a specification of the former in eastern and southeastern Turkey, focusing on sites of 'difficult heritage' (Macdonald 2009) such as the former Armenian/contemporary Kurdish villages scattered throughout rural Turkey. The chapter provides a narrative of marginalization manifested through multiple and overlapping histories of migration, population engineering and exile in the country. In simultaneously providing a historical account of brutal nation-building processes in the area and the more contemporary encounters and exchanges between Armenian visitors and local Kurds, the chapter identifies both the human and non-human components of the physical landscape and invites readers to think through what still remains 'as Armenian' in the century following the 1915 Genocide.

The fifth chapter, entitled 'Building Homes of Unity', is based on my ethnographic work in the central Istanbul neighbourhood of Kurtuluş, as well as archival research in the housing and property database of the local municipality. This chapter offers the history of a neighbourhood where nation-building processes resulted in the Turkification of street names and other public places, as well as of its residents. Although there are no official numbers, it is widely believed by community members (including priests working in the churches in the area) that Kurtuluş is, and long has been, home to the greatest number of Armenians in the city of Istanbul (see also Kaymak 2016). This chapter demonstrates the links between local and much wider processes of Turkification and their direct and indirect impacts on resident Armenians. In addition, it analyses some of the particular Armenian responses to these Turkification processes. For this, my research concentrated on apartment names, which are displayed publicly on nameplates at the entrance to each building. These inscriptions demonstrate how Armenians negotiated their difference from the imposed category of 'Turk' and reproduced or rejected altogether such impositions. By looking at the (re)construction of apartment buildings in the period after the 1955 Pogroms, I create a taxonomy of building names and identify owners of particular apartments named 'Birlik' (lit. unity). At the same time, I propose a taxonomy of the names of the people who live in these apartments, often as extended families. As almost all buildings with such names were built (i.e., financed and designed) by non-Muslims, this chapter investigates both the material and political conditions behind the naming of buildings in Istanbul.

The sixth chapter, 'Taking the Slow Boat to Istanbul', is based on my research on the boats en route to Kınalıada, an island off Istanbul that is widely imagined as 'an Armenian island' (Kaymak 2016). Before going into detail about ethnic demarcation between Armenians and Turks with Muslim backgrounds on the island, this chapter accounts for differences among its residents in terms of the time spent both on the island throughout the year and on the way to the island. I suggest a primary level of distinction between permanent and temporary island residents (i.e., those who reside there throughout the year and those who live there only in summer), which is specifically discerned in the time spent waiting for and travelling on boats. I explore speed and slowness in multiple ways, first in relation to the overall enterprise of going to the island, which can be time-consuming, and second in relation to the relative speeds of different types of boats that operate between the island and Istanbul. I argue that boat schedules, waiting, unexpected delays and time spent aboard create a multiplicity of temporalities through which islanders claim particular relationships to the island. Hence, I argue that the making of Turks and non-Turks is also a temporalizing process in Turkey, in which everyday conceptualizations of 'the islander' are very much embedded in the making and covering of distances between the island and Istanbul proper.

The final chapter, entitled 'An Island That Is No More', primarily considers the everyday relationships among Armenian and non-Armenian residents on the island. It investigates how and why this island is stigmatized as a 'foreign country' (in Turkish: *yabancı ülke*) in popular Turkish imaginary. At one level, this situation arises from the stigmatization of non-Muslims as 'foreigners' in Turkey, as the predominantly non-Muslim islands are usually imagined accordingly. However, at a more crucial level, my ethnographic findings reveal that the island is a place where the distinction between the public and private spheres collapses, where it is no longer possible for Armenians to hide their differences from the imagined and crafted category of the Turk. As opposed to the anonymity provided by mainland Istanbul, it is not possible to hide differences based on particular exclusive definitions of Turkishness from the public gaze on the stigmatized island (cf. Duru 2013 and Kaymak 2016).

The main departure point for my research was to critically engage with the old and emerging orthodoxies within the wider disciplines of migration and diaspora studies. Instead of solely focusing on state-minority and majority-minority relationships, I had a scholarly concern to comprehend the dynamics of Armenian practices of place-making (which could also be thought of as distance-making or border-making) that go well beyond relationships with majority Turks. At one level, limited perspectives run the risk of ignoring the production of the category of the Turk in the last century and the diversities of populations generally referred to with this term. They also run the risk of taking Turks, Armenians and others around them as ontologically different. At another level, I believe such limited perspectives also reproduce and historicize Armenians as a minority, a monolithic community and a population of 'foreigners' in the post-genocide landscape of contemporary Turkey. In many ways, a predetermined and uncritical focus on the social marginality of Armenians following majority-minority and centre-periphery dichotomies serves the Turkish nationalist discourses that silence Armenian pasts and presents, gloss over the body of politics that label Armenians as 'foreigners' and vehemently deny the 1915 Genocide. The islands of my informants in that sense define the imagined and physical spaces that came into existence as a direct result of the politics of marginalization in Turkey and Armenia. However, as this book aims to demonstrate, these islands are also sites where 'antidotes to master narratives' (Seremetakis 1991) and 'tools for destabilizing central authority' (Tsing 1993) are constantly articulated.

On 'getting there'

I started my research with an agenda of studying everyday relationships between Armenian citizens of Turkey and undocumented Armenian migrants in Istanbul. However, as I proceeded, I found a fragmented Armenian social life in the city: the relationships between Armenians from two different nation-state settings were limited, and both Armenian groups in the city were diverse to such an extent that it was impossible to suggest any distinct community based on a generalized definition of identity or a fixed disposition of locality. Research and analysis at the level of community proved to be of little use; I realized I needed to come up with a second and much more comprehensive level of analysis and a novel approach to 'framing my informants'. However, in the process of writing, I was to understand that there was something inherently problematic about that.

At a very specific and thus far under-analysed level, it seems it is our research design that becomes problematic in understanding the diversity of issues we tackle in ethnographic research. In a book chapter on holism, George Marcus (2010) revisits his earlier call with Michael Fischer for ethnographies of 'whole systems' (Marcus and Fischer 1986). He argues that back in the mid-1980s the target of critical anthropology was the reductionism and essentialism of textual representation within the field, whereas now we should pay attention to the 'problem of organizing inquiry on moving ground and time according to scales and a temporality appropriate to its objects of study' (Marcus 2010: 33).

Marcus (2010) elaborates the two most important problems anthropologists face: a simultaneous urge to produce 'better or more adequate descriptive-analytic accounts of ethnographic subjects in a changing world' and critical engagement with 'the media of knowledge production in ethnography, from inception, without obvious or conventional bounds' rather than 'providing analytic frames for the messy experiences of contemporary fieldwork' (28). Here, by following this line of thought, it appears that holisms in relation to representation of ethnographic data are inherently in tandem with holisms relating to research design: what was formerly understood as 'a burden of ethnographic representation' is now 'constitutive of core relations that define critical argument' (33). As a result, a vicious circle of academic production that involves consecutive steps of 'preliminary thinking-research design-final data' ends up justifying the validity of its own components. It is also in this sense that the research itself does not bear any transformative qualities for the researcher herself, which would also have important effects on the anthropological data collected during fieldwork.

> If our misunderstandings of ethnographic data are a function of the analytical assumptions we bring to them, then it would follow that overcoming our misunderstandings must involve rethinking the assumptions that led to them.
> (Holbraad 2010: 83)

In the above quotation, and similar to Marcus (2010), Martin Holbraad considers one of the most challenging aspects of ethnography: how data potentially end up justifying the research design and reflecting conformity to analytical thinking. It is the pre-research clustering of groups of people into analytical categories that is problematic, and this is why once the research is done, it becomes futile to attempt to re-cluster informants. However, this task of self-criticism and discussion for the purposes of research is a very difficult one. Consequently, I wonder how we could understand anthropology necessarily as a science of critique (Marcus and Fischer 1986; Marcus 2010) by recognizing at the same time our very limited capacities in critically engaging with holisms (and reductionism) during the pre-research, research and post-research periods. In other words, how are we going to critically engage with our subject matter and informants not during the post-research write-up but during the research itself? Is such a task possible, and to what extent?

Here I provide some reflections from my own research, although I am well aware of my limited capacity in accomplishing the above-mentioned mission of eliminating reductionism and holisms in research design. I should note here that when I realized this it was already too late to change the primary focus of my research design; that is, I had already departed for research focused on Armenians from two different nation-state settings in Istanbul. However, during the fieldwork, I realized I still had the option to reconsider the ways I would approach and contextualize the locations in which I conducted my research, that is, my fieldwork site and the *roads* that led to it. This option of not reframing informants but redefining the fieldwork site is best explained in James Clifford's words:

> Localizations of the anthropologist's objects of study in terms of a "field" tend to marginalize or erase several blurred boundary areas, historical realities that slip out of the ethnographic frame. [...] The means of transport is largely erased – the boat, the land rover, the mission airplane, etc. These technologies suggest systematic prior and ongoing contacts and commerce with exterior places and forces which are not part of the field/object. *The discourse of ethnography ("being there") is too sharply separated from that of travel ("getting there")*.
> (1997: 99–100, emphasis mine)

Although my first attempts at understanding relationships between Armenians from Turkey and Armenia failed as the scope of everyday encounters was very limited, I articulated another level of ethnographic focus that would become much more comprehensive: my research focus shifted from studying Armenian *inter-*community relationships in Istanbul to the wider lens of Armenian dwellers and travellers en route to Turkey. I started by locating some diverse Armenian groups and individuals in contemporary Istanbul in relation to their respective, constantly in-the-making, and sometimes overlapping social and physical environments. As I increasingly came to see fieldwork as a 'travel practice' of the researcher (Clifford 1997), I revisited my fieldwork notes, and what had previously appeared as 'offshoots' in research and/or matters concerning 'travel literature' became central tropes in my ethnographic writing. More than anything else, travel, as a daily practice, defines 'the common ground' between my informants and myself and points at the various configurations of place where I met or encountered them. Here is a partial list of how we both travelled:

First: travelling on foot. Michel de Certeau writes (1984) that 'walking manipulates spatial organizations' and 'creates shadows and ambiguities within them' (111). As I construe the strategic versus tactical relationships of power portrayed in de Certeau's analysis of space, walking is primarily a relationship of power situated against the state-imposed structurings of the physical landscape. Those shadows and ambiguities mentioned by de Certeau as inherent to spatial organization compose, I believe, a lumpy amalgam of physical historical signs scattered around a vast diversity of places inhabited or abandoned by the contemporary population of Turkey (see again Parmentier 1987 for a distinction in defining different historical signs in physical space). This is why, when I first arrived in Istanbul, I began my fieldwork by simply walking and taking notes in different historical Armenian neighbourhoods. In a post-genocide context like that of Turkey, these neighbourhoods had been home to local Armenians to different degrees. Similarly, Saybaşılı (2008) notes that it was through walking that her own fieldwork site, the Tarlabaşı neighbourhood of Istanbul, emerged as a location that spontaneously came into being through flows of interrelated spatial practices and intricate webs of unpredictable connections (131). Hence, walking is both a 'medium and outcome' as a spatial practice (Tilley 1994: 29). In other words, it is creative of spaces, although often at the expense of the 'destruction' of others. This is why, from the very beginning of my fieldwork, by walking, I expected to explore particular ethnographic data at the expense of not noticing others. My failure to notice the Birlik/Tahtaburunyan apartment building during the initial years of my research in Istanbul is best understood as a natural shortcoming of walking as a particular mode of place-making.

Second: travelling on buses. In my research among undocumented migrants from Armenia, I always had difficulties in establishing relationships with them for the trust-related reasons to be explained in the following pages. This is how and why I decided to conduct research beyond the borders of Istanbul in the first place. By travelling on the buses that transported migrants, shuttle-traders and other travellers between Istanbul and Armenia, I anticipated getting to know possible new informants on these 40-hour bus journeys. I travelled between the two countries a dozen times, not always with a return ticket. With the great majority of my fellow passengers, companionship was temporary. However, I was able to form more lasting relationships with a number of people who became important informants. I followed them between Istanbul and their homes in Armenia and observed the processes of migration and informal transnational trading they were engaged in. It was during these long and sometimes unbearable bus journeys that I started to think about approaches that could reveal the hidden structures specific to displacement and migration (Saybaşılı 2008). As a result, what I formulated as a research practicality not only transformed into an essential fieldwork site but also provided this book with a comprehensive thematic framework to combine the multiplicity of narratives on homes and homelands in relation to the physical dimensions of transnational migration.

Third: travelling on boats. I spent much time on the boats that connect mainland Istanbul and the Prince Islands Archipelago, where I conducted research among Armenians with summer homes on Kınalıada. As already mentioned, these islands are usually imagined and portrayed as a 'foreign country' in Istanbul (Brink-Danan 2012). While I continued my research on the island, boats opened up as essential sites to observe how Armenians from Istanbul engaged with the diverse islander population around them in a very particular on-the-move public space. There was a particular *temporalizing* aspect to boat travel as well, which posited itself in the time invested en route to the island: distinctions between 'natives of the island' (in Turkish: *adanın yerlisi*) and the broader category of 'islanders' (in Turkish: *adalılar*) were widely put in place according to one's capacity to travel to the island by (slower and faster) boats as much as the 'actual time' spent on its soil. On this subject, Avner Wishnitzer in his historical account of time in the late Ottoman Empire, *Reading Clocks, Alla Turca* (2015), writes that starting from the second half of the nineteenth century, as ferry lines in Istanbul increasingly 'wove together hitherto loosely connected localities into well-integrated systems, growing parts of the city were gradually subjected to a clock-based temporal order which dramatically rearranged daily and nightly routines' (124). Although I conducted my research some one and a half centuries after the first passenger boat to the islands operated in 1846, boat trips still had a profound effect on the organization of some twenty-first-century urbanites' daily routines in Istanbul. It is in this context of sea transportation that what initially appeared to me only as a mode of commuting for some (and a means to break away from the city for others) was a fundamental practice of articulating genealogies vis-à-vis the island.

In a book that is heavily invested against locating Armenians in Turkey and Armenia within a framework of 'imaginary coherence' (Hall 1994: 224) or writing up a history that privileges an ethnoreligious component of what people from two different nation-state settings share, I wish to put forward an argument that focuses on the commonality of places (and the roads between them), which came into existence in the wake of particular histories of genocide, survival, exile, migration and community rebuilding. As the core chapters of this book will reveal in detail, this is where I find travel a challenging yet promising concept for mapping these historically and physically networked places – and patterns of everyday behaviour. However, this is also where I expect the undeniable 'taintedness of the term' (Clifford 1992: 100, 1997: 39) to help us grasp the universalizing effect of another term, 'displacement' (Kaplan 1996: 132–3; cf. hooks 1992: 173).

Throughout this book, I deal with diverse conceptualizations of travelling, which go beyond defining the 'smooth movement' of people and things in which they 'retain an authenticated relation to an original dwelling' (cf. Lury 1997: 78). I do not take the traveller as a tourist; rather, I find the latter a particular embodiment of the former. I also do not find the experiences of travelling in direct antagonism to those of migration and homecoming (cf. Chambers 1994: 5), and I again search for a possible way to understand what they have in common. My goal is not to find a new umbrella term that bears the risk of silencing the violence embedded in historical movements of people, as in the slave trade; rather, I aim to think through various subject positions blended in the ways Armenians move in and en route to Turkey, and to account for the impact of past dispersions on their contemporary movements. By firmly holding on to a 'dwelling perspective' (Ingold 2011: 10) while writing about travelling, my enquiry shifts from studying *where* they arrive to *what* they make of that place.

If my informants from both Turkey and Armenia had visited villages wiped off the map by violence and massacres in various corners of Anatolia, looking for ancestral homes, relentlessly comparing old and new photographs of toppled monasteries or cursing treasure hunters found digging up long-forgotten burial places, then *what* was there to pursue in the 'old homeland'? I expand on this question while writing about my informants from Armenia who had entire neighbourhoods destroyed by the earthquake in Gyumri or Vanadzor, who lived in migrant enclaves in Istanbul, called people in Moscow online, and constantly went back and forth on international buses via Georgia: *what* was there to call 'home' in Armenia? I can expand on my question even more when I think about my informants from Turkey who migrated from rural Anatolia as late as the 1960s, who demolished old houses and rebuilt middle-class family apartments in Istanbul neighbourhoods, wrote letters to Paris, went to the airport to welcome friends and relatives from Los Angeles, bought or rented summer houses on an 'Armenian island' and waited to get on a boat despite delays: *what* was there to be 'left behind' in Turkey for? There is no single answer for each of the three questions I raise here, but they should point at different processes of place-making in the wake of various forms of displacement, always because of displacement and sometimes in spite of displacement. I am seeking an approach that can simultaneously illuminate the intertwined experiences of loss and gaining of place. Modern Armenian history of the past century has been almost exclusively studied from the perspective of the former, whereas I understand that this is an outcome of no random situation but rather of deportation, extermination and genocide. I also take responsibility in accounting for the making of place even in the aftermath of 'total loss' of and rupture from place. This should explain why I prefer 'travelling' over 'displacement'; I believe the former has greater capacity in reflecting the balance between what is lost and what is gained. This is also why, in this book, I never make use of 'travelling' in full isolation from wider connotations of stasis, dwelling and various forms of immobility (Clifford 1997; Ingold 2011; Khan 2016). However, I generally do not vocalize a celebratory tone about the 'positive impact' of displacement in connecting otherwise distant places and people. Rather, I explore the ways in which my informants take pride in and feel fascination about their own mobility and histories of dispersion (see Rapport and Stade 2007 for a discussion of the 'cosmopolitan turn' in mobility studies; see Glick-Schiller, Darieva, and Gruner-Domic 2011 for recent discussions on 'diasporic cosmopolitanism').

Native anthropologists and anthropological natives

As the careful reader should have already noticed, one of the main departure points of this book is to discuss how epistemologies (of people and places, and their histories) are shaped in the wake of particular methodological interventions. This is why it is critical to note that issues of access to my informants reflected themselves in particular ways. Over the course of the years that I conducted this research, I never had a 'cock-fight moment' or a moment that broke the ice in the way Clifford Geertz experienced in Bali (1972). In most cases the ice never melted, and, when it did thaw, the situation was always prone to restoring itself to where we first began. This was directly related to my background from a Turkish-speaking Muslim family. Although I had relatively fewer problems in accessing Armenians from Turkey, I was often perceived as a source of insecurity by migrants, shuttle-traders and other travellers from the Republic of Armenia. The insecurity, as I understood from my informants, was not only based on our constantly reproduced positions as the imagined victims and perpetrators of the 1915 Armenian Genocide. In the hundred years following the Genocide, Armenians in both Soviet Armenia and Kemalist Turkey were subjected to direct state surveillance, although in different ways and to different degrees. One of the first questions I encountered in both countries, sarcastic yet demanding a solid answer, was whether I was a spy working for the Turkish state. A significant number of times in Armenia, my informants believed that they were being followed by intelligence agents after they met me. Anthropologists are often mistaken for spies, and within the specific contexts of Turkey and Armenia, my personal baggage pushed the limits of my ethnographic research to the extent that it revealed the wider relationships between people and their states. In Turkey, the threat I posed to my informants was based on century-long state practices of violence and the impunity of perpetrators. In Armenia, the threat I posed had less to do with the Turkish state, as many informants feared being blacklisted by the Armenian National Security Service for being in contact with a Turkish citizen.

Ohnuki-Tierney (1984) wrote that ethnographic observation tends to become a sort of 'negotiated reality' between informants and the anthropologist, at least until the anthropologist's presence becomes less conspicuous (585). However, as hinted above, I was never invisible or fully integrated with my informants. Although I was from Turkey, I never qualified as an 'insider anthropologist' during the part of my research conducted in Turkey. As Narayan (1993) once noted, 'native anthropologists' were usually perceived as 'insiders' regardless of their complex backgrounds, and the differences between them were usually ignored in the discipline (677). This was why Appadurai (1988) criticized the concept of the 'native anthropologist', as he found that it was deeply buried in an ideology of authenticity (cited in Narayan 1993: 676). Similarly, Clifford (2013), referring to Sven Haakanson, Jr. (2001: 79), invited us to think about why the 'native anthropologist' was always, in effect, required to speak from an 'emic' rather than an 'etic' position (251).

However, there still remains an important question to ask: was I ever 'native' during my research? Similar to what Navaro-Yashin (2002) experienced as a Jewish person of 'minority' status in Turkey (14), I was simultaneously native and foreign in my fieldwork (cf. Aras 2014). In Turkey, particular definitions of Turkishness reflect the ways in which 'natives' (in Turkish: *yerli*) and 'foreigners' (in Turkish: *yabancı*) are imagined domestically. As portrayed earlier in this introduction, religion is a central component of the definition of Turkishness (Cagaptay 2005), which has led to a situation in which non-Muslims (such as Greeks, Jews and Armenians) are often imagined as 'foreigners' in their own country. It is in this sense that I was a 'native' in Turkey, and perhaps a 'wholie' in Abu-Lughod's (1991) understanding of the term. However, my informants also understood differences between us through this constantly reproduced definition of Turkishness in which Armenians were always 'foreigners'. Consequently, what separated both Navaro-Yashin and me from the people in our respective fieldwork sites was the same particular definition of Turkishness that incorporated differences of religion into the making of 'natives' and 'foreigners' in the country. In other words, both Navaro-Yashin and I, as individuals from Turkey, were outsiders to the people we studied, who were also from Turkey. However, her position as an 'outsider' was related to the ways that Jews were perceived as 'foreigners' in Turkey, thus making her a 'not-too-native anthropologist' (Navaro-Yashin 2002: 14), whereas I was probably a bit-too-native anthropologist for my Armenian informants from Turkey. My position as a 'native' of Turkey was understood vis-à-vis the historical process in which my informants were denied such an affiliation.

The problem of 'we' in contemporary Turkey (and Armenia) also repeats itself in the particular terminology I use to address the people I encountered during my research. As opposed to an 'imagined community' (Anderson 1983) in harmony, 'we' as a contested community of natives and foreigners in Turkey is probably also paralleled in the denial of 'we' in the sense of 'authorship' to anyone but the researcher in social sciences in general. For me, the issue of authorship is not about the levels and distribution of ownership of data among the people who contribute to research. Instead, it directly points at the separation of the researcher from 'the people' in the field and the silencing of the relationships between the two. Here I believe the issue is not limited to deciding what terminology to use in addressing 'the people' at the centre of the research, but also how the researcher and 'the people' are widely understood as distinct analytical categories of ethnographic enquiry at a more fundamental level – a distinction similar to the way 'natives' and 'foreigners' are imagined in contemporary Turkey. Consequently, in this book I do not necessarily problematize whether to use 'informant', 'interlocutor', 'respondent' or 'participant' (and so on) but demonstrate greater concern in the distinction between the researcher and the unspecific terminology that defines 'the people', simply because such a distinction reproduces hierarchies in the ways knowledge is produced and shared. In this regard, I believe application of new terminology does not address the question of power between the researcher and the people in focus.

Following Said (1989), I am concerned with 'the noise' of 'the people' without necessarily spending energy on how to define them with particular terminology. He wrote:

> [T]he kind of scrubbed, disinfected interlocutor is a laboratory creation with suppressed, and therefore falsified, connections to the urgent situation of crisis and conflict that brought him or her to attention in the first place. It was only when subaltern figures like women, Orientals, blacks, and other "natives" made enough noise that they were paid attention to, and asked in so to speak.
>
> (210)

Although at that point Spivak (1988) had already noted that it was impossible for the subaltern to speak as the research was always embedded in the colonizing project of studying 'the other', I nevertheless depart from Said's (1989) invitation to introduce the 'noise' of informants to research (and text) and 'convert them into topics of discussion or fields of research' (210).

Said does not directly show us the way, but there are options. Nancy Scheper-Hughes in *Death without Weeping* (1992) asks whether it is possible to be both *anthropologa* and *companheira* in research. Following Mikhail Bakhtin (1981), she argues that ethnography is 'more dialogic than monologic, and anthropological knowledge may be seen as something produced in human interaction, not merely "extracted" from native informants who are unaware of the hidden agendas coming from the outsider' (Scheper-Hughes 1992: 25). On the one hand, her suggestion on 'companionship' and her argument for 'dialogue' between researcher and informants are in line with how I envisaged research and how I formulated particular modes of travelling and dwelling and ways of being 'natives' and 'foreigners' in the later stages of writing this book. On the other hand, for Said (1989), the emphasis on the Bakhtinian dialogue between the researcher and the informant is merely 'a domesticated result' of a long debate on how and whether to locate interlocutors as 'outsiders' (210).

Clearly, for Said, the 'noise' of the interlocutor has more to offer than 'dialogue' in the field. In his understanding, dialogue does not necessarily eliminate the 'whitewashing' of the colonial (and colonizing) relationships between the researcher and the interlocutors, a relationship that primarily rests on the presupposed 'otherness' of the latter. For instance, in particular response to Marshall Sahlins's *Islands of History* (1985) and Eric Wolf's *Europe and the People without History* (1982), Said (1989) asserted that the lack of 'noise' even in the works of these resourceful anthropologists is directly related to how 'culture' is approached from a 'vantage point' (212–16) – or a 'mountaintop', as suggested by Clifford (1986b: 22).

This is how in the end I use the term 'informant' in most of the book, with the exceptions of sections on physical mobility that deal with bus travel and boat travel, respectively. In doing so, I also have great hope not to be mistaken for imposing a hierarchy of authority or voice. In the first half of the book, I widely refer to 'the people' as 'travellers' and often simply as 'travel companions', and in the second half of the book I refer to them as part of a larger group of 'protagonists' among particular non-human actors like winds, waves and boats that shape a particular regime of urban mobility on the sea. In addition, although I do not make a clear-cut distinction and do not necessarily follow a consistent definition, at times I also refer to as 'friends' the people I am still in contact with to date.

More on terminology

This book aims to complicate the relationships between enclosures of places and people. In doing so, it contends that there is not only a spatial but also a temporal aspect in the making of place, especially evident in the further making of distinctions in the lexicon of affinity. In Turkey, 'foreigner' (*yabancı*) has many different layers of meaning, yet one should not miss the structural frameworks in which the term has endowed meaning that is unique as the term is widely applied to otherize non-Muslims from the country. This is undoubtedly a direct outcome of the particular historical conditions of 'statecraft', a term I loosely borrow from Navaro-Yashin (2002), in such a way as to account for the brutal nation-building processes in the country while also deliberately looking for a less state-centric metanarrative. However, if there is an epistemological regime of dualities in Turkey as this book argues, there is a significant component of it that concerns the production of time (not to be directly assumed as history). I sense that the various distinctions that are at play among people – in Turkey and perhaps elsewhere – tend to mark and stress a moment of contact from 'outside' (as in the arrival of strangers), a situation which is both based on and reproduced by the presupposed temporal anteriority of one category of belonging over another. This is why I wish to discuss how human movements to and within contemporary Turkey are situated within a context of 'temporal pollution – matter not in its correct temporal place' (Stewart 2017: 135 paraphrasing Douglas 1966).

If 'a place on the map is also a place in history' (Rich 1984: 212), I am inclined to speculate on how people travel between places through travelling in history, and vice versa. However, this is not to simply reiterate that places are first and foremost 'geohistorical locations' with particular histories (Mignolo 2000: 184); rather, I want to pay attention to the human practices that are simultaneously productive of time and place. As I acknowledge that 'movement in the world always involves a loss of place, but the gaining of a fragment of time' (Tilley 1994: 27), I suggest that the Armenian Genocide has a double effect of disconnecting Armenians from their personal/family pasts and places while simultaneously providing them a greater narrative to connect to wider times and places within a framework of 'Armenian history'. If 'place is logically presupposed in the category of *displacement*' (Axel 2001: 14, emphasis original), I find an opportunity in thinking through what people gain in their loss in order to understand this double effect of the Genocide. I argue that it does not merely mark a moment of 'rupture' from times and places, but also a remaking of them. On the orthodox efforts to represent the remains of the Genocide, David Kazanjian (2018) writes:

> Armenian nationalist visions that circulate in the diaspora often invent the tradition they seek to have recognized and restored, projecting a normative, contemporary ideal of what was lost into the past and then chasing its return in an impossible and endless game of repairing that which never existed in the first place. Inevitably, the normative ideal is held together by Islamophobia, racism, heteronormativity, and gender conformism. The figures of the invariably murderous Turk, the inevitably righteous Armenian Church, the passively victimized Armenian woman, the tragically heroic Armenian man, and the broken heterosexual family populate diasporan narratives that *purport to show how an ancient nation was destroyed and must be restored, just like the famously ruined churches in Ani.*
>
> (224, emphasis mine)

The argument presented above invites us to think about an idealized past that is a direct outcome of the rupture produced by the Genocide. In Armenia and the diaspora, the Genocide is usually defined in terms that almost 'idealize' this catastrophic event to the extent that the diverse narratives of survivors are silenced for historical coherency (Altınay 2014). In Turkey, where public discussions on the history of genocidal processes targeting Armenians (and other non-Muslims in general) are vehemently suppressed by the state, the conflict between 'what was' and 'what must have been' before the Genocide is less dramatic. This situation is related to the fact that for Armenians in Turkey, knowledge about the past is based on experience and transmitted between generations only through personal communication (Suciyan 2015: 18). In this sense, they rely on what they hear and see from their own families and friends in learning about their own past, which is not necessarily defined as 'Armenian history'. If 'past' refers to 'everything that happened in the past time' and 'history' refers to 'the representation of the past' (Stewart 2012: 3 paraphrasing White 1981), without formal recognition of and education on the Genocide, in Turkey the past is always positioned somewhere in between Turkish and Armenian official histories – despite the voices seeking recognition.

In *The Historiographic Perversion*, Marc Nichanian (2009) discusses the history of the multiple names of 'the event' that referred to the extermination of the Armenians of the Ottoman Empire. He writes that in a time period before the word 'genocide' had been invented, without a name for the event, the survivors did not need to be persuaded of the fact that they had been the collective targets of a project of massive extermination (8). However, it is at the centre of Nichanian's intellectual project that without an emblematic name – perhaps like the *Shoah* or the *Naqba* – there will be no possibility of fully expressing what happened to Armenians in 1915. He writes that there can be no question of using the word 'genocide' to designate or describe a 'fact' that could be qualified as 'genocide' in a space where historical authority is already contested (3). This is why Nichanian expects that such an emblematic name will eventually replace the generic name of 'the Genocide' or 'the Armenian Genocide' (10). In an earlier work that involved an exchange of letters with David Kazanjian, his expectations from the future in defining the past are clearly put into words:

> Of course it is a past event. But it does not belong to *our* past. It defines the past of the future. A past event that is still to happen? How is this possible?
>
> (Nichanian and Kazanjian 2003: 128, emphasis original)

And he hints at an answer in the following lines:

> This is to say that we are only on the eve of an age when perhaps an understanding of and for the Catastrophe will be possible.
>
> (ibid.)

Nichanian (2009) expects that an understanding of 'the event' will come in an unexpected way, pointing to Derrida and his conceptualization of the future anterior, the *à venir* or the unpredictable future (10). Here Nichanian implicitly refers to *Of Grammatology* (1974), where Derrida makes a distinction between two different types of futures, one constituting 'normality' through its predictability and another proclaiming 'monstrosity', coming into full capacity for change and transformation through its unpredictability (5). Taking direction from another work, I want to turn to *Force of Law* (1992), where Derrida emphasizes that it is the particularity of each event that makes it impossible to have justice *at the present time* simply by following the rules (24–5). In other words, justice is only possible in a future that does not follow the rules and emerges in an unexpected way. I believe it is with similar yearning for particularity that Nichanian writes against the generic name of the Armenian Genocide, for which justice will never be done without its own emblematic name and thus without its own particular history. It is in this sense that the Genocide is a past event that is still to happen (Nichanian and Kazanjian 2003: 128). As Nichanian puts it, 'it will have come back to us' (2009: 10).

As the research behind this book was conducted before the future recognition of a past event as history, I find what remains unnamed until then posing a great challenge to work through. All throughout the text I refer to Turkey as a 'post'-genocide context, and my application of this term might seem contradictory to the ways in which I have defined the 'past' in the above paragraphs. For instance, is there any possibility that I end up in a sort of denial every time I attempt to acknowledge the Genocide by defining Turkey as a 'post'-genocide political context? What if I miss what the future could possibly bring? I see that the current debates on the politics of the naming of the event are stuck here, because we find ourselves in a situation in which we are made to choose between the representation of the event and its past – and this is a political choice in contemporary Turkey as much as a philosophical one. Perhaps this question also concerns how genocides are universalized across time and space by simply placing a 'post' before their generic names. This is why the name that Nichanian so desperately looks forward to arriving in the future has a transformative capacity in the making of the past. For him, it is a unique name that will 'rescue' Armenians from striving to prove their own deaths (Nichanian and Kazanjian 2003: 127).

If, unlike history (a representation), the past is yet to happen (to be fully understood), here the discussion comes full circle back to the beginning of this section: the question of *when* an event happens is inherently linked to *where* it happens. This is most evident in the complexity and the diversity of the ways 'post' is utilized as a device for historical critique and representation in the recent decades, and I am inclined to follow the discussions that point at the similarities and the differences between the ways the term functions in defining 'what' comes after colonialism and socialism (Chari and Verdery 2009; Rogers 2010; Mignolo and Tlostanova 2012; Koobak and Marling 2014). In this sense, I do not necessarily find that '"post-" will always privilege a temporal language and agenda over a spatial one' (cf. Kaplan 1996: 21). We can almost never think about 'the post-socialist' beyond the borders of states that once had socialist governments (Rogers 2010: 4–6), while we can still apply 'post-colonial' to denote an epistemological periodization in intellectual history (Shohat 1991; Hall 1996). For instance, we can make use of a colonial (and postcolonial) perspective in analysing power relationships around the world, but this would not be possible in the case of socialism (Etkind 2011; Tlostanova 2018). However, in both cases the prefix has profound effects in universalizing different political contexts, whether in thinking about the connections between Kenya and India (Shohat 2006) or between Poland and Uzbekistan (Tlostanova 2018).

This is where the 'post-' in 'post-genocide Turkey' tends to blur the lines within two particular dimensions. First, it does not locate early twentieth-century Turkey (which, in fact, did not exist at that time) in relation to other places and periods where similar genocidal processes took place. Second, it does not specify what comes 'before' and what follows 'after'. In the case of Turkey, the prefix also hides the ongoing effects of the Genocide on the present political organization of the country and everyday lives of its Armenian citizens because of its authority in compartmentalizing time (see Suciyan 2015: 21–2 for a scholarly discussion).

This discussion leaves me obliged to clarify how the terminology is being used in this text. Everywhere I refer to 'Genocide' with an uppercase 'G', I refer to the Armenian Genocide, which I take to have occurred from April 1915, when the Ottoman Interior Ministry ordered the arrest of Armenian political and community leaders, to November 1918, when the Temporary Law of Deportation of May 1915 was repealed, although the vast majority of Armenians had been deported and perished as early as the first half of 1916 (Kévorkian 2011: 3). However, it should be noted that various genocidal processes against Armenians had already been in place since the late nineteenth century and continued targeting them until the early 1920s, the evident impunity for each of those violent events paving the way for the next (Dadrian 2005 [1995]: 11; Hovannisian 2007: 5). Anywhere in this text where I do not intend to stress the particularities of the extermination of Ottoman Armenians in early twentieth-century Anatolia, I refer to the concept of genocide with a lowercase 'g' as a more general term. The term also appears frequently in adjective form as in 'post-genocide', again with the lowercase 'g'. Although I refer to 'the Genocide' to denote the diverse events that eventually led to the annihilation of Ottoman Armenians and their mass exodus from their ancestral places of origin within a specific time period, I refuse to deploy such a term as 'post-Genocide' with the uppercase 'G'. This is not merely grounded in a stylistic or grammatical choice in which I try to differentiate the term in noun and adjective forms. Following the discussions in this section, I see 'the Genocide' as a historical event, a representation of the genocidal processes of early twentieth-century Anatolia. However, in the lexical juxtaposition of genocide with 'post', I sense that we need room for ambiguity until the emblematic wording that Nichanian (2009) waits for appears from the future. If 'post' works towards periodization in such a way that imposes a clear historical moment of termination of 'the event', the lowercase 'g' signifies that we still have time to fully understand the past of our present. I see these reflections as contributing to the ongoing debates on temporality, representation of the past and the politics of naming in the contemporary scholarship on Turkish and Armenian studies.

A PRELUDE: LOST IN GEORGIA

In the early spring of 2012, I went to Armenia for a short visit. I had been invited for an NGO meeting between various partners collaborating on a local history project from Turkey, Armenia and Germany. I travelled to Yerevan on a bus from Istanbul for about 40 hours and decided to go back to Istanbul by airplane. At that time flights between Yerevan and Istanbul with a return were as expensive as 600 US dollars: due to the blockade by Turkey and Turkish Airlines, a monopoly of private companies charged high prices for the two-hour flight. Hence, for most passengers travelling between Armenia and Turkey, the fastest and most reasonably priced option was to travel first to Tbilisi, the Georgian capital. Passengers travelling from Yerevan arrived in Tbilisi in shared taxis and marshrutkas, the minibuses that dominate post-socialist landscapes, a five-to-seven-hour overland journey, and then took a flight to Istanbul. Going in the opposite direction, passengers travelling from Istanbul arrived in Tbilisi by airplane, then took shared taxis or marshrutkas to Yerevan.

When I went to book a flight from Tbilisi to Istanbul, all the flights were full on the days I wanted to travel. However, I had two other possible places to fly from: Batumi, on the Georgian side of the Georgia-Turkey border, and Hopa on the Turkish side. I booked the flight from Hopa as it was three times cheaper than a flight from Batumi. Hence, my plan was to leave Yerevan for Tbilisi in a shared taxi, then take another shared taxi to the Georgian border town of Batumi, and finally take a private taxi to the Turkish border town of Hopa. However, when I left Armenia and entered Georgia, I realized that flights from the Turkish border town of Hopa were in fact operated from Batumi. The distance between the two cities was only about 30 kilometres, and there was no airport in Hopa at all.

This situation brought about various complexities in terms of border crossings between the two countries, especially for passengers who were short of time or money. Passengers travelling from Hopa to Istanbul were required to take a shuttle-bus from the Hopa town centre to the Batumi airport. They were taken directly to the specific gate of departure without any passport control or customs checks, although they physically crossed the Turkish-Georgian border. Moreover, checked baggage was accepted for the aircraft at the port of departure indicated on the ticket. This was how it was guaranteed that passengers from Hopa, who were travelling on far cheaper tickets on a domestic flight, and passengers from

Batumi, who were travelling on more expensive tickets on an international flight, were separated. In this sense, the port of departure for any passenger was not where they physically boarded the plane, but where they had their baggage checked in by the authorities. This was a practical solution that prevented goods smuggled from Turkey into Georgia from arriving at or departing from the Batumi airport.

As a result of all this, it would have been impossible for me to catch my flight, but I missed my flight from Hopa for another reason. Earlier that day, I had taken a shared taxi from Yerevan's Kilikia Bus Station for Tbilisi. Similar to many other shared taxis and marshrutkas I had travelled in between the two countries, the passengers had different mother tongues and citizenships. I occupied a seat in the last row of the vehicle, a large Mercedes that was probably more than twenty years old. Sitting next to me was a Kurdish-speaking teenage boy from Armenia, and next to him a Russian soldier. The row in front of us consisted of an Armenian woman who had migrated to Los Angeles, a Dutch tourist and a Kurdish man from the predominantly Kurdish province of Van in eastern Turkey. As we were stopped twice by Armenian police asking for bribes, the strangers inside the shared taxi started a conversation about whether we could make it to Tbilisi on time. A commotion started when the Dutch tourist asked the Armenian woman sitting next to him in English about what had happened. She briefly responded in an American accent that she had no idea as she wasn't listening to the conversation between the police officer and the driver. Following that, she turned back to the row behind her and repeated the Dutch tourist's question to the Kurdish boy sitting next to me, this time in Armenian. The same exchange of questions and answers repeated itself several times in English, Armenian, Russian, Kurdish and eventually Turkish – when the Kurdish men from Turkey could not communicate with the Kurdish boy from Armenia due to differences in dialects and pronunciation, they finally turned to me and I translated for them from Armenian to Turkish and from Turkish to Armenian.

The Kurdish men were surprised by my presence as they never imagined running into a Turkish man on the road between Yerevan and Tbilisi. While it was a huge generalization, I felt that as Kurds from Turkey, they had no reason to trust a Turkish man they met on the roads of Armenia. The violent history of nation-building in post-Ottoman Turkey resulted in the making and marking of differences between Muslim Turks and Kurds and popularized those differences in the form of stereotypes about Turks, Kurds and others. This was probably why I first appeared to them as someone to approach cautiously, until I made them sure about my own political stance vis-à-vis the Kurdish issue and the violent history of Turkey. I was already six months into my fieldwork and, by that time, it had already proven very difficult to persuade informants from/in Turkey, Armenia, and elsewhere that I was not a spy or someone with an affiliation with the Turkish government. However, after several questions about who I was and jokes about politics in Turkey, the three of us became friends two hours into our journey. I learned that they were also on their way to Hopa to catch a bus back to Van, so we agreed to share a taxi together for the rest of the journey.

We arrived in a central square in Tbilisi, where I was arriving for the first time in my life. There were no taxis leaving for Batumi, from where we had planned to take another taxi to Hopa. As most taxi drivers in this particular part of Tbilisi were Armenians working as drivers en route to Armenia, it was possible for me to communicate in Armenian. One taxi driver offered to take us to where most taxis for Batumi departed, but he was not interested in taking us to Batumi himself. Meanwhile, my new Kurdish friends were busy buying painkillers from a pharmacy nearby. When they came back, I explained the situation. The three of us agreed to take a shared taxi to Batumi from another part of Tbilisi, and we got into a city taxi to go there.

Ten or fifteen minutes after entering our third mode of transport of the day, I realized that I had forgotten my bag in the shared taxi that had brought us from Yerevan. My laptop, camera and field notes were inside the bag, and I had to find it. I tried to explain the situation to the taxi driver and asked him to bring us back to the public square in central Tbilisi we had arrived at earlier in the day. However, the driver did not understand what I meant, partly because he was not from Tbilisi. It was extremely difficult to communicate with him, as he was not Armenian as the previous two drivers were and I did not know any Russian or Georgian. I heard something like '*Turk?*' When I responded in the affirmative, he made a sudden U-turn. When I saw the building that we were approaching, I understood that he was taking us to the main bus station of Tbilisi, Ortachala, and he finally brought the taxi to a parking lot nearby full of other taxis. The driver left the car, approached the other taxi drivers and explained something that made one of the other taxi drivers approach our car and talk to us. It appeared that all taxi drivers in this particular part of the Ortachala bus station were Azeri speakers from Georgia. I understood that the taxi driver brought us there knowing that the Azeri and Turkish languages are very closely related. I explained the situation to the Azeri taxi driver, he explained the issue to his friends, and one of them 'volunteered' to help find my bag (and at the end of the day charged me 60 Georgian laris, equal to 25 US dollars). He asked me about where the taxi from Yerevan to Tbilisi had dropped us off, and I responded that I simply didn't know. At that point, my Kurdish friends remembered the receipt from the pharmacy where they had purchased their pills. We presented the receipt to the Azeri taxi driver, and it became clear that it was a pharmacy at the nearby Ablavari Metro Station. My Kurdish friends waited at Ortachala with our Georgian taxi driver from Batumi, and I set off on another journey with this Azeri taxi driver through the streets of Tbilisi.

The Azeri driver took me back to Ablavari Metro Station. However, our driver from Armenia had already left with new passengers en route to Yerevan. There were other Armenian drivers waiting for passengers; I told them what the car and the driver had looked like. They knew whom I was talking about based simply on my description and called the driver to ask him to leave the bag somewhere specific on the road so that I could find it. The driver responded that he would leave my bag at the tomato stall of Gregory in the border village of Shulaveri. Following that, the Azeri taxi driver took me to the border village, asked for my bag from tomato stall to tomato stall, found Gregory and my bag with nothing touched or lost, and took me back to my Kurdish friends, who were still waiting for me at the Ortachala bus station in Tbilisi. When I asked the Azeri taxi driver whether we would have followed the Armenian shared-taxi driver all the way to Armenia if he hadn't dropped my bag off in the border village, he responded that Armenians would have killed him if he had attempted to enter their country – a definitive no!

In the end, after a good four hours of chasing my bag through the streets of Tbilisi and Georgian border villages, I already knew that I was going to miss my flight. We finally arrived in Batumi a couple of hours after midnight, and I decided to cross the border into Turkey by road with my Kurdish friends. By the time we arrived in Hopa in another taxi, the sun was just about to rise. The three of us had some lentil soup in a restaurant frequented by exhausted truck drivers in this border town. Then my Kurdish friends asked me whether I was coming with them to the bus station. I checked flight schedules and prices and decided to take a flight from Trabzon in the afternoon, instead of booking another flight from the Hopa/Batumi airport, so the three of us went to the bus station. I took a two-hour bus journey to catch a flight to Istanbul while my Kurdish friends embarked on a 700-kilometre bus journey to their side of Mount Ararat. With the delays on my part, border crossings and bribe-seeking Armenian policemen, it took them about 30 hours to reach home, a journey of only 200 kilometres had the overland border between Turkey and Armenia been open. As the first core chapter of this book starts to unfold in the following pages, the borders in this part of the world necessitate an expansive look at the (im)mobility regimes that have been in operation since the fall of the Iron Curtain.

Chapter 1

TAKING THE BUS ON THE WAY FROM HOMES

[H]owever different the reasons were, the result was the same: wherever the flexible borderline between East and West shifts, Armenia and/or the Armenians are in some mysterious way right there, as if waiting to become intermediates between the newly distributed East and West. Usually this happens against their will, Armenians are as if doomed to become intermediates.

(Levon Abrahamian, *Armenian Identity in a Changing World*, 2006: 348)

The border towns of Hopa in Turkey and Batumi in Georgia enjoy increasing mobility between the two countries. As of December 2011, Turkish and Georgian citizens are able to travel between the two countries with national identity cards, or, in other words, without a passport. In 2011, Batumi was amongst the most popular travel destinations for Turkish citizens; approximately 750,000 visited the city for its casinos and nightlife (1 October 2012, *BBC Türkçe*). Similarly, in 2015, despite the decrease in the total number of foreigners visiting Turkey, the number of Georgians increased, and they constituted the second largest group of visitors, after German and before Bulgarian nationals (28 January 2016, *Hürriyet*). In 2015, the Georgia-Turkey and Bulgaria-Turkey land crossings were the third and fourth busiest Turkish borders after the Istanbul Atatürk and Antalya International Airports (27 May 2016, *TRT Haber*). An additional 1.6 million people also visited Turkey as day-trippers (in Turkish: *günübirlikçi*) from these neighbouring countries to shop and trade in the border towns (28 January 2016, *Hürriyet*).

This increasing mobility between Georgia and Turkey should be understood in relation to the increasing partnership between the two countries. However, this partnership between Turkey and Georgia should also be located within the current political map of the post-socialist Caucasus that is being shaped in the shadow of the unrest between Turkey and Armenia, and similarly between Georgia and Russia. The contemporary Caucasus constitutes a fragmented zone of closed borders, autonomous regions, de facto independent states and invaded territories. Both internationally recognized and unrecognized borders within Georgia prevent or constrain travel to Russia at specific locations, such as the regions of South Ossetia and Abkhazia, while the borders of Armenia and Azerbaijan are disputed regarding the Nagorno-Karabakh region, which is internationally recognized as part of Azerbaijan. I suggest that these conflicts create a unique regime of mobility among the various independent and unrecognized states of the South Caucasus. It is these conflicts that have brought about trade opportunities since the collapse of the Soviet Union (Humphrey 2002; Marsden 2017), subsequently leading to the emergence of particular towns and border crossings as nodal points where people from countries in conflict mix and mingle. Hopa is one such nodal point.

The north-eastern border of Turkey (with Georgia, Armenia and the Azerbaijani enclave of Nakhichevan; see Figure 3 below) was shaped by two treaties in 1921: first with the post-revolutionary Russian Soviet Federative Socialist Republic in March in Moscow and then with representatives of the Georgian, Armenian and Azerbaijani Soviet Socialist Republics in October in Kars.[1] Until 1937, the border between Hopa and Batumi was very porous, allowing locals to visit family, shop and trade on either side (Akyüz 2017: 24–35). However, with the intensification of Stalinism (and as an indirect protest against the Montreux Convention in 1936 that permitted Turkey to remilitarize the Bosphorus and the Dardanelles), the border was closed, becoming one of the most rigid borders of the Soviet Union (Pelkmans 2006; Gültekin 2007) until its reopening in 1988 (Akyüz 2017: 24).

The transformation of the Turkish-Georgian border from an impermeable line into a zone of interaction contrasts with the history of the Turkish-Armenian border. As opposed to the popular view and public memory on the issue in Turkey and elsewhere (with the exception of Armenia), the border between the two countries has not always been closed. It was open from 1927 to 1993, connecting Armenia's second largest city, Gyumri, to the Turkish city of Kars; this was the only

Figure 3 A Map of Conflicted Zones in the South Caucasus (with some major roads connecting and detouring them).

functioning border crossing between the former Soviet Union and Turkey.² It is in this historical context that the politics centred around the Genocide between the two countries did not result in the closing of the border by Turkey. In fact, Turkey was amongst the first states to recognize the independent Republic of Armenia in 1991 (Goshgarian 2005). However, with the intensification of the Armenia-Azerbaijan conflict regarding the redistribution of territory in the Karabakh region in 1993, Turkey sided with Azerbaijan and closed its border with Armenia in protest and as a way to blockade the transportation of goods into the country (see the next chapter for more on the impact of the ongoing dispute on the recent political and economic history of Armenia). However, as the rest of this chapter reveals in detail, despite the closing of the border since 1993, Armenians nevertheless found ways to go to Turkey for trade and travel, and 'the generalized image of the Turkish enemy' never stopped them from getting involved in trade expeditions and buying Turkish goods (Abrahamian 2006: 251).

The map above illustrates the fragmented political nature of the South Caucasus very well. In Hopa, during more than a dozen border crossings between Georgia and Turkey, I observed truck drivers from Turkey, Georgia, Azerbaijan and Armenia waiting in the same line. Buses en route to Baku, Yerevan and Tbilisi all arrived there with passengers bearing Russian, Georgian, Armenian or Azerbaijani passports. Private cars, taxis and minibuses were mostly involved in short-distance travel between Georgia and Turkey, between towns close to the border. Hopa served as a meeting point for many people who did not have much access to travel *elsewhere*. It is in this context of political fragmentation that I consider Hopa, at the westernmost tip of the post-socialist Caucasus region, as a place where historical relationships between ordinary people are constantly being reproduced, re-established and reinvented. In order to explore this north-east corner of Turkey and its relationship to the world beyond, I find Sarah Green's elaboration of the Balkans to be a good departure point:

> The problem of the Balkans, as they are constituted in hegemonic terms, is not too much fragmentation, as many suggest, but too much connection, too much relationship; the Balkans always seem to generate ambiguous and tense connections that ought, in modernist terms, to be clearly resolved separations.
> (Green 2005: 129)

My purpose here is not to suggest that the Balkan case can be directly supplanted onto the case of the Caucasus. Nevertheless, it should be stressed that both regions are post-socialist and post-Ottoman (the Caucasus to a lesser extent than the Balkans). Both regions have resonated with political and ethnic conflict since the late imperial era (Romanov, Ottoman or Habsburg), and this has continued into the nation-state and post-socialist eras. Moreover, as we will see in Chapter 5, it is from both regions that hundreds of thousands of Muslim refugees moved into Turkey in various waves of migrations in the twentieth century to become Turkish citizens and eventually 'Turks' (Bora 1998; Cagaptay 2005). Hence, both regions pose historically significant connections with contemporary Turkey and its nation-building enterprise. The historical diversity of these two regions neighbouring contemporary Turkey and, as Green (2005) puts it, the abundance of relationships among their diverse populations are difficult to grasp in modernist thinking. This chapter aims to illustrate some of these complexities ethnographically, to unpack how these multi-layered and contingent affiliations with people and places are lived by Armenians among these contested national settings.

In the following pages, I approach political fragmentation as part of the relationships among people in order to account for the constitution of 'mobility' in relation to 'stasis' (Clifford 1997). In Hopa, I observed that the closed border between Turkey and Armenia resulted in particular modes of living and travelling: people were on the move as much as they themselves and others around them were restricted from moving. I suggest, through presenting the account of my travel companions from Armenia en route to Istanbul, that the increasing mobility between Turkey and Georgia is intimately related to the restrictions on residents of these three countries from travelling to third-country contexts. This adds to the observation that mobility is being realized at the expense of many others who cannot move or are stopped from moving (Glick-Schiller and Salazar 2013).

In this chapter I contextualize two major issues in contemporary anthropology by asking how we define mobility in relation to stasis and how we should make sense of ongoing *immobilities* vis-à-vis globalist paradigms of increasing free movement. It is for this reason that here and all through the text I define 'movement' specifically as the physical transportation of humans and non-humans (goods, animals and money) between two localities. I use 'mobility' and 'movement' interchangeably, but only in the 'singular' case of the former term. What I understand and conceptualize in this book as 'mobilities' and subsequently 'immobilities' refer to particular juxtapositions of 'travelling' and 'dwelling' as defined by Clifford (1997). Thus, for instance, my attempt is to move beyond how 'anthropology frequently dealt with immobility as a cipher for assemblages of blocked, stuck and transitional movement' (Khan 2016: 93). There is an additional non-physical dimension to (im)mobilities with an emphasis on the transportation of discourse and its constant deconstructions and reconstructions. Both terms refer to a general historical condition of travel, migration and displacement of people and their ideas, traditions and know-how. Thus, as opposed to the physical dimension of movement, mobilities and immobilities stress (or are at least based on a search for) a human condition shared universally.

I undertake this task by focusing on three ethnographic settings. I have already revealed the first of these: the land crossings at the national borders between Armenia and Georgia and between Georgia and Turkey. In the following section, I attempt to locate a particular bus station in Istanbul in relation to other neighbourhoods of the city, in addition to networks of transnational post-socialist mobility and formal and informal forms of the global economy. Subsequently, I present ethnographic data from my research on 40-hour bus journeys between Armenia and Turkey, and I portray the dynamics of contemporary travelling between the two countries. In each of these three settings, I find that academic and political discourses marginalize particular narratives of mobility and create hierarchies between them. A prime example of this tendency is particularly the underrepresentation of women's accounts within the literature on travel and mobility. By portraying a case that specifically locates femininity as a component of mobility, one of the purposes of this chapter is to contribute to the literature on the gendered nature of international mobility (Morokvasic 1984; Kaplan 1987; Enloe 1989; Wolff 1993; Hoving 2001; Pessar and Mahler 2003; Bloch 2017). In doing so, it does not take gender to observe 'how men and women move differently', but rather to capture the socially, culturally and historically constructed relations between the sexes that 'inflect the texture of mobility, and vice versa' (Elliot 2016: 76). Although not directly realized in this chapter, this book, particularly in Chapter 3, contributes towards understanding women's sexuality in migration contexts beyond a sexual objectification framework (Cheng 2010: 22).

A bus station as a departure point

The Emniyet bus station, although located in the very centre of Istanbul, is not widely known amongst the general public. However, it serves as a major hub for travel between the post-socialist world and Istanbul. The adjacent cargo terminal makes the trading of goods possible for relatively well-off traders who can afford the services of freight companies. However, traders who can afford to do so often use other more comfortable forms of transport than buses. Most traders travelling on the buses departing from the Emniyet station are involved in small-scale trade; they are shuttle-traders (in Armenian from Russian: *chelnoki* and in Turkish: *bavul tüccarı*), and they carry the goods they purchase in Istanbul back to their countries of origin themselves. Since the collapse of the USSR, shuttle-trading has been a common practice among the citizens of former socialist countries (Yenal 2000; Humphrey 2002; Yükseker 2007; Reeves 2014; Bloch 2017).

Not all passengers frequenting this bus station are directly involved in trade. For many of the passengers, trade is not the primary incentive for travel. There are people arriving in Istanbul with a one-way ticket in search of work, as well as people leaving Istanbul – some leaving for good after making some money. Students and tourists also use the bus station. There are in-transit passengers travelling between Turkey's eastern and western neighbours. Despite their different reasons for making use of the station, almost all passengers leaving Istanbul carry goods purchased in the city, whether as gifts to friends and family or goods to be potentially sold in their city of arrival. Many carry olive oil to be given as gifts, detergent to be sold to shop owners, and textiles intended for gifts and for sale. Others, such as students or tourists, buy more textiles than they personally need in case these can be sold to traders or shop owners back in Armenia. In this context of travelling between the post-socialist world and Istanbul, a gift is often a potential good to be sold, and vice versa. The articulation of long-distance travelling and contacts in this region only through perspectives of economic interest is a very limited framework (see Helms 1988: 5); trading – at least in the context of the buses between Turkey and Armenia – takes many forms.

This small pocket of the post-socialist world around the Emniyet bus station is situated on the southern shore of what is now called Istanbul's 'historical peninsula' (in Turkish: *tarihi yarımada*),[3] acknowledging its status as a UNESCO World Heritage Site. However, there is a juxtaposition between this global stage (and the mass tourism that goes with it) and the marginal and almost invisible activities going on in its shadow. As Bloch (2017) calls it, 'the Russian district' (32) of Istanbul does not attract the attention of the international tourists who visit the nearby museums and monuments. The Emniyet bus station and its surroundings have come into existence as a result of a business other than tourism, namely textile production and trade. There have been textile workshops here since the 1980s and even earlier periods, and over time, most workshops have established storefronts where the purchase of goods on the spot is possible. With the collapse of the USSR these workshops attracted many shuttle-traders from former socialist countries, which have resulted in a boom of low-budget hotels in the area. I conducted research in a triangle that consisted of three neighbourhoods within walking distance of each other: Samatya, where the bus station is situated; Laleli, where most shops and hotels are located; and Kumkapı, where more hotels are scattered and where many post-socialist migrants live. It is important to note here that historically both Samatya and Kumkapı were neighbourhoods with considerable Armenian populations, not only until the Genocide but also up until the 1960s. Both neighbourhoods still have functioning Armenian churches and other Armenian public institutions.

The common characteristic of these three neighbourhoods is that they display a vivid picture of contemporary globalizations and mobilities taking place with different speeds, legal frameworks and physical settings. The informal economy of textile production in workshops and its trade is based on networks of relationships between producers, shopkeepers and traders, as well as hotels and landlords, bus and cargo companies, and local authorities. Eder and Öz (2010) note that the intensive deregulation of the Turkish economy since the 1990s has created a fertile environment of informalization in manufacturing and subsequently trade (83). It is in this framework that the country became an attractive destination for shuttle-traders, as the liberalization of the economy paralleled the emergence of informal trade as one of the essential sources of GDP in Turkey (ibid.; see also Kirişçi 2005). As a result, this particular micro-economy in the city is maintained through an informal transnational network of business. In the case of the transnational trade between Armenia and Turkey, the closed border and the lack of diplomatic relationships between the two countries add another layer to the informality of business, simultaneously resulting in advantages and obstacles for traders.

Different parts of the city have different micro-economies, and the neighbourhoods of Laleli, Samatya and Kumkapı, whose historical particularities informed the placement of the Emniyet bus station, are engaged with the economies of post-socialist countries and the rest of the city in multiple ways through diverse human actors. Perhaps they could be best understood as epitomes of 'global scaling' at different levels (Glick-Schiller and Çağlar 2008), scales that require combinations of formal and informal economies (see Keyder 1999), people with different skills and legal entitlements under different citizenship and migration regimes, and various mediums of exchange (whether e-money, banknotes, gifts or even barter) and services. These three neighbourhoods are neither the final nor the initial 'localities' where goods, people, money and information leave or arrive. To the contrary, the movement of goods, money and information should be understood as circular. It is in this sense that globalization, as Anna Tsing (2000) once noted, should not be understood as a contradiction between 'global forces' and 'the local', nor as merely an interaction that is reduced to the relationships between the two (338). Tsing's criticism targets the globalist paradigm at two levels. At one level, it attacks the portrayal of movement of goods and people as taking place only between developed and developing economies by underestimating the extent of mobilities within the latter. At another level, it attacks how the 'local' as well as the 'locality' are reduced to a 'place' where global flows are consumed, incorporated and resisted (463).[4]

In order to understand global circulations and simultaneously reject globalist frameworks, Tsing (2000) proposes to study globalization from below, which for her comes to mean studying non-Western, local or transnational understandings of the term. I find the Emniyet bus station in Istanbul both a physical and a mental departure point to engage with this alternative framework of globalization and circulation. Although not united by language, religion or experiences of violence, I suggest that Armenians from various parts of Turkey and Armenia share a common element in their understanding of mobility and dispersion and demonstrate a particular narrative of global circulation. This shared understanding is difficult to define, though it points to how histories of migration, exile and long-distance trade have led to a normalization of mobility. Similar to what Sarah Green observed more than a decade ago in Greece (2005), I also observed during my research that Armenians in Armenia took movement for granted: although some of them were not even migrants or 'on the go', for them family histories of dispersion, exile and relocation always signified further and future mobilities (see Dink 2000). The quotation by Levon Abrahamian at the beginning of this chapter is intended to account for the centrality of physical movement within the lives of past and present Armenians.

Based on my research, I hypothesize that post-genocide global dispersion is one of the major cultural tropes that Armenians believe they share with each other. Although the initial formation of the Armenian diaspora precedes the Genocide and should be considered in relation to earlier histories of diasporizations and re-diasporizations, many Armenians I met (especially from Turkey) did not know much about the historical Armenian trade networks and diasporas that once stretched from Madras to Amsterdam (Panossian 2006; Aslanian 2011). Nevertheless, almost everyone I encountered through fieldwork articulated dispersion as an important element of being Armenian. Their past, present and future are shaped in light of what I have so far defined as mobilities. Both in Istanbul and in Armenia, people had multiple places of origin and family histories of various waves of displacement. They had family members and friends in a multiplicity of cities, and they had a contingency plan for leaving – just in case. It is in this context that mobility was a fundamental component in providing a sense of what they shared as Armenians, which, I believe, also epitomizes a particular account of globalization from below, a system of mobilities and circulation that has its own internal logic and organizational structures.

Michael Lambek (2007) asks whether we could consider the past and present connections between distant localities as constituting a common 'region' or even a 'system' (xiv), as opposed to the networks of exchange between interdependent 'centres' and 'peripheries' presented by Wallerstein (1974) three decades earlier. As Marcus and Fischer (1986) wrote, in the 1970s Wallerstein 'directly challenged the failure of the development theories of the 1950s and 1960s and proposed within the ahistoric and separated disciplines of political science, economics, and sociology to explain what was happening in the third world' (80). Nevertheless, Wallerstein's accounts of how particular places were historically constituted as 'peripheries' were overly limited (Roseberry 1989). Critical scholarship following Wallerstein has primarily focused on closing those gaps between the separated disciplines, employing a more holistic look towards world history. Subsequently it was revealed that what were labelled as 'centres' and 'peripheries' in Wallerstein's theory did not reflect how restructurings in the global economy historically occurred when '*players who were formerly peripheral* begin to occupy more powerful positions in the system and when *geographic zones formerly marginal to intense interactions* become foci and even control centres of such interchanges' (Abu-Lughod 1989: 334, emphases original).

For anthropologists, increasingly historicized ethnography should be understood as 'corrective to its own ahistoric past and a critique of the ways Western scholarship has assimilated the "timeless" cultures of the world' (Marcus and Fischer 1986: 78). Following the same line of thought, I wonder whether contemporary patterns of circulation, travel and place-making can be recognized as part of historically constituted systems. However, my intention here is to go beyond a political economy framework in accounting for the endurance of these systems (see Ortner 1984) by also recognizing their historical transformations. I wish to take account of historical dispersions of languages, religions, traditions, etc. in the making and development of these systems.

Much social science literature consistently defined culture as 'the shared, the agreed on, and the orderly' – whether styled as 'the functionalist glue making social cohesion possible', 'the abstract code enabling societal communication' or 'the domain of shared, intersubjective meanings that alone make sense of symbolic social action' (Gupta and Ferguson 1997: 4). Here, my intention is to look for a definition of culture that is less orderly, without denying the 'fundamental assumption that people are always trying to make sense of their lives, always weaving fabrics of meaning, however fragile and fragmentary' (Ortner 1997: 9; also quoted in Hoffman 2009: 421). Following this, in my understanding of the terms, 'the shared' and 'the agreed on' as described by Gupta and Ferguson should not necessarily constitute mutually inclusive components of culture. As following chapters will demonstrate in detail, 'dispute' can provide a basis for people to articulate what they share in common. It is in this sense that culture can be understood as 'a moving territory' of constant articulation, which is creative and transformative of people, things and discourses (Deleuze and Guattari 1987).

If we are going to look for a definition somewhere, I suggest that we can understand culture 'as a site of travel' (Clifford 1997: 25) that embodies 'practices of travel' and 'zones of contact' for various insiders and outsiders.[5] However, it should not be limited to those aspects of physical movement in which external relationships are negotiated. On the contrary, it should involve the core constitutive elements within the group itself – perhaps, as indicated earlier, positing a point of 'dispute' yet 'something taken for granted' (in the sense of Green 2005) by my travel companions on the road between Armenia and Turkey. I suggest that taking mobility for granted reflects a 'diasporic moment' (Fortier 2000, quoted in Ekmekçioğlu 2016: 102, footnote 2), which expresses the sharing of particular everyday practices by people located at different nodes within transnational networks of dispersed 'communities'. These practices circulate within a system of exchange (and travel), yet they may be disconnected and isolated from one another and occur simultaneously in different places in different forms (Fortier 2000: 142). Here, following the footsteps of Ekmekçioğlu (2016), it is essential to note that the 'diasporic moment' does not necessarily refer to a moment experienced in a diasporic setting. Therefore, the term does not intend to define what diaspora is. It does not aim at analytically distinguishing between the term and 'the homeland', either. Instead, the term emphasizes a shared component in everyday practices of life despite transnational dispersion. In this vein, the term works towards capturing what Armenians possibly share in common without the imposing tone of 'culture' and replaces it with an emphasis on 'a system of exchange' (ibid.).

Here I do not intend to replace 'culture' with 'system' and reintroduce the term as an order, but rather to reiterate one of the former's promises in providing a sense of commonality – whether or not disputed – for Armenians dispersed around the globe. Whether considering themselves 'diasporic' or not, I find that diasporization as a historical process is a central trope in the articulation of what Armenians share in common. The dispersion of Armenians and the formation of diasporic centres date from well before the 1915 Genocide (Panossian 2006; Tölölyan 2010). Based on Boyarin's conceptualization of the contemporary Jewish diaspora (referred to in Clifford 1997: 248; see also Boyarin and Boyarin 1993), I suggest similarly that the diaspora as we know it today can be thought of as the result of various waves of diasporizations and re-diasporizations, stressing the multiplicity of nodal points in Armenian global networks. In such extended networks, the idea of shared commonality cannot be expected to be determined by relationships between 'the homeland' and the host country (cf. Safran 1991), but rather by the independent quality of multiple links between individual nodes within the network (Heller 2004: 202).

Khachig Tölölyan (2000) argues that given the processes of diasporization and the multiplicity of diasporic centres, and the extent to which diasporic centres such as Paris, Los Angeles and Beirut have increasingly claimed vitality as much as ancestral lands, globally dispersed Armenian communities are being transformed into a 'transnation', a term I believe specifically stresses the shifting hierarchies between homelands and diasporic centres. It also informs us about the formation of a system of mobilities among Armenians as depicted earlier. Although Tölölyan specifically focused on the roles of elites and institutions in the making of this transnation, my enquiry is based on analysing how a system of circulation is understood by my travel companions in and en route to Istanbul. This is how I wish to account for the particular ethnographic narrative of globalization from below in the next section.

Earlier histories, other languages

I met Luiza, a woman in her mid-fifties from Armenia, in the summer of 2012 on one of the buses that departed from Istanbul in the early morning. She was carrying a dozen blankets and two huge suitcases filled with textiles to be sold in the markets of Yerevan. She would not be directly selling these items herself; she was bringing the goods to Armenia to sell to shop owners and other traders in the country. She lacked the financial means to rent a space in one of Yerevan's large public markets and could not afford to take her business enterprise to another level. Similar to many other shuttle-traders, she did not pay cargo companies to ship the goods she acquired; the things she purchased in Istanbul consisted of whatever she could physically carry herself.

As I began chatting with her, she told me that she was born to a family of Genocide survivors who were from different parts of the Ottoman Empire. I learned that she used to work as a school teacher before the collapse of the Soviet Union. She lived with her husband in Yerevan at the time I met her and her son had been living in the United States for over a decade. The way she spoke Armenian made everyone on the bus respect her. Unlike the other passengers, she spoke without a provincial accent, and without 'foreign influences' like Russian or Turkish. Her Armenian was *makur*, or 'clean', and she had the authority to tell me that she liked the poetic and 'old-fashioned' way I spoke (Western) Armenian. During my numerous bus journeys between Turkey and Armenia via Georgia, I met many women who shared Luiza's profile – retired women in their fifties who had to find a new way of making a living after the collapse of the USSR (see also Bloch 2017). These women, with their work experience and education levels, composed a particular group of travellers different from the younger generation of passengers who were children when the USSR collapsed.

On our long bus journey from Istanbul to Yerevan, we talked about various issues. I asked her about the language she used to communicate with the owners of textile workshops in Istanbul. I expected to hear Russian, Armenian or even Turkish as an answer. Much to my surprise, she responded that she communicated only in Polish. She told me that after the collapse of the USSR, she immediately got involved in business in Poland, shuttling goods between Lodz and Warsaw. She told me that Poland was a relatively easier destination for Armenians to do trading back then. She also had some distant family members in Warsaw, which made it possible to base herself in the city for that time period. However, I still did not believe that shop owners in Istanbul could communicate in Polish. She explained that in the beginning of the 1990s Turkey had attracted shuttle-traders from all over the post-socialist world, including Poland. This was how some of the workshop owners had learned sufficient Polish to conduct business and thus were able to communicate with Luiza in Polish in Istanbul.

Luiza's account challenges the ways we often see the contemporary mobility of people and goods. In line with Tsing's critique (2000) of the globalist paradigms that reduced 'locality' to 'place', in Luiza's case there is no singularity of direction of movement. In other words, her present mobility between Armenia and Turkey is made possible by earlier histories of mobility, which for her (on the road to Poland following the collapse of the USSR) and for her earlier family members (in their forced exodus from ancestral homelands) encompassed different time periods and political contexts. When I met her again at her home in Yerevan, I expressed how amazed I was by her ability to do business in Polish. What seemed to me extraordinary was very normal for her. She simply said that *kyanky indz berets ajstegh* (lit. life brought me here). She was indeed among those who took mobility for granted. As noted, she was born in Soviet Armenia to a family of Genocide survivors. If there had not been the Genocide, she would not have been born in the USSR. As a result, her attempt to make a living through shuttle-trading in the then-collapsing socialist regimes of East Europe also depended on her family's history of migration and exile from their ancestral lands in Turkey. Counterintuitively, the main reason for her to do business in Turkey also appeared to be the closed border. The lack of means of direct travel between the two countries resulted in a market situation in which Turkish goods were in high demand in Armenia.

Contemporary Armenia is not merely landlocked; its eastern and western borders are impermeable due to the military conflict with Azerbaijan and the blockade by Turkey, respectively. It is for this reason that the country is highly dependent on transportation of goods exported and imported via Georgia and Iran. Although the goods exported from Turkey do not constitute the bulk of total Armenian imports (energy supplies from Russia constitute the majority), the export-import imbalance between the two countries clearly shows that Armenia is dependent on trade with its western neighbour. For instance, in 2015 the volume of imports from Turkey was 134 million US dollars, while export volume to Turkey in this period was only 2.4 million US dollars (Inan and Yayloyan 2018: 8). However, what is missing in these statistics is the main 'pull' factor as vocalized in almost all of my interviews with shuttle-traders like Luiza: the quality of goods, especially textiles, produced in Turkey.

Luiza's mobility within the context of travelling between Armenia and Turkey is made possible at the intersection of various histories of mobility that involve Turkey and the Genocide, Soviet Armenia, Poland and the collapse of socialism, and the more recent history of the closed border between the two countries. Hence, an analysis of her mobility between the two countries should be based on a wider understanding of the ethnographic context presented here. When I asked her why she didn't continue doing business in Poland, she responded that with the country's accession to the EU it became impossible for her (for a confirmation of this situation in other post-socialist contexts see Bloch 2017: 60; see also Eder and Öz 2010: 90). Hence, it was capitalist globalization processes that limited her mobility and consequently prompted her to seek new destinations for trading. As opposed to the promises of globalist discourses celebrating easier movement of people and goods under capitalism, it was new immobility regimes of globalism that led her to seek alternative routes made possible by other histories and regimes of mobility. Luiza's narrative continues, and is complemented by that of Anahid, in the next section, with respect to the narratives of the people who make a living on the buses and offer a perfect example of 'dwelling-in-travelling' (Clifford 1997).

On the road

As indicated in the introduction of this book, when I first decided to travel on buses between Yerevan and Armenia, it was due to practical concerns: it had proved difficult for me to meet post-socialist Armenian migrants in Istanbul. Over time, the bus journeys became essential sites for ethnographic enquiry. One of the main reasons for this development in my research was that I gradually noticed how issues of 'alternative routes' were constantly negotiated by the passengers on these buses. I observed how 'tactics' (formulated as opportunistic and often defensive momentary actions to creatively resist organizational power structures by de Certeau in 1984) were crafted and applied against the always-in-the-making physical and non-physical borders of nation-states.

Many Armenian women trading in Turkey stated that at first they had had serious concerns about coming to Turkey. When I asked Luiza and others I met on the road why they had chosen not to go to Russia, where it is estimated that at least 125,000 Armenians live in Moscow alone (Arutiunian 2006; Galkina 2006; see also Light 2010 who notes that these numbers are usually exaggerated and expressed in millions), their answers were various. Some stated that there were already too many Armenians in Moscow. Others preferred taking a bus to Istanbul instead of taking a flight or a bus to Moscow in terms of fares and what they could carry back as goods to be sold in Armenia. Some believed that there were many design options for clothing in Turkey, whereas in Russia 'all the clothes looked the same'. There were some other emerging destinations like Dubai, but Istanbul proved to be the primary destination for those who opted for bus travel, where it was possible to carry goods without extra transportation charges. Finally, some women said that they came to Turkey for the adventure (see also Bloch 2017: 10).

All viewed Turkey as a relatively desirable place to do business as shuttle-traders and to work as permanent migrants or sojourn occasionally. Based on this observation, here I direct my enquiry towards understanding immobilities in the era of globalization at two different levels of analysis. First, as already described through the story of Luiza, I attempt to understand the 'home' contexts in which Turkey became a desirable place for my travel companions. Second, I explore *everyday* tactics and strategies of place-making through an ethnography of the road connecting the two countries. Here, the emphasis indicates that for shuttle-traders and other frequent travellers, bus journeys are not exceptional situations but rather a significant element of everyday life.

One woman who constantly travelled between Armenia and Turkey was Anahid, whom I met on the way from Yerevan to Istanbul in the spring of 2012. Anahid was in her mid-fifties and had, at the time of research, been working for more than a decade as an attendant on a bus owned by her husband. Her husband, a Turkish man with (Islamicized) Armenian origins from Turkey, was the driver of the bus. Together the family also owned a small office in Istanbul's Kumkapı district, in walking distance of the Emniyet bus station, where it was possible to book tickets or send goods, letters, money and even passports to Armenia. Their small bus company was primarily a family enterprise. They both had dual citizenship, which enabled them to maintain their business between the two countries. Unlike most Armenians from Armenia who lived in Turkey as undocumented migrants, Anahid was a naturalized Turkish citizen. I travelled with her three times, once from Istanbul to Yerevan and twice in the opposite direction.

When Anahid first saw me on the bus after our departure from Yerevan, she understood that I was a first-timer and told me that I could trust her during the bus journey. With a louder voice she said in Turkish: *Hepimiz insanız sonuçta, Türk Ermeni fark etmez* (lit. we are all human beings after all, Turkish or Armenian, it doesn't matter). While welcoming me, it was clear that by speaking in Turkish she was also letting others around me know that there was a 'stranger' on the bus. A few hours after our departure, it was lunch time. I had thought we would stop somewhere on the road; however, we would not be stopping anywhere until we arrived at the Georgian border. When Anahid noticed that I didn't have anything to eat, she told me to wait a moment and with sudden moves she confiscated food and drinks from other passengers, prepared a *lavash* wrap (a form of unleavened flatbread widely consumed in Armenia and neighbouring countries, including Turkey) with cheese and some herbs, and poured some orange juice. Suddenly my tray table was full. She told me to eat and enjoy the rest of the journey.

Anahid was truly a charismatic woman and she was respected by her passengers, the majority of whom had already travelled with her several times. During my many bus journeys, I observed that many passengers kept travelling with the same bus companies so that they could feel secure in a familiar environment. This situation resonates with what Magnus Marsden (2015) observed regarding Afghan traders conducting business in different parts of the post-socialist world. He wrote that trade relationships are 'often long term and durable' and 'maintained even while those who play an active role in them embark on highly mobile lives' (1029). As I would find out later, Anahid was a master of dealing with practical problems on the bus, as well as more bureaucratic problems in border crossings between Armenia and Georgia and between Georgia and Turkey. She could easily calm down passengers complaining or fighting each other, and she was also adept at persuading border officers in Armenia and Georgia that no one was smuggling goods from Turkey. She always gave instructions to first-timers on how to pass through borders and how to pack things so that the border police would not suspect any signs of smuggling. During border crossings, she made announcements to passengers about where to wait for passport queues, which forms to fill in, and what stamps to ask for.

In addition, Anahid was a pivotal figure in the organization of the daily schedule of shuttle-traders once they arrived at their destination. She advised them on where to shop and eat in Istanbul. On one occasion, I noticed that she even provided menus of some restaurants in Istanbul and took orders for lunch and dinner two days before the bus arrived in the city, so that the shuttle-traders could maximize their time for shopping in the city. For shuttle-traders, who would be coming to Istanbul for only three days a week (as the buses spent two days on the road in each direction), Anahid's instructions were very useful.

The trust Anahid built around her persona was very much based on her charisma as a powerful but generous woman, and as an authority figure on the bus. If at one level her authority reflected itself through her capabilities in dealing with disputes among passengers or with the border police, at another level she marked her own and others' territories on the bus by having the final say on seating arrangements. She would often change the seats of passengers during the journey without consulting them when she found it necessary. For instance, during one of our journeys she changed the seat of a teenage girl who started crying when she found out that her seat did not recline. The person whom Anahid instructed to replace the young woman was an elderly woman who couldn't go against the conductor's authority. Similarly, she publicly humiliated men who smoked inside the bus or slept on the bus floor. I never heard any opposition against her.

It was in relation to her penchant for public announcements that when Anahid found out that I was Turkish, she expressed loudly that, for her, every person was first and foremost a human being, not Turkish or Armenian. At first I did not understand why she was talking in such a manner in which everyone could hear what she was saying in Turkish, although without necessarily understanding her. However, she likewise always talked loudly at particular people about issues arising, especially when she wanted to make it clear that everything was under control or there was nothing to worry about, such as thieves on the bus or single men travelling without family. In this way, she warned her passengers about suspects and similarly built trust through her public announcements.

In many ways, Anahid's responsibility went beyond the tasks of an ordinary bus attendant. While providing services to her customers, she also maintained relationships with the 'outer' world on their behalf. This necessitated a detailed organization of space and relationships among the passengers on the bus. Travelling on buses between Turkey and Armenia is difficult and complicated, as the Georgian authorities want to make sure that goods brought from Turkey are not sold in their country. This is why, for instance, the Georgian border police tape over the undercarriage of every bus entering the country and check meticulously whether the tape was damaged while the buses leave the country. They are the only ones authorized to untape the undercarriage. For buses coming from Turkey, the border police in Georgia (and also in Armenia) often check every single item carried on the bus, causing hours of delay for the passengers on their way back home.

Maintaining a good level of communication with the border police was a delicate issue on bus journeys. This was where Anahid's and her team's professional experience about how to deal with authorities was needed. Three times during my journeys from Yerevan to Istanbul, bus companies initially refused to issue me one-way tickets on the grounds that Georgian border authorities did not accept one-way transit passengers going all the way to Turkey, although there was no legal framework for such practice. However, people working at these bus companies came up with practical solutions every time.

Before my first bus trip from Yerevan to Istanbul, I went to Anahid's company's ticket office, located in Yerevan's Hrazdan market. She was not there as she was travelling back to Istanbul, but there was another woman in her mid-fifties behind the ticket desk. She was fluent in Turkish and I later learned that she was a very good friend of Anahid's from the time they worked together as undocumented migrants in Istanbul. After Anahid married and set up the bus company with her husband, they needed someone they could trust to work for them in Yerevan. As she was the only person in the tiny office, I asked her about the departure dates and prices. When she refused to issue me a one-way ticket to Istanbul, I insisted, and she told me that she would think of something, asking me to come back the following day with my baggage before the bus departed for Istanbul. However, she didn't promise me a seat on the bus. When I came back the following day, she told me there were two other men who wanted to travel with one-way tickets. They were not going all the way to Istanbul. The first was travelling to the Black Sea town of Trabzon and the second to Ankara. Thanks to these other passengers who also wished to go one-way, I was permitted to take the bus along with them.

Each time I travelled on one-way tickets, our bus passed through the Armenian side of the Armenian-Georgian border easily but stopped a few hundred metres before the Georgian side. On each occasion, the other one-way ticket passengers and I were bustled into a taxi in order to enter the country as if we were travelling individually, before returning to our seats on the bus a few kilometres after the border crossing. Such measures were never taken by bus companies when the buses entered Turkey from Georgia, or on the way back into Armenia.

As Armenian and Turkish nationals do not need a visa to enter Georgia, I wondered why the Georgian authorities did not let anyone enter from Armenia on a one-way ticket. I quickly realized that it was specifically buses en route to Turkey that were perceived as problematic by the Georgian authorities, as I was never refused one-way tickets when travelling in the opposite direction from Istanbul to Armenia. During my various attempts to communicate with Georgian border police to understand why this was the case, I never obtained a satisfactory answer. They were either unwilling to talk or the language barrier did not allow us to communicate. Only once, a busy officer expressed that they, the border guards, had so much responsibility over those Armenians taking the long detour via Georgia to enter Turkey that if something went wrong they would have to cover the basic expenses of those passengers, including meals and transport back home. At that time, I did not fully understand why this was the case. However, during an interview with a government official from the Ministry of Internal Affairs based in Tbilisi and in the exchange of emails that followed, it was explained to me at length.

In February 2012, Turkey changed its entry requirements for foreign nationals entering the country as tourists (in compliance with the decision of the Council of Ministers dated 10 October 2011, no: 2011/2306). The new requirement grants Armenian nationals visas for 30 days on arrival with a limit of staying in the country for 90 days in total in a 180-day period. In other words, with the new regulation, Armenian nationals can stay in Turkey for three months and then need to wait another three months before re-entering the country. This is in marked contrast to the past, when the regulation was vague regarding the time period it defined. Armenian nationals could stay up to 90 days within any time period (instead of 90 days within 180 days), thus making it possible to obtain unlimited numbers of visa renewals by re-entering Turkey.[6]

When I first started my research between June 2011 and February 2012, it was common practice for undocumented Armenian migrants to leave Turkey and re-enter for visa renewal. Hence, the number of Armenians who overstayed their visas was minimal, as the legal system in Turkey allowed them to renew their tourist visas simply by leaving and re-entering the country. The new regulation made it impossible for migrants to renew their visas every time they entered Turkey. However, several months after the regulation had come into effect, there were still many Armenians who did not know about it. This was why many Armenians who had already stayed in Turkey for the maximum amount of time allowed by the new regulation (without even knowing it) could not re-enter Turkey when they attempted to do so. In those cases when Turkey denied them entry, it was the Georgian authorities who had to assist Armenians to return to Armenia. Therefore, one of the measures taken by the Georgian authorities to reduce this burden was to ensure that everyone had a return ticket.

As the buses between Yerevan and Istanbul went through three countries with different migration regimes and two border crossings where different legal practices were in effect, bus crews' expertise was much needed by the passengers. In many ways, Anahid and her team resemble what Mary Helms (1988) terms 'long-distance specialists', or the well-travelled and most experienced people in their societies who lead the way for future travellers.[7] Anahid was among the first wave of Armenians who came to Turkey to find a job right after the collapse of the Soviet Union. She therefore had considerable experience in Turkey and was fluent in Turkish. Her husband was an Islamicized Armenian man, providing her not only Turkish citizenship but also critical connections with the police in Istanbul and Hopa, the border town where her husband came from. During my bus journeys with different companies, I met several other younger women who either were married to or had relationships with men from Hopa. Their relationships and marriages helped them build transnational bus networks between Turkey and Armenia via Georgia.

A woman's constant movement

For Armenians, the only feasible way of travelling to the rest of the world by land is via Georgia. Frustration about the closed border with Turkey is often expressed in mythical terms. I was told several times by fellow passengers about a bus that had directly entered Turkey despite the closed borders. It was believed that there was a secret bus company run by an unnamed Armenian oligarch, for which a ticket was very expensive and difficult to get. Among the people who travelled between Armenia and Turkey, no one I encountered had met anybody who had booked a seat or knew how and where to get a ticket on this mythical bus. It is because travelling to Turkey is mystified in Armenia that women like Anahid were often recognized by passengers as undertaking a huge responsibility and contributing to the wealth of their society, unmatched by anyone else.

In Anahid's case, such responsibility and contribution came with a maximization of the amount of time she could possibly devote to her job. Like most other bus conductors, she spent four days a week on buses (two nights and one day from Istanbul to Armenia, and two days and one night from Armenia to Istanbul). She spent two nights a week in a hotel room in Istanbul with her husband, a place where most of her passengers also stayed. She spent another two nights at her house in Yerevan. One day on the bus when I asked her where she lived, she responded with a smile, pointed to the seats around us and told me that she lived on the bus and never left home. Similar views among long-distance traders were also shared by Osella and Osella (2007) and Marsden (2017), who demonstrated that people not only made homes on the way but also expressed that they never left home when they travelled. I find that these views should also be in line with Ahmed's long-celebrated understanding of home, which, for her, emerges at the centre of relationships between 'those who stay, those who arrive and those who leave' (1999: 340; also referred to in Kasbarian 2009: 372). In the case of Anahid, who almost never stays at her primary home in Yerevan but follows a pattern of travelling without taking a break, I find that it is the specific repetitions of movement, or rather its consolidation as a form of dwelling and perhaps even stasis within the repetitive cycles of her travelling, that makes her call the bus a home.

As critical scholarship on mobility has suggested, we must go beyond understanding mobility as identical to freedom, involving a free floating of people between different nation-state settings (Salazar and Smart 2011). To the contrary, mobility is made possible through practices and experiences of immobility (Clifford 1997). At one level, various forms of borders and bordering practices, as well as the legal and political frameworks of power, determine the extent of networks of movement (Navaro-Yashin 2012). This is why Nina Glick-Schiller and Noel Salazar (2013) call our attention to 'regimes' of mobility, highlighting the role of individual states and changing international surveillance administrations that affect individual mobility. The closed border between Turkey and Armenia and the subsequent tactics employed by bus companies to navigate this situation exemplify such practices, frameworks and relationships. At another level, the mobility of some is made possible thanks to others who either do not move or stop moving (Osella and Osella 2007) and often at the expense of others who cannot move (Glick-Schiller and Salazar 2013). Yet Anahid's is a nuanced story, because it is the story of a woman who does not stop moving. It is her ability to *move constantly* as a *woman* that makes her central to the subject matter of this chapter.

The three emphasized words in the previous sentence ('move', 'constantly' and 'woman') indicate the three significant aspects of a particular form of mobility that are important to unpack here. First: movement. Rouse (1991) argues that although migration has had the potential to challenge established and fixed spatial images, it has commonly been treated as (a) movement from one set of social relationships to another, (b) a shift from one significant environment to another and (c) a movement between groups identified with distinct ways of life (11). Literature following Rouse has demonstrated that no natural and unbreakable link necessarily exists between identities and places (Gupta and Ferguson 1997), and identities are outcomes of processes (Bowman 1993; Sökefeld 2006). Places do not determine who we are, yet place-making and the formation of identities are intimately related processes (Tsing 2000). It is in this sense that I am inclined to search for definitions of 'place' and 'place-making' that necessarily go beyond totalizing the relationships between people and places. 'Movement' (i.e., the physical aspect of mobilities) is one such key point of entry.

I am also not inclined to define 'place' as a necessarily physical location. Anahid's account, rather, is informed by a 'non-place' (Augé 1995) where not only do particular relationships intersect but these relationships are transmitted through the very mobility of the physical setting. However, her account contradicts Augé's notion, as the moving bus is the key site of her place-making activities. The movement of the bus is itself positioned within vast networks of mobility, such as roads, bus stations, hotels and booking offices that operate under the supervision of 'long-distance specialists' like Anahid. In a different vein, the bus is a 'territory' as in the work of Deleuze and Guattari (1987), which connects and transforms discourse. It is not only in-the-moving but also a site where (im)mobilities of past and present Armenians are discussed and put into perspective. The bus is also a site of dwelling, as depicted below.

This brings me to the second aspect of Anahid's centrality in this chapter. There is a temporal aspect to her movement. She does not merely move; she moves *constantly* and her place-making should be located in relation to the time she spends on the roads. I suggest that Clifford's (1997) formulation of 'travelling-in-dwelling' and 'dwelling-in-travelling' should help us to understand the aspect of time in place-making while travelling. He introduces the former concept in order to refer to the circulation of cultural narratives and representations, and the ways these are negotiated, adapted, co-produced or rejected by individuals living in a certain locality. In this sense, travelling-in-dwelling could be understood as any form of creolization, formulation of transnational affiliations, consumption of imported goods and so on. The latter term, dwelling-in-travelling, refers to maintaining a life in constant physical movement. As I construe this particular juxtaposition of stasis and mobility, there is a nuance in what it defines vis-à-vis nomadism. I find the latter term to imply specifically the 'regular and frequent movement of the home base and the household' (Salzman 2004: 18; cf. Braidotti 1994: 5; see also Bauman 1993: 240 for a discussion on what the term implies in relation to other metaphors of travel). However, with dwelling-in-travelling the emphasis shifts from the spatial displacement of home to its spatial diffusion. In other words, home is not confined to being a place to depart from and return to; its location should not be reduced to place (Tsing 2000). Instead, its location emerges as 'a *series* of locations' (Clifford 1989, quoted in Kaplan 1996: 168, emphasis original). I believe it is this second formulation of mobility that is epitomized by the 'long-distance specialists' of the bus journeys between Armenia and Turkey, although Clifford himself conceded that he did not elaborate upon this second notion well enough.

As described above, Turkish immigration law changed in effect from February 2012. The introduction of limits on the number of days during which a tourist could visit Turkey made it impossible for migrants and shuttle-traders to renew their expired visas by exiting and re-entering the country. The change brought about different challenges for different groups of Armenian citizens. People who intended to overstay their visas and seek work as undocumented migrants in Istanbul were no longer able to visit their families in Armenia until they decided to return permanently. For those who made a living through constant travel between the two countries, the situation necessitated new tactics. For Anahid and other Armenian women working on the buses, their relationships with Turkish men introduced them to new possibilities of mobility (see the next chapter for more on this). By marrying these men, women like Anahid maintained their mobility and businesses. Most bus companies already had bus drivers with Turkish citizenship, or hired bus drivers interchangeably to avoid visa restrictions. In sum, under the new regime, some people maintained their mobility while others could not.

The bus challenges notions of an ethnographic setting tied to a particular physical place. On the contrary, the bus itself becomes both a site and a mode of a particular form of relationship that is tangible and physically traceable along the road between Armenia and Turkey, produced and maintained by the people who frequent it. Buses, I suggest, could be understood as physical mediums for transmitting long-distance relationships, as well as settings in which these relationships are created and relocated. In this context, we need a framework that does not define circulations of people, objects and ideas either as inflows or outflows – terms denoting unidirectionality of movement between fixed localities. It is for this reason that I suggest thinking through 'travelling' in relation to studies of mobility.

In many ways this book is an attempt to reconsider – if not to directly revitalize – some old and heavily tainted terminology in making sense of places and the literal ways through which people approach and affiliate with them. One cannot deny that 'travel as a literary genre' (i.e., travel literature) is historically embedded within the particularly gendered history of European colonialism, which has evolved into defining a very privileged way of looking at movement that has been increasingly defined as tourism. However, I find it relatively easier to work through 'travel as a comparative method' provided that we separate 'travel stories' from 'travel literature' *(a la* Clifford 1997) and that the former is articulated as a form of narrative of movement in which we can detect the simultaneous constitutions of 'here and there', 'now and then', 'local and foreign', 'difference and affinity', and 'native cultures and cultures of translation'. This is a promising yet dangerous attempt as travel has historically emphasized a departure from an imagined locality (Wolff 1993: 232).

I fear that more than two decades after Rouse's (1991) criticisms of studies of migration and mobility, movement is still imagined through its penetration into stasis, positing the former as active and the latter as passive. Clifford's (1997) notions of 'travelling-in-dwelling' and 'dwelling-in-travelling' help disrupt this binary. In this formulation, travelling is as much a part of dwelling, stasis or immobility as it is of movement. As Janet Wolff (1993) suggests, such an articulation of travel operates in two ways; it is literal in the sense that both the researcher and the subject of research are on the move, and it is epistemological as it describes knowledge in a different way, as contingent and partial (226). As a result, travel bears the possibility of de-essentializing both the researcher and the subject of research, namely cultures and communities (ibid.). In this respect, travel stories go beyond being a genre of individual travelling, tourism or visiting exotic 'distant' places. Instead, they shed light on accounts of dispersed populations (and field experiences of researchers), as part of wider mobility regimes (Glick-Schiller and Salazar 2013).

Here, my goal is to stress the circularities within Armenian women's historical and geographical/physical movement by way of introducing travel as a form of place-making, and perhaps even in such a way as to include those experiences that can be only vocalized as displacement and exile. As already noted in the introductory chapter, my conceptualization of travel has been to account for the making of the roads that have unmistakably connected my informants (who well deserve the title of travel companions) and myself. If the taintedness of each and every notion of movement and belonging becomes much clearer in their particular juxtapositions between one and another, I cannot suggest a better terminology to think through the connections and separations that make us believe in and identify with people, places and things that are scattered over short and long distances. I offer a hypothetical list of possible new terminologies to see and hear how they put forward issues of relationality and positionality between and among people and places: exile-in-dwelling and dwelling-in-exile, dwelling-in-displacement and displacement-in-dwelling, home(coming)-in-diaspora and diaspora-at-home, belonging-in-place and (dis)placement-in-belonging, exodus-in-exile and diasporization-in-diaspora, and so on. They all break down to nuanced meanings of 'here' and 'there', but I sense that they do not inform us well about the more general historical conditions of 'movement' and '(im)mobilities', which I have defined as referring to processes of transportation and transformation, respectively.

Lastly, there is a gendered aspect of Anahid's constant movement that needs to be critically unpacked. As a prime example of dwelling-in-travelling, she does not merely constantly move; she is a *woman* in constant movement. As Susan Hanson

(2010) notes, there have been two general strands in the geography literature on the relationships between gender and mobility. The first strand takes gender as the cause of mobility but construes the latter in highly generalized terms and misses the details about movement patterns and reasons for movement (9). The second strand takes mobility as the cause, but simplifies the differences between men and women (11). It is crucial to note that both strands similarly end up demonstrating that men move more than women without much contextualization. Similarly, Janet Wolff's (1993) feminist critique of travel literature targets construction of travelling as a predominantly male phenomenon (232; see also Pratt 1992: 171 for a similar discussion). Although there is nothing inherently or essentially masculine about travel, the discourse of travel typically functioned as a 'technology of gender' that transmitted, inculcated and reinforced patriarchal values and ideology (Abbeele 1992: xxv–xxvi; also cited in Wolff 1993). Consequently, departure from the imagined locality reveals embodied discourses on men and women.

Similar to the historical constitution of travel literature, globalization discourses often tell very selective stories of mobility. This is why, on the one hand, specific histories of travelling such as labour migration, pilgrimage and tourism need to be articulated along gender lines (Clifford 1997). On the other hand, more specifically, the feminist critique of travel also needs to acknowledge two important issues:

> First, that what is to be criticized is (to retain the geographic metaphor) the dominant centre; and secondly, that the criticism, the destabilizing tactics, originate too from a place – the margins, the edges, the less visible space. There are other metaphors of space which I find very suggestive, and which may be less problematic, at least in this respect: 'borderlands', 'exile', 'margins' – all of which are premised on the fact of dislocation from a given, and excluding, place.
> (Wolff 1993: 235)

Here, Wolff introduces a dimension into the earlier discussion on the limitations of defining migration as movement between two fixed and inherently different localities. Again, in her formulation the physical locality is not much of a problem in the analyses of migration, but the dominant discursive centres that make us comprehend localities only as physical are. She directs our attention to the power structures, epistemological regimes and historical processes that have 'created' similar discourses on place and gender. In this view, the feminist critique should work towards redefining the male-dominated narratives on travelling. However, in search of new definitions, our task is to avoid not only reproducing the sexism (as well as other imperializing moves such as racism) hidden in academic research and writing (Kaplan 1987: 194), but also setting up a new gender normativity (Braidotti 1994: 31). Although this chapter has focused specifically on the historical and physical conditions that have made the movement of Armenian women en route to Turkey possible, not on gender on a broader level, I take Judith Butler's (1990: 7–8) question literally: 'Where does the construction of gender take place?' If embodiment is a spatial practice, and vice versa (Bourdieu 1977: 163; Massey 1984: 52; Creswell 1996: 9), I believe that answering this question would help us to understand the historical and the contemporary arrangements of gender and mobility without privileging or under-analysing one versus the other (Hanson 2010).

If mobility reconfigures gender relations in already gendered contexts (Mahler and Pessar 2006: 42), I find that the physical places depicted in this chapter emerge as 'locations in contradiction' where different push-and-pull factors make people not only encounter other people but also their norms and their embodiments of those norms (see Brah 1996: 204 on her notion of 'locationality in contradiction', which she defines in relation to Rich 1984). As a result, I take one of the prerequisites of gender seriously, namely its 'repetition' (Butler 1990; Creswell 1999; Elliot 2016), and I propose to focus on *where* it is repeated as much as *how many times* it is repeated. I find it impossible to define a universal category of gender and mobility based on Anahid's experiences with men and other women on the buses, at the bus stations and across borders. However, I find it valuable to examine what kinds of places she travels to – or, in other words, what kinds of places she makes through travelling. As a negotiator of the relationships with the wider world at the border crossings, bus stations and stops, hotels, stores and workshops, Anahid is a translator of not only language between Turkish and Armenian in and en route to Istanbul, but also of the roles, norms and expectations between men and women. However, in doing so, what kind of a world is she bridging to?

As noted above, this is an already gendered world. I argue that the way we imagine place explains a lot about the relationship between gender and movement. Here, I find Ingold's (2011) distinction between the world as 'surface' and the world as 'meshwork' useful. In a world of meshwork, things are instantiated as their paths of movement, whereas a world of surfaces should imply that they are only objects located in space (162–3) (see also Massey 2005 for a discussion on the reduction of space into surface). It is important to note here that for Ingold people acquire knowledge not through transmission (143) but only through movements that make them '*grow into it*' (162, emphasis original) – which could only happen in a world that is understood as a meshwork of relations and intertwined paths (ibid.) If moving is knowing and gender is repetition, there is a fundamental aspect of Armenian women travellers' accounts of dwelling-in-travelling in which they are also repeatedly exposed to other people's understanding of normative gender and subsequently negotiate their own roles in light of the knowledge they acquire. This is not to imply that there could be true or false, real or distorted acts of gender that would be revealed as a regulatory fiction (Butler 1990: 141) between Armenian women and the Turkish men (and equally women) they would encounter on the streets of Istanbul. Instead, it implies that gender is performed *despite* its repetitions in everyday life.

In all these places Anahid travels to, I find a 'subtle but fundamental correlation between exterior movement and interior transformation' of the traveller that 'opens up the conceptual possibility of imagining *mobility as a form of gender in its own right*' (Elliot 2016: 85, emphasis mine; see also Elliot 2012). I believe this is a subtle yet remarkable move within the discipline, as it enables us to enrich the link between stasis and mobility, between what have been historically imagined as two separate domains of the female and the male, respectively. Following this line of thought, we should comprehend those dominant discourses that set apart women from men, and similarly movement from stasis, and recognize the diversity of places that become visible vis-à-vis their relationship to power – such as borderlands, exile and margins, as suggested by Wolff (1993) above. As this chapter has attempted to show, this list can be extended to stress that people who cannot move and people who cannot stop moving are part of a wider regime of (im)mobilities. If all the roads that lead to Armenia give the country its unique political and physical shape as a landlocked 'island' in one of the world's most contested zones of conflict and war, there is more ethnographic room to explore how this shape is understood, maintained and altered inside the country. This is why, in the next chapter, I will discuss how the border between the two countries points at the practices of transgression as gendered, which I believe comes to light in relation to the contemporary modes and conditions of female migrancy and the historical experiences of women during the Genocide.

Chapter 2

EXPANDING OUTSIDES IN ARMENIA

It does not matter if we accept it or not, we have become distant from our religious faith. Religion is now of secondary importance to us. If speaking Armenian makes someone Armenian, then there are many Muslims who speak Armenian better than I do. Are these people Armenians? [They say] 'my grandmother was an Armenian...' And [I respond that] your grandfather was Muslim. Whose blood are you carrying? The Armenian is in unity with his/her religion. If you want to be Armenian, you are supposed to come [to the church] and be baptized, become a member of the Armenian church, then you can say 'I am an Armenian'. Wars happened for that faith, it is for that faith that we sacrificed many people in the beginning of the 20th century.

(Archbishop Aram Ateşyan, 25 February 2012, *Agos*; my translation)

In late 2014, I came across the headline 'Registered as Muslim, Funeral in the Church' (in Turkish: *Nüfusunda İslam Yazıyor, Cenazesi Kiliseden Kalktı*) in the Turkish newspaper *Sabah* (17 December 2014; see also *Radikal* and *Agos* published on the same day). Ferman Gez, aged eighty-four, sparked a controversy upon his death. As the newspapers indicated, his eleven children were conflicted over his faith. While seven of them insisted that he was a devoted Muslim, four of them claimed that he was an Armenian Christian and had converted to Islam only on paper because he was afraid of living as a Christian in his native village in the Turkish province of Batman (historical Sassoun). After negotiations between the Armenian Patriarchate of Turkey and the Directorate of Religious Affairs, the latter a branch of the Turkish government, the decision was left to the deceased man's wife. In the end, Ferman Gez was buried in an Armenian cemetery in Istanbul.

For people with no familiarity with the scope of Armenian affairs in Turkey, such news may seem incomprehensible. Similar stories make the headlines at least a couple of times a year, portraying dispute amongst a deceased person's relatives. In cases where relatives of the deceased did not previously know that their beloved grandparent or parent was Armenian, the information comes as a shock. In cases where they already knew, as with Ferman Gez, the dead person's Armenian background prompts conflicts among relatives. While some family members are comfortable with their Armenian origins, others are not happy about the sudden exposition of their hidden family background to the wider public. Many people struggle to accept their Armenian heritage. These include (i) Armenian parents or grandparents who converted to Islam during or after the Genocide and lived as Muslims until their death, (ii) Armenian parents or grandparents who converted back to Christianity, (iii) children or grandchildren who continued living as Muslims and (iv) children or grandchildren who converted back to Christianity.

Accounting for the heterogeneities of these post-genocide families in contemporary Turkey looks like an impossible task. Conversion to Islam emerged as a common strategy for various Armenian communities before the Genocide and peaked after it as a means to avoid annihilation (Dadrian 2005 [1995]; Akçam 2006). It persisted to avoid discrimination after the emergence of Turkey as a nation-state (Özgül 2014). However, the extent of ambiguity regarding what defines a person as Armenian and the number of Armenians in contemporary Turkey is revealed when we consider Armenian women and children who did not convert to Islam willingly. Many children, for instance, were forcefully taken by Muslim families during the Genocide and raised as Muslim Turks or Kurds without knowledge of their own Armenian ancestry.

Talin Suciyan (2015) argues that a fundamental aspect of being Armenian in Turkey is based on the exchange and circulation of 'autobiographical knowledge' – knowledge that is based on experience and transmitted from one generation to the next only through personal communication (18). In cases where the transmission of autobiographical knowledge to subsequent generations has been interrupted due to the silence or death of older generations, people are not aware of their Armenian ancestry in Turkey. I did not conduct research with Genocide survivors who, whether forcibly or voluntarily, continued their lives as Islamicized Armenians. Thus, this chapter is not intended to account for this debate, or to suggest an approximate number of people with possible Armenian ancestry in the country. The analysis provided here is based on my research in Armenia, among 'travellers' to Turkey in Armenia, including return migrants, deportees and shuttle-traders. In a move to expand more and reflect on what I have argued in the preceding pages, my intention here is to account for current popular understandings regarding post-genocide Turkey as an ancestral homeland by way of locating those in relation to my informants' specific personal histories of (im)mobility. In other words, if the previous chapter located movement within larger systems of mobility, this chapter considers how these (im)mobilities are reflected through articulations of a bond with the 'remaining Armenians' in post-genocide Turkey. The ambiguities regarding people's origins in post-genocide Turkey add another layer of confusion for Armenians from Armenia in imagining cultural and historical proximities between people in Turkey and their own country.

Based on my research in Armenia, this chapter explores how Armenian 'travellers' (in the broad sense of the term explained previously) located themselves in relation to people in their ancestral homelands, in what is now Turkey. I provide narratives of women I met in the Armenian cities of Hrazdan and Gyumri. As the text unfolds, these women's terminated or irregular mobilities are presented as significant for understanding their personal approaches towards the post-genocide context of Turkey. In addition, the transformation that Armenia experienced as a post-socialist nation-state in the last three decades – impoverished by closed borders, economic blockade, the 1988 earthquake and an energy crisis – is introduced as the backdrop to these women's narratives of place-making in a changing world.

Moving ground, shaking foundations

Ozinian (2009) and Körükmez (2012) note that the majority of Armenian migrants in Istanbul are from former Soviet industrial cities in Armenia, not from the capital city of Yerevan. This was a pattern I also started to notice over the course of my bus journeys between Istanbul and Armenia. Apart from a few shuttle-traders from Yerevan, my informants in Istanbul were from smaller former industrial cities and towns, such as Gyumri and Vanadzor. I noticed that while the collapse of the USSR had had profound effects on their lives, the devastating earthquake of December 1988 was an equally crucial turning point. That earthquake, which hit the northern parts of the country with a magnitude of 6.8 on the Richter scale, resulted in 25,000 fatalities; another 50,000 were injured and 530,000 were left homeless (Schott and Kalatas 2014: 77–8).

Right after the earthquake, the Soviet government requested relief from the international community (Schott and Kalatas 2014). This came as a shock to many Soviet citizens, as it was visible in the media for the first time that the government could not handle a situation on its own. As a good friend who worked for civil society organizations expressed during our visit to an exhibition on Armenian media in Yerevan, 'the earthquake shook the foundations of the Soviet Union'. The earthquake in Gyumri brought a marked shift in Soviet policy, as the same friend explained: 'even in the nuclear disaster of Chernobyl, Soviet citizens were never informed about the extent of such catastrophes and the state's limited ability to handle the situation'. The earthquake is widely understood as a turning point in recent Armenian history as it disturbed the image of linear evolution that was formerly based on Soviet ideas of modernization and progress (Shagoyan 2010).

The foundations of the Armenian Soviet Socialist Republic were shaken in 1988 not only physically but also politically. In February of that year, roughly ten months before the earthquake, Armenians in the tiny city of Stepanakert (the official Soviet name then), located in the Nagorno-Karabakh autonomous oblast within the Azerbaijani Soviet Socialist Republic, started to demonstrate for the self-determination of the region and its subsequent merger with the Armenian Soviet Socialist Republic. 'An island of territory' (de Waal 2013 [2003]: 10) formally established in 1923 and surrounded by Azerbaijan, the oblast was populated predominantly by Armenians, with 75 per cent Armenians and 25 per cent Azerbaijanis at the time the protests started (12). The demonstrations in the region quickly spread to Armenia and triggered a series of political rallies throughout 1988. The oblast had long constituted a priority within the political agenda of Armenians, and whenever there was a major political thaw or shift in the USSR, the Armenian government sent letters and petitions to Moscow for the area's 'return' to Armenia (16).

The Karabakh movement, like the Gyumri earthquake, was foundational in the making of independent Armenia (Suny 1993a; Verluise 1995; de Waal 2013 [2003]; Panossian 2006; Libaridian 2007), and the most recent episode of war over that territory in 2020 transformed diaspora-Armenia relationships as the country further consolidated its centrality as a homeland (Kasbarian 2021; cf. Pattie 2005). When the Karabakh movement first emerged, it was the first time in the history of the Soviet Union that people attempted politics from below by calling for changes to internal borders (de Waal 2013 [2003]: 11). Although the movement did not initially have anti-Soviet sentiments and sought political transformation through the existing system, persistent refusals from the Soviet authorities in Moscow to transfer Karabakh to Armenia infused the country with nationalism and growing anti-Soviet sentiments (Suny 1993b: 128). The Gyumri earthquake entrenched this shift in political temperaments.

The Gyumri earthquake and the Karabakh movement had similar transformative impacts on Armenia and complemented each other in catalysing political change (on the emergence of new forms of politics in the aftermath of catastrophes, see Bode 1989; Klein 2007; Simpson 2013). These events triggered discussion and dissent in Armenia and ultimately led to independence. In the years following 1988, Armenia declared independence, went to war with Azerbaijan over Karabakh and helped seal the dissolution of the USSR. The newly independent nation-state found itself amidst a huge political crisis, exacerbated by isolation due to Turkey's decision to close its borders in support of Azerbaijan's claims to Karabakh in 1993.

Ishkanian (2002) notes that in the late 1980s, just before the onset of this catastrophic era, Armenia was the third most industrialized Soviet republic. In 1990 the USSR ranked 26th out of 130 countries in the UN Human Development index, making it a 'high human development country' (UNDP 1990: 111). Just two years after independence, in 1993, Armenia ranked 93rd in the same index, implying a sharp decrease in terms of living standards (UNDP 1996: 28). In the same year, per capita income in Armenia was only equal to that of its 1960s' level (3). By 1994, the country was suffering from 2000 per cent inflation and a negative annual growth rate of -16 per cent (18). Between 1988 and 1994, the country's gross national product underwent a five to sixfold decline (Platz 2000: 123). By 1994, only 30 per cent of the country's industry was functioning (ibid.).

Thus, in less than a decade, as natural and political catastrophes followed one another, the once very industrialized Armenia transformed into a de-industrialized country (Dudwick 1997; Platz 2000; Ishkanian 2002). As many of my informants from Armenia noted, the early 1990s were an extremely difficult period in terms of sustaining a basic standard of living. In addition to the lack of employment opportunities, cuts in electricity and gas and the collapse of telecommunication services drastically changed the course of everyday life (Dudwick 1997; Platz 2000). The era is widely remembered as a historical moment of isolation for Armenians in the newly independent state. Not only were many Armenians deprived of their means to communicate and physically get together with friends and family in the country and abroad, but it was also a moment in which Armenians started to leave the country en masse. It is estimated that the population shrank by at least 30 per cent in a decade due to emigration (Ishkanian 2002). The majority of these emigrants went to Russia, while others were dispersed across post-socialist countries, the EU and the United States (Körükmez 2012). Hence, the migrants and petty-traders who chose to come to Turkey constitute only a small percentage of the people who left the country.

Expanding outsides, shrinking insides

In Armenia, there is a variety of everyday explanations for the transformation the country has experienced in the last three decades. In the previous chapter, I explored how tales of a mythical bus that supposedly crossed directly into Turkey reflected a desire among Armenians for the reopening of the border between the two countries. In addition, I came across a large variety of myths, conspiracy theories and popular jokes that were critical of the country's governing and economic elites, its economic and military dependency on Russia, and NGO, IMF and World Bank employees (Barsegian 2000; Platz 2000), but such tropes are not unique to Armenia. Returning to Levi-Strauss (1955: 429), how are we to explain why such narratives resemble one another around the world?

The answer is that these stories or myths widely end up 'as specific histories with pointed meanings in current political struggles' (Clifford 1997: 190). At the time of my research in the first half of the 2010s, Armenia had been an independent country for two decades. The disastrous impacts of the late 1980s and early 1990s were still visible in the infrastructure and buildings in various cities and towns, and in the organization of everyday life. As one of my informants put it during a meeting in Gyumri in 2013, independent Armenia found itself 'an island in the middle of one of the world's most mountainous regions', surrounded by economic blockade, international conflict and restrictions on mobility. In the context of this landlocked country, I suggest that the island metaphor operates at two distinct levels. At one level, it demonstrates the isolation of the country in relation to the changed map of the three trans-Caucasian post-socialist independent states of Georgia, Azerbaijan and Armenia. At another level, the metaphor hints at how this isolation prompted 'the reconfiguration of basic categories of space, time and practice' that further 'urged the re-articulation of personal and national identities' (Platz 2000: 116). As noted by many of my informants, the new Armenia seemed significantly more distant from the outside world than Soviet Armenia, an irony given that Armenian independence had been driven by a desire for the opposite. Regarding the energy crisis of the 1990s, Stephanie Platz wrote:

> In wintertime, without electricity, it became dark indoors by 5:00 P.M., and families would gather around a single candle or lamp along with a single heat source or sit in total darkness to conserve resources. The length of the day

was cut in half, and night time passed unnoticed by recorded time, as activity and sight ebbed with the sun. Whereas a 1986 poll showed that 90 per cent of Armenians depended on television for news, now, without television and radio, access to news was limited, particularly because energy shortages also presented obstacles to the regular printing and distribution of newspapers. The absence of these media, which would otherwise connect Armenians to the outside (*durs*), to international time, and to each other, made distances greater both within and outside of Armenia and in making the past seem farther away in time. Where *outside* had once been the term used to refer to every place outside the former Soviet Union, it now came to include all former Soviet territories outside of the Republic of Armenia. Armenians, 'inside', felt cut off from the 'outside' world and from each other. With phone lines down and without transportation, relatives on the other side of the city, in the nearest village, or abroad were equally far away and inaccessible. Because a transcendent connectedness had been essential to Armenian identity, changes to the familiar distances binding people, places, and things eroded perceptions and experiences of identities.

(Platz 2000: 130, emphasis original)

Almost ten years after Platz published on the shrinking insides of Armenians and twenty years after she conducted that research, I similarly came across various forms of place-making based on rearticulating the configurations of notions of distance and proximity between Armenia and the outside world. As I will contextualize in the following sections, one of the most common themes that appeared during conversations with informants in Armenia was the tendency to point out the Armenian ethnic background of historically and internationally famous personalities. Such personalities included Leonardo da Vinci, Lady Diana, Steve Jobs and former Turkish President Abdullah Gül. I sense that these popular remarks account for the 'small nation' (in Armenian: *poqr azg*) situation that developed in the wake of the Genocide and the massive political and economic transformations in the twentieth century (Shirinian 2018: 49).[1]

Clifford (2013) invites us to decipher experiences of loss and renewal, shifting past and present attachments and the social, cultural and political strategies that are active in the rearticulations of the bonds between people who claim anteriority in relation to imagined landscapes (68–9). As I explore now, a particular aspect of place-making in Armenia works against a shrinking Armenian universe, a process that precedes the collapse of the USSR. The Genocide of the early twentieth century, the period of isolation under Soviet rule and the energy crisis in the wake of the collapse of the USSR mark different historical periods in which Armenians came to understand that their connections with the world around them were cut – or, as Platz (2000) suggested, 'shrunk'. It is in this historical cycle of shrinking (after the Genocide), expanding (during the Soviet era) and reshrinking (after independence) insides that I find circulating myths to be a cultural translation of a desire of openness for a re-expanded inside or an accessible world among the citizens of Armenia. Based on the accounts of mobility of women in two cities in contemporary Armenia, the next two sections attempt to account for a reflection of these popular demands for openness and accessibility to the wider world.

Gyumri

I arrived in Gyumri on one of the coldest days of winter in early 2012. Gyumri, Armenia's second largest city with an official population of 120,000, felt like a deserted town, with empty squares and streets. In contrast to the modernist Soviet architecture of Yerevan, Gyumri's layers of building styles reflected the city's history as an urban centre that well exceeds that of the capital (Shagoyan 2011). However, again in contrast to present-day Yerevan's gleaming centre, the centre of Gyumri resembles an impoverished town, with uninhabited and collapsing buildings, dusty roads, and almost no hotels, shops or cafés. Once an important urban industrial setting, Gyumri was among the cities worst hit by the earthquake of 1988. Located near the Turkish border in north-eastern Armenia, Gyumri's pre-earthquake prosperity stemmed in part from the fact that, during the Soviet period, it hosted the only functioning border crossing in the South Caucasus.[2] There were no border crossings between Turkey and Soviet Georgia, making Gyumri a key node in the transportation of goods and people during the Soviet era. As noted earlier, the border was closed in 1993.

It was in Gyumri that I observed the concurrent impacts of the 1988 earthquake, closed borders and depopulation, processes that have characterized Armenia's transformation since 1990. When I visited Ani in her miniscule Soviet-style apartment on Tigran Mets Avenue in the city centre, she was busy heating the room where she lived, cooked and slept with her gas stove. There was no central heating in her building anymore and she had no other way of dealing with the freezing cold. Although only in her mid-sixties, Ani looked much older. She had sought work in Istanbul about a decade before we first met. She had lived in Istanbul as an undocumented migrant for five years before being deported back to Armenia in 2009. Before the collapse of the USSR, Ani had worked at a Soviet holiday resort for an Armenian workers' union. When the business shut down in the early 1990s, she had been lucky to find employment in Gyumri as a local guide for the influx of American bureaucrats and international development professionals. However, this job was not sufficiently lucrative and did not last long. As a result, she left for Istanbul in the early 2000s in order to earn the money required to provide medical care for her then dying husband. Although at the time Ani could have travelled between Turkey and Armenia relatively easily, the cost of his medication meant that she did not return to Gyumri even once during her first five years in Istanbul, in order to avoid spending time and money on renewing her ninety-day visa.[3] When she finally decided to visit her husband after five years in Istanbul, she was deported from Turkey as she had overstayed her visa. She expected deportation; however, what she did not know was that she was never to return. Following deportation, Ani fully expected that she would be denied re-entry into Turkey for a specific period of time, but she did not expect the fine she would need to pay if she wanted to re-enter. This prohibitive fine prevented her from returning to Turkey after what had been planned as a short visit to Gyumri. When her husband eventually died of his terminal disease, she gave up on the idea of going back to Istanbul for good. In the ten years since she had first travelled to Istanbul, Ani was only able to take care of her husband and was not able to save any money; this was the main reason for the serious financial hardships she faced at the time of our meeting.

When I asked her how she had decided to go to Istanbul in the first place, Ani explained that it was the cheapest option. All she needed to do was get on a bus that cost less than 100 US dollars at the time of her travel. She had a couple of friends who had left for Istanbul, and, after consulting them, she too decided to seek work in the Turkish metropolis. It did not take long for Ani to find a job in Istanbul. When she moved in with her friends in Kumkapı, she was introduced to a network of employers and employees; in less than a week, she found a job at a restaurant for shopkeepers (in Turkish: *esnaf lokantası*) in Istanbul's Grand Bazaar. The restaurant was owned by a Kurdish man who was himself a migrant from south-eastern Turkey. Ani told me that she waited tables, chopped and peeled vegetables, and delivered lunch or dinner to the stall and workshop owners in and around the Bazaar. She quickly gained the trust of those she worked with, so much so that shop owners would leave the keys of their businesses with her to open and close the shops or ask her to transport jewellery or money between shopkeepers. Eventually, one of the shop owners asked Ani to work as a full-time housekeeper in his home, a multi-storey building that consisted of apartments that belonged to different members of his family. Ani accepted the job, which also allowed her to save on rent and utilities as she was able to stay in the building with the family.

Ani told me that this marked the beginning of her best time in 'Constantinople' (see the similarity with the narrative of another informant portrayed in the next chapter). Upon using Istanbul's former name, Ani looked into my eyes and asked whether I had heard the word Constantinople before. She explained that before the Genocide, the city boasted more Armenians than any other in the world. Turks, Ani went on, changed the metropolis's name to Istanbul after they had killed the Armenians and sent the Greeks into exile. She added that I should keep in mind the fact that Istanbul was still home to the largest concentration of Armenians in the world; in the streets, there were millions of them. Most did not know about their Armenian origins as they were Islamicized after the Genocide, but this didn't matter as it was in their blood. This presence was the main reason why Ani always felt comfortable and secure in Istanbul; every time she looked into people's eyes she could feel an affinity in their faces. For her, these were Armenian faces.

In her new job Ani had very little free time. Nevertheless, she was highly satisfied with her employment as a live-in domestic worker. She no longer needed to think about rent, utilities or food. Moreover, she had a very good relationship with her employers. Ani felt a sort of affinity with them from the first moment she met them. She identified them as an Armenian family from Rize, in the north-east Black Sea region of contemporary Turkey. As she talked, two things caught my attention. First, it was apparent that none of the members of the family she worked for had Armenian names. The man who hired her was called Yusuf, his brother was Süleyman and another brother was named Mustafa, all Quranic names. Their father had passed away years ago, their mother's name was Ayşe and they all married women with Muslim names from the same region. However, from the beginning Ani made it clear that this was an Armenian family. When I voiced my confusion – why would an Armenian family have Muslim names? – Ani provided more evidence. The mother of the family, she explained, attended an Armenian church on some Sundays, as well as for Easter and Christmas services, but her sons never did. She owned a Bible written in Armenian, while her sons had Bibles in Turkish in their bedside drawers. However, the entire family also practised salah (in Turkish, via Farsi: *namaz*, or daily prayers), one of the five pillars of Islam and an obligatory religious duty for all Muslims, at home and at mosque (especially on Fridays), and fasted during the holy Islamic month of Ramadan. For Ani, the family were devoted Christians only; to me they seemed to have mixed religious practices.

By the time Ani told me that she had attended the Islamic circumcision ceremony of her boss's son in their village of origin in Rize, I already had an extended list of the family's blend of diverse religious practices in my notebook. Clearly they practised Islam in public; however, their religious practices did not necessarily follow a private-public divide. The mother of the family went to church, and the entire family continued praying five times a day and fasting in the month of Ramadan even when they were out of other people's gaze. One possible explanation is that this family was an Islamicized Armenian family that converted after the 1915 Genocide. Another possibility is that they were Hemshins, an Armenian-speaking Muslim population from the Black Sea region of Turkey that has confounded academic and popular attempts to define what it means to 'be Armenian', both in Armenia and in Turkey (see Benninghaus 2007; Hovannisian 2009; Kaya 2014). When I asked her whether the family was officially registered as Muslim or Christian (the Turkish state continues to retain the religious affiliation of individuals in its databases), Ani did not know the answer, while at the same time reminding me that they were nevertheless Armenians. Ani never asked the family about how they identified themselves, but she had her own precise point of view. I will analyse her point of view only after I introduce Mariam in the next section, who lived in Hrazdan at the time of research.

Hrazdan

The city of Hrazdan was founded at an altitude of 1675 metres in 1959 on the site of the former village of Akhta. Built on principles of Soviet urbanism, the city resembled a clustering of villages centred around the Kentron neighbourhood with Soviet-style apartment blocks and administrative units. When I first travelled there on a cold spring day in 2012, it took me roughly an hour from Yerevan by bus. Many people, especially university students, commuted between the two cities every day on buses and marshrutkas. The commuter trains that once operated between Sevan and Yerevan with a stop in Hrazdan no longer ran, and the train station was dilapidated. However, unlike most other post-industrial towns I visited in Armenia, Hrazdan still had some industry. Some factories were abandoned, but the skyline was dominated by the smoking chimneys of cement and chemical factories and a thermal power plant.

I was introduced to Mariam, a young woman in her mid-thirties, through my friend Parandzem, who was also from Hrazdan. Both Mariam and Parandzem lived in the southern districts of the city, a residential zone largely comprising small houses with gardens. Like most people from Hrazdan, their families had arrived in Armenia as Genocide survivors. Before 1915, they had lived in a provincial town on the other side of the Armenian-Turkish border, facing Mount Ararat from the south-west. Parandzem was now a student at Yerevan State University and lived with her parents and sister. Mariam, also single, lived with her parents on the same street as Parandzem and, at the time of research, had recently started shuttle-trading. I had met Parandzem at a meeting of journalists from Armenia and Turkey in Yerevan, where she was employed as a translator between Armenian and English, and from time to time she helped me with translations during interviews I conducted for my research.

Mariam wanted to meet me at Parandzem's house. However, before our first face-to-face encounter, she requested over the phone that I keep the fact that I was about to interview her a secret. She didn't want anyone else to know that she had agreed to meet a foreign man at her friend's house. As I was waiting for Mariam, Parandzem's mother started to prepare some food, snacks and dried nuts, and poured us some vodka. Like other hosts I met in Armenia, Parandzem's mother was very hospitable and kind. When she finally took her seat at the table, she told me that she was impressed by the way I spoke Armenian. I thanked her and she responded that she was particularly surprised that I had learned Armenian in Istanbul. Prior to our meeting, she noted, she had not known there were Armenian schools in Istanbul or Turkey. In response, I told her while there were indeed Armenian schools in Istanbul, I had studied Armenian in London. She asked me why I had preferred London to the Armenian schools of Istanbul. I told her I had learned Armenian for my London-based PhD research and added that, as a non-Armenian, I wouldn't have qualified to study at an Armenian school in Istanbul. My answer shocked her. Parandzem then joined our conversation from the other side of the table and asked me whether I was *really* not Armenian. At the time of our meeting at her house, she had known me for more than a year. I thought I had been clear and honest about my Turkish background throughout my research. At least that was my impression. Something was wrong.

At that point Parandzem's father and sister joined us and we switched from Armenian to English. She told me she thought I had an Armenian grandmother, *like almost everyone else in Turkey*. When I said that this wasn't true in my case, she became upset. She remembered a scene in which I had been talking to friends from a circle of university students in Yerevan. She quoted me speaking of the diversities of being Turkish in contemporary Turkey, with me saying that most Turks did not know about their own family histories. I remembered the conversation she was referring to and realized that my efforts to account for the diverse ways of being Turkish had produced confusion about my own family background. Parandzem's assumption of my Armenian origins was related to how contemporary Turks and Turkishness are perceived in Armenia. In first-time encounters, I often found myself being asked, 'Are you *really* not Armenian?' or 'Are you a *real* Turk?'

There was a multiplicity of ways in which the question was formulated, but the most common was whether I was a 'pure' Turk (in Armenian: *makur Turk es?*). People responded variously upon finding out that I was a real or 'pure' Turk. In Parandzem's case, she treated me with her usual care for the rest of the day but turned down all of my future requests to meet; I have not seen her since.

Mariam showed up in Parandzem's kitchen just in time for our scheduled interview. My first impression was that she was a modest woman in her late twenties, wearing a very simple outfit. She seemed distant and a bit nervous. We made our way into the living room, in Parandzem's company, taking our seats around a tiny table set with a pot of tea, dried fruits and nuts. The homemade apricot vodka and a small bowl containing different brands of cigarettes were left behind on the kitchen table, where the rest of the family, including the father, remained seated. As we started to talk, Mariam again wanted to make sure that this interview would be kept secret among the three of us. Very few people around her knew that Mariam was shuttling goods between Istanbul and Armenia. Only a few friends and close family members knew about her transnational trading enterprise and she clearly wanted to keep it that way. Mariam would tell people that she was visiting her sister in Yerevan for a few days when she was in fact travelling to and from Istanbul. She explained that in a small city like Hrazdan, most women shuttling goods between the two countries were subject to various forms of suspicion. There were rumours about female shuttle-traders who had suddenly become rich; everyone believed that their fortunes were a product of sexual relationships with Turkish men rather than entrepreneurial skill. This is why Mariam never sold the goods she purchased from Istanbul in Hrazdan. She had contacts with a couple of shop owners in Yerevan and would always consult them about what was needed before departing for Istanbul.

When I asked Mariam whether she felt comfortable in Istanbul, she said that the city filled her with anxiety. Similar to Ani, whom we met above, Mariam believed that many people in Turkey were of Armenian origin, even if they didn't know it. However, unlike Ani, Mariam did not see familiar faces in Istanbul. Although she believed that many Turks were unconscious or amnesiac Armenian converts to Islam, this particular account of history did not translate into contemporary affinity. She explained that the primary reason she did not feel comfortable in Istanbul was Turkish men. During her frequent stays in Istanbul, she always found herself fearful of their eye contact and avoided verbal communication on the streets. She was not comfortable communicating with the men who worked in the textile shops she visited, either. She often found physical contact with these men, unintentional or otherwise, difficult to bear. In many ways, Mariam intentionally minimized contact with others, pretending she was talking on the phone, for instance, so that men would not bother her during her visits to Istanbul.

At the time of research, Mariam was relatively new to the business of shuttle-trading and only visited Istanbul once a month, though she believed that she would need to visit more often in the near future. Similar to the other female shuttle-traders I met, she had very limited time in Istanbul and only stayed for two nights each visit. However, even if she had more time, she was quite uninterested in anything besides business. When I asked her whether she had visited Kumkapı, she looked very disturbed. She knew about the neighbourhood as the place where most Armenian migrants lived and had been advised by other female Armenian shuttle-traders to avoid it (see previous chapter). She believed that the people who lived there were dangerous and prone to taking the 'wrong path' (in Armenian: *skhal janabar*) in life, an expression with a moral connotation that goes beyond the meaning of 'going off the rails' in English. While her expression reminds me of Ingold's (2011) perspective on the 'way of life' that people follow, which is 'a prescribed code of conduct, sanctioned by tradition, that individuals are bound to observe in their day-to-day behaviour' (162; see Tilley 1994: 30 for a similar analogy), I find that there is a physical and temporal aspect of travelling behind her moral sentiment. Laleli, the shuttle-trading hub in walking distance of Kumkapı, was the only place Mariam visited in Istanbul; it was there that she stayed (at hotels with other business women) and visited the shops that mostly operated within networks of business between Turkey and the post-socialist world. Her approach to maintaining a physical and moral distance between herself and Armenian migrants in Istanbul was similar to that of other shuttle-traders I met en route to Turkey.

I argue that the main reason for shuttle-traders like Mariam to claim that the migrants were more prone to going astray lies in differences in terms of their mode of travelling to Turkey. For instance, Mariam's experience within the urban landscape of Istanbul was rather limited in terms of time and space in comparison to more settled migrants. Like most other shuttle-traders, she only spent a few days at a time in the city, albeit at regular intervals. As portrayed in the previous chapter, for all shuttle-traders, these business-oriented journeys required meticulous calculations and management of time. However, they all noted that they deliberately avoided both Kumkapı and the migrants who lived there.

I observed that Armenian shuttle-traders positioned themselves as moral beings by constantly comparing themselves with migrants, articulating a sense of difference from them. Their emphasis on their own morality was often a reflection of how they made sense of wider transnational politics, dispersions and shifts in the world economy (Wanner 2005; Osella and Osella 2009; Marsden 2015; Bloch 2017). This is how and why their articulations and expressions of morality should be viewed within larger frameworks, by following what Caroline Humphrey and Ruth Mandel (2002) advised on taking into account longer and earlier histories of production and trade (reflected in the sexual division of labour and local entrepreneurial traditions) in studying 'transition' from state communism to capitalism (4). As noted in the previous chapter, the collapse of the USSR and emergence of new borders created opportunities for trade (Humphrey 2002; Marsden 2017), which emerged as a source of income, especially for women (Dudwick 2002: 239). The departure of men searching for work in urban centres led post-socialist women to look for economic opportunities elsewhere (Heyat 2002: 30). Women's secondary position in the labour market within the former Soviet Union paradoxically made them more flexible in adapting to petty trading in the new capitalist economic framework (Dudwick 2002: 238). However, post-socialist women who trade 'often articulated a sense of shame about the ways in which their new professions had forced them to make fundamental philosophical changes in their lives' (Bloch 2017: 64). In the context of post-socialist Bulgaria, Kaneff (2002) observed that an individual's moral stance towards trade was shaped by her employment before the collapse of the Iron Curtain (47). For instance, farmers were more easily inclined to find new ways of making a living through trade than low-ranking bureaucrats like former teachers. In post-socialist Russia, the acute confrontation between capitalist trade and socialist values has played an important role in defining citizens as moral (Humphrey 2002: 72–3). In post-socialist Moldova, for example, Bloch (2017) noted that traders have had to unlearn, or at least disregard, the rules for being good socialists in the process of becoming 'good capitalists' (58). As in the case of Mariam in contemporary Armenia, Bloch's informants often hid the fact that they regularly left Moldova for business (88).

Each of the aforementioned accounts, from different corners of the former socialist bloc, also traces differences between older and younger generations. In post-socialist Armenia, I observed how the collapse of the USSR resulted in a diversification – if not divergence – of moralities between older and younger generations. I argue that these differences should be viewed in relation to ongoing discussions on how to 'be' and define an Armenian (see also the next chapters on how such discussions extended and were materialized among Armenian migrants in Istanbul). It is in this context that moral frameworks divide Armenians and paradoxically still bear the capacity to bring them together within the framework of public discussion. While divergence from and compliance with those moral frameworks can take many forms, they reflect wider practices of place-making. For shuttle-traders like Mariam, the shame of getting involved in transnational trade is always mixed with the pride of being hard-working and not abandoning 'home' despite the hardships of life (see also Kaneff 2002: 41; Bloch 2017: 67). As many shuttle-traders noted, they, unlike migrants, did not leave their families behind.

Through imagining and frequently vocalizing their moral superiorities over migrants, the Armenian shuttle-traders expressed pride in simultaneously working hard abroad and taking part in the division of labour within their families in Armenia. Due to their extended periods of absence, migrants are not seen by shuttle-traders to contribute as much to the well-being of their families. Migrants are also seen as 'investing' far less in the common good of their own nation, which, in contemporary Armenia, is widely understood as an extended family (on the notion of nation as family see Abrahamian 2006: 146–7; Shirinian 2018: 49–50). However, it has to be acknowledged that many Armenians take mobility for granted as a result of earlier histories of dispersion, diasporization and sojourning, as explored in the previous chapter. In other words, in Armenia, where both physical mobility and travelling-in-dwelling are a part of everyday life, how do we account for the articulation of moral differences between those who left and those who stayed? I suggest that there has to be a particular element of travelling to Turkey that triggers discussions of morality among Armenians. Similar to what

I presented earlier, discussions that conjoin personal ethics and travel should be understood as a form of place-making. The morality associated with the more temporary movement articulated by shuttle-traders is, I suggest, a way to make sense of and express the wider political and economic changes Armenia has gone through since the collapse of the Soviet Union. Moreover, as the next section will suggest, women's travel to Turkey has to be put into perspective within the earlier histories of mobility and especially that of the Genocide.

An ambiguous enclosure

When do imagined historical affinities translate into sources of trust? Both Ani and Mariam believe that there are millions of (Islamicized) post-genocide Armenians in contemporary Turkey. Their differences of opinion as to whether those they encountered in Istanbul were proximate or distant others index two trends among the wider cohort of my informants. In Ani's case, it has to be underlined that she used to live with a family with mixed religious practices in Istanbul. Over the course of the time she spent with this family, she closely observed how the family maintained a delicate balance between public performances of mosque attendance on Fridays, fasting during the Muslim holy month of Ramadan, and circumcision ceremonies in their village of origin and church visits in secrecy on important Armenian religious days. Based on her experience with this family, Ani's faith in the invisible bond of shared blood was reinforced. She trusted in the Turks-as-former-Armenians.

Mariam did not feel as comfortable as Ani. In addition to the limited amount of time spent in Istanbul, her anxieties should be viewed from a historical perspective in which the practices of kidnapping, rape and detainment of Armenian women by Muslim men were essential components of the Genocide and the Islamicization of Armenian women in the subsequent period (Sarafian 2001; Bjørnlund 2009; Tashjian 2009; Ekmekcioglu 2013; Altınay and Çetin 2014; Kurt 2016a). To date, intimate relationships with a Muslim man and specifically with a Turk have been understood as part of the genocidal processes in which forced marriages also took place (see Libaridian 2014). This is how the public memory of the Genocide plays a crucial role in shaping relationships between Turkish men and shuttle-trader women from Armenia.

I argue that the gendered nature of the Genocide and the particular modes of displacement – as epitomized in the death marches of women and children, and their kidnappings – generated the primary lens through which travelling is conceived by Armenian women en route to Turkey. For people in Armenia, this is not simply an act of migrating or conducting trade in just any country, and this is why my informants expect and accordingly act with a certain stigmatization that comes with travelling to Turkey. In this context, the mobility of women does not always work in a positive, liberating way on gendered power relations (Scott 1986; Braidotti 1994; Gilbert 1998; Hochschild 2000; Mahler and Pessar 2006;

Westin and Hassanen 2013; Gaibazzi 2015; Elliot 2016). This is because the public memory of the Genocide plays a crucial role in shaping relationships at two levels: first between Armenian women who travel and who do not travel to Turkey, and second between Turkish men and shuttle-trader women from Armenia. Here, especially concerning relationships among Armenians, the 'shame' of genocide and survival, which otherwise bonds them together (Nichanian 2009: 118), catalyses the emergence of a moral rift in the context of travelling to Turkey. In addition, I suggest that such moral confrontation among Armenians is possibly linked to the recent history of transformations that Armenia has gone through and its relocation within the wider world as an independent country.

In Armenia, different definitions and understandings of morality work in parallel ways in relation to making sense of a place that has been physically shaped by the Genocide and the collapse of the USSR. As Shirinian (2016) notes, two different concepts in Armenian, *aylandakutyun* (moral perversion) and *aylaserutyun* (sexual perversion), are in tense relationship. As she suggests, tracing this relationship 'through multiple sites of anxious expression can help make sense of political-economic transition as it affects nation' (23). As I construe this relationship and its immediate impact on Armenians travelling en route to Turkey, I find that it helps Armenians navigate their roles, routes and positions in an imagined cartography that has been materially shaped by the major political as well as natural catastrophes of the long twentieth century. In other words, what otherwise looks like a public discussion on what is socially acceptable and what is not tends to guide Armenians in a changing world. This is how different understandings of moral decay in contemporary Armenia – whether specifically pointing at the corrupt behaviour of bureaucrats or sexual perversion of ordinary people – 'circle back on one another' (52). In many ways they are inseparable.

In referring to the relationships between Armenian women and Turkish men, moral disapproval emerges as a 'strategy' to cope with the stigmatization that is deeply connected to travelling to Turkey. In constantly positioning themselves as morally superior to other Armenian and post-socialist women, I understand that this 'strategy of distinction' works on rhetorical and practical levels. On the more rhetorical first level, it justifies their movement between the two countries by reinstating normative gender frameworks. On the more practical second level, it guides them in 'a context of uncertainty' (Biehl 2015) by helping them position their roles as strangers, friends and business partners in an imaginative roadmap of making a living (see also Yükseker 2004 and Bloch 2017 and their conceptualization of 'strategic intimacy' between post-socialist women and Turkish men). For instance, for Anahid, presented in the previous chapter, there was a component of practicality in her moment of indirectly but publicly announcing that there was a Turkish man on the bus. She warned her female passengers from Armenia so that they could act accordingly if and when they needed to. However, for Mariam, as presented in this chapter, it appears that her 'strategy of distinction' was based on a combination of 'place-making-through-moral-justification' and a genuine concern about encountering men en route to Turkey.

Papazian (2020) notes that for Armenians from Armenia 'the Turkish "Other"' is 'reproduced and somehow further nourished' by going to Turkey (220). As noted above, the particular modes of Armenian travelling to Turkey should not only define the extent of direct relationships with the wider population of the country but also inform a gendered pattern in sensing what sets people apart. Many of the young and unmarried Armenian women I met en route to Turkey expressed concerns about meeting Turkish men in Istanbul. Within the post-socialist informal economic hub of Istanbul, most migrants and shuttle-traders from the former Soviet Union and Eastern Europe feel that they are widely perceived as hypersexualized by Turkish men (Gülçür and İlkkaracan 2000; Bloch 2017). Armenian women en route to Turkey are no exception to this and many of them note similar concerns about meeting Turkish men and conducting business in Istanbul or elsewhere in the country. I believe that, for Armenian women, crossing the border between the two countries introduces another layer in the ways these women fear that they will be perceived as 'sexually transgressive' (see Parla 2009; Bloch 2017). This is because the 'borderness' of the Turkish-Armenian border, or its border-like qualities in altering the realities it marks (Green 2012: 581), is primarily informed by the Genocide in relation to its female victims. The duality of this gendered aspect of travelling to Turkey, defined from both outside (by Turkish men) and inside (by Armenian women themselves), sets the tone of relationships between Armenian women travellers and the wider Turkish public.

The way my informants understand the post-genocide population of Turkey should reflect how they were critical of the emergence of the nation-state of Turkey (as a country of Turks), but does it necessarily reflect whether different ethnic, cultural and religious components are incorporated in their own imagery of Armenians? Ayşe Gül Altınay (2014) noted that the general tendency among Armenian elites, intellectuals and institutions in Turkey, Armenia, and the diaspora has been to follow a very narrow definition of what makes a person 'Armenian'. Language and religion have been imagined as central in this definition, although diasporic centres in the Middle East and the West prioritized them differently in relation to the political and social contexts of their host societies (Panossian 2006: 299–300). In this way, what was once a polyglot community was reshaped into a monolingual community (ibid.) and converts to Islam (and possibly to other schools of Christianity) were denied becoming Armenians. Altınay (2014) writes that narrow imaginations about the Armenian nation were based on views that took conversion to Islam and adoption of Armenian women by Muslim families as forming part of the Genocide (202). She notes that converted survivors began to disappear from historical narratives specifically in the second half of the twentieth century, when Armenian national history came to be framed around the concept of the Genocide (201).

However, what I observed in Armenia among returned migrants, deportees and shuttle-traders was not always in line with the official historical narratives that defined a person as 'Armenian'. It seems there is at least an element of ambiguity that depicts a process of 'ethno-ethnicization' (Mandel 2008), a construction of a native theory in Armenia in relation to the post-genocide Muslim population of Turkey. As a process of marking off relations in opposition to one another (Comaroff 1992: 51), detecting the historical transformations in the definitions of ethnicity consequently promises to account for the everyday practices of place-making in contemporary Armenia.[4] Following this, I argue that identifying Turks-as-former-Armenians emerges as a way of locating contemporary Armenia in historically (and perhaps future-oriented) wider worlds (including an imagined greater Armenia), with a wider inside as opposed to an enlarging outside and increasing insularity (as depicted by Dudwick 1997; Platz 2000). In contemporary Armenia 'ethno-ethnicization' reflects an 'inside-out situation' in which the direction of what 'ethnic enclosing' hints at seems to be misleading: it does not work towards an exclusive nation of Armenians and it does not work towards an inclusive community, either. Instead, it works towards even more ambiguous boundaries – a situation that in turn brings about expansion of 'insides' in politically and economically isolated and landlocked Armenia. In this case, 'the inside' does not refer to the inside of the ethnic community or the nation; it defines zones of accessibility, intimacy and connectedness among Armenians in distant places (as defined by Platz 2000).

In this context of expanding and shrinking insides, the borderlines separating the two countries could be understood 'as tidemarks that are traces of movement, which can be repetitive or suddenly change, may generate long-term effects or disappear the next day, but nevertheless continue to mark, or make, a difference that makes a difference' (Green 2012: 585; see also Green 2011). From the perspective of people in Armenia, the border with Turkey (and elsewhere) seems to be unsettled for various reasons. This is also why, in closing this chapter, I suggest utilizing the term 'diasporic native'. As construed by Clifford (2013), the term attempts to account for the constantly shifting poles of autochthony (which echoes in *we are here and have been here forever*) and diaspora (which echoes in *we yearn for a homeland*), which cannot be always mutually exclusive (76).[5] In swinging between the two poles, the metaphor of the island (and practices of mythical thinking, and desires for openness and access to the wider world) reflects a political context in which diasporization has been a historical condition of place-making in Armenia. This is not to acknowledge or suggest that a politically defined territory is home to a diaspora with a monolithic experience of diaspora formation. This is not to impose hierarchies of knowledge between myth and fact, either. To the contrary, the approach presented here attempts to show how at times nativism or claiming anteriority is heavily laden with earlier processes of displacement and subsequent settlement of others in ancestral lands (see Suciyan 2018 for a discussion on diasporization as a possible theoretical lens to locate Armenians from Turkey in relation to their history of dispossession).

In the next chapter, I continue to analyse the processes of marginalization through which notions of place-making are defined, this time by focusing on the accounts of migrants who resided in the Istanbul neighbourhood of Kumkapı at the time of research. The chapter extends the ethnography of mobility (and post-mobility) in relation to recent histories of urban decay, marginalization, earlier histories of exile and waves of migration in the context of post-genocide Turkey. Again, an important point of entry in the analysis of ethnographic material will be a very particular debate (and a dispute) on norms and values, which endows Armenians with a general 'guideline' in approaching people and making sense of the places around them in their everyday lives.

Chapter 3

MAKING CENTRES AT THE MARGINS IN TURKEY

There are two Kumkapıs in Constantinople: Inner Kumkapı and Outer Kumkapı. There are two types of news in the *Masis* [newspaper]: domestic [*nerkin*, lit. inner] and foreign [*ardakin*, lit. outer] news. One has to be careful in distinguishing the inner from the outer in the news in the *Masis*, for sometimes a woman giving birth to triplets in America could be portrayed as 'domestic' news. However, in other newspapers, if the donkey of the bread seller brays in the streets, it will be 'domestic' news. If the donkey brays inside the Patriarchate [of the Armenian Apostolic Church, located in Kumkapı] it will be community news. There is no such distinction for the people of Kumkapı. The ones 'inside' [inner Kumkapı] are never seen 'outside' [outer Kumkapı], and the ones 'outside' are never seen 'inside'. (Hagop Baronyan, *Stroll through the Neighbourhoods of Constantinople*, 2014 [1880]: 18) (my own translation from the Turkish edition and the original text in Armenian)

In the above excerpt from *Stroll through the Neighbourhoods of Constantinople*, the famous nineteenth-century Armenian satirical writer Hagop Baronian ('Baronyan' above in Turkish transliteration) deliberately confuses his readers with his concepts of inside and outside. One can translate his concepts to our contemporary thinking in at least three ways. First, his concepts refer to a distinction between Armenians and non-Armenians. Second, the concepts refer to the spatial dimension of distinction between the physical centre of the neighbourhood of Kumkapı, where the Armenian Patriarchate is located, and its immediate surrounding area where Armenians live. Third, the concepts are also based on a distinction between the local level (news concerning ordinary Armenians) and the community level (news concerning the clergy).

Rachel Goshgarian (2018), in her literary analysis of Baronian's work, writes that the author 'insists upon the distinctions between Armenians living in various neighbourhoods' of the Ottoman capital and 'ultimately paints a picture of Istanbul that is anything but uniform' (2). His account of this diverse city and heterogeneous population of Armenians reflects a specific time period in which 'inhabitants of the city experienced a series of changes, conversations and reactions related to the "modernizing" reforms' (1) that secularized and thus repositioned the Empire's non-Muslim communities in relation to their respective clergy classes (Kiliçdağı 2010: 234). It was in this context of political transformation that Baronian was amongst the first group of intellectuals who publicly criticized the religious institutions that were traditionally at the top of power hierarchies within the Ottoman political system (Goshgarian 2010). His concepts of inside and outside should thus be understood in the wake of the historical processes in which Armenians of the Ottoman Empire sought new ways of coming together as a community (see Chapter 5 for more on this political system based on faith groups).

This is how, I assume, at the very end of his paragraph Baronian sarcastically moves to assert that no such distinction exists between the inner and outer zones of Kumkapı. The distinction is in his own satirical thinking, which he purposefully puts forward in his critique of the elitism of the clergy. For him, the acknowledgement of the distinction presupposes everyday practices of encounters between the clergy and ordinary Armenians. However, in his account the inside and the outside stand worlds apart, to the extent that their occupants are almost uninformed about, and show no interest in, each other. As there is no contact between the residents of inner and outer Kumkapı, they are simply unaware of each other and of their own positions as insiders and outsiders.

Some 130 years after Baronian published his work, I observed how the contemporary residents of Kumkapı, including members of the Armenian clergy based in historical religious institutions and more recent migrants from post-socialist Armenia, are similarly positioned in various insides and outsides. As Alice Elliot (2012) notes in her PhD thesis on the conceptualizations of 'outside' in the context of central Morocco, such concepts can be considered in light of Foucault's notion of 'discursive formations' (1972), which include ideas, norms and a wider array of reference points with different meanings for different subjects but are still shared at the level of everyday communication (Elliot 2012: 72). In the context of my enquiry into the neighbourhood of Kumkapı, I propose to explore particular spatial concepts, including 'community' and 'homeland', and to account for their different meanings. As this chapter demonstrates in detail, the disputed meanings of these concepts do *not* preclude individuals from conversation with each other or the exchange of ideas. In line with the theme of the previous chapter, in the following pages I aim to explore the remaking of people (as individuals and communities) as they travel and places (as social constructions of affiliations and shifting 'borderlands' between various insides and outsides) once they are travelled to.

A 'repopulated cosmopolis'

As briefly mentioned in Chapter 1, Kumkapı is located in the south of Istanbul's 'Old City Peninsula' (Su forthcoming).[1] It is within walking distance of various neighbourhoods of different economies of tourism, wholesale trading and manufacturing. It is also within walking distance of the Emniyet bus station from which buses for Armenia and other post-socialist destinations depart.

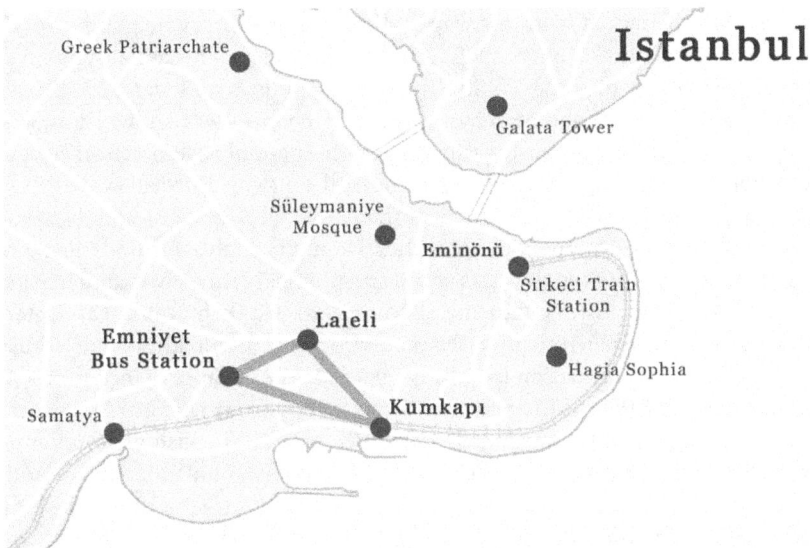

Figure 4 A Map of Istanbul's 'Old City Peninsula', with the Emniyet Bus Station, Kumkapı and Laleli.

Similar to what Baronian noted in the 1880s, the neighbourhood today still portrays sharp dichotomies. It is famous for its fish restaurants and taverns, scattered along pedestrianized cobblestone streets around the suburban train line station.[2] However, behind this façade of well-maintained tiny streets, there is another Kumkapı that is poverty-ridden and home to crumbling or abandoned buildings, closed Armenian schools, and migrants from a variety of post-socialist and post-colonial contexts. Although the neighbourhood is not geographically peripheral or classifiable as a slum, today the greater part of the neighbourhood is highly marginalized within the social topography of Istanbul.

Baronian's satirical work still resonates with the spatial organization of the contemporary neighbourhood of Kumkapı and its location(s) vis-à-vis other Istanbul neighbourhoods. One of the fundamental issues raised by Baronian's book is that insides and outsides often have a multiplicity of meanings that occasionally contradict and replace each other. As I observed in Kumkapı during my research, for instance, the Patriarchate is and is not a centre of the neighbourhood. Although it is located physically at the centre of Kumkapı, it does not have that much centrality in the lives of local or migrant Armenians. Similarly, migrants from the Republic of Armenia living in the area are and are not marginal in relation to local Armenians in the city. As many of them also claim ownership to Armenian ancestral homelands, they are involved in place-making in a particular way. The neighbourhood of Kumkapı is no different in this perspective; it is both centrally and marginally located in Istanbul and is implicated in both the 'domestic' (in Armenian: *nerkin*, lit. inner) and 'foreign' (in Armenian: *ardakin*, lit. outer) affairs of Armenians in the city. It is in this way that the contemporary neighbourhood is not a 'marginal margin' (Green 2005). On the contrary, its marginality is very much 'related to hearts of things' (ibid.) in terms of politics and wider historical processes of social and economic change. As this chapter will show, Kumkapı reveals itself as central to urban transformation in Istanbul with a century-long history of nation-building in the country, the still-ongoing Kurdish war in the south-eastern provinces, and the collapse of the USSR.

Kumkapı shares its destiny with the other Istanbul neighbourhoods located around it. Despite having been the city's social and political centres over much of its Byzantine and Ottoman history, these neighbourhoods lost their political and later their social centrality in the transition from empire to modern nation-state (Çelik 1986; Keyder 2008). This situation is directly related to the collapse of the Ottoman Empire and the relocation of the new state's capital city from Istanbul to Ankara in 1923. As the state institutions left the city and the new Turkish governments channelled funds to the construction of the new capital, Istanbul entered a period of decay and neglect that would last well into the early 1980s (Danielson and Keleş 1985; Heper 1987; Keyder 1999). The marginalization of Istanbul in relation to Ankara also brought the marginalization of neighbourhoods dispersed around the old Ottoman institutions located throughout Kumkapı. However, the decline of Kumkapı is also related to the changing demographics of the city. As non-Muslim populations such as Greeks, Jews and Armenians left the city – especially after the 1950s due to state-sponsored violence targeting them – many Istanbul neighbourhoods with considerable non-Muslim populations also entered a period of decay (Mills 2010; Soytemel 2014). However, unlike its neighbouring districts involved in production, Kumkapı has remained a predominantly residential area for migrants (Biehl 2015), again primarily due to its particular engagement with the city as well as the economy. Kurdish immigrants from eastern Turkey increasingly replaced Christian minorities in the neighbourhood from the 1980s onwards. In Kumkapı large houses formerly belonging to the Ottoman Armenian bourgeoisie were split into smaller apartments to house a growing number of Kurdish migrants and sojourners. This was in contrast to the neighbouring districts where former residential buildings were mostly transformed to house textile production and later the boom in the service economy (i.e., tourism, catering and entertainment). Today migrants from diverse places of origin live in such converted buildings where apartment sharing is the most common practice (ibid.).

The main reason why Kumkapı emerged as a migrant neighbourhood is related to the changing demographics of Istanbul in general. The contemporary population of the city has been formed by various different waves of migration over the last century, some of which I hinted at above. Until the end of the First World War, Istanbul's population experienced steady growth. As the capital of the Ottoman Empire, the city attracted large numbers of people from the provinces, so much so that population control in the city was on the priority list of its Ottoman rulers (on the macro- and micro-scale policies of demographic engineering in the Ottoman Empire, see Inalcik 1954; Zürcher 2005; Şeker 2007; Öktem 2008; Eldem 2009). As we see in Baronian's volume on Istanbul neighbourhoods, as well as in his other satirical works, the changing demographics of the city were also reflected in the constitution of social and spatial hierarchies between its residents. Istanbul in the second of half of the nineteenth century experienced a population boom and tensions between local residents and immigrants from the provinces were translated into rigidities between these aforementioned insides and outsides (Goshgarian 2010: 9).

The population of the city continued to increase during the first two decades of the twentieth century and peaked at 1.2 million following the end of the First World War. In the same time period, the total number of the Armenian population in the city reached 120,000, which included post-genocide refugees from various provinces (Johnson 1922: 18, cited in Ekmekçioğlu 2016: 4, footnote 14). This is how, unlike in the rest of Ottoman Anatolia where the Armenian population was exterminated or forced to leave, the Armenian population of Istanbul *increased* following the 1915 Genocide.

In the Republican period numerous different but chronologically overlapping waves of migration shaped Istanbul's demographic composition. To begin with, especially between the early 1940s and the late 1960s, the vast majority of the non-Muslim populations of Istanbul increasingly left for other countries. As we will see in Chapter 5, this exodus primarily developed as a response to the nationalist Turkification policies in the country, which marginalized non-Muslims economically and socially. Among these policies, the 1942 Wealth Tax, the 1955 Pogroms and the 1964 forced exile of Greeks probably had the most extensive impact on the future of these non-Muslim Istanbul populations (see Aktar 2002; Güven 2006; Suciyan 2015). In addition, a sophisticated patchwork of laws and regulations restricted former Ottoman and Turkish citizens (i.e., survivors of the 1915–16 Armenian Genocide and the non-Muslims who fled the country in the post-1923 Republican era, respectively) from settling back into their former places of residence (Akçam and Kurt 2012; İçduygu and Aksel 2013; Kurt 2016b).

For the Jews, Greeks and Armenians who remained in Istanbul, the exodus implied movement within the city. As opposed to their former dispersion all around the city, non-Muslims began to concentrate in particular neighbourhoods (see Chapter 5). In addition to the social and economic marginalization imposed by the state vis-à-vis non-Muslim populations in this era, physical marginalization produced by massive construction projects in the Old City Peninsula in the 1960s also made non-Muslims leave their historical neighbourhoods behind (Keyder 1999; Akpınar 2016), including the predominantly Armenian Kumkapı. It was following this period of physical marginalization of these neighbourhoods, and their abandonment by their former residents, that they became a source of cheap accommodation for other marginalized people from the rest of Turkey, especially Kurdish migrants fleeing political and economic instability in eastern and south-eastern Turkey (Biehl 2015; see also Yükseker 2004 on the impact of Kurdish displacement in the transformation of the neighbouring Laleli district).

I conducted research in a time period in which not only Kurds but also post-socialist migrants sought cheap accommodation in Kumkapı. As we will see later in this chapter, stigmatization of Kurdish migrants from eastern Turkey resulted in the decrease in the demand for accommodation in the neighbourhood. However, historically, this would not have been possible if the local Armenians had not left the neighbourhood for the diaspora or other Istanbul neighbourhoods in the previous decades. As local Armenians left and Kurds settled in the neighbourhood, a small number of women involved in shuttle-trading between Turkey and Armenia in the immediate aftermath of the collapse of the Iron Curtain found cheap accommodation here. From the late 1990s onwards, the neighbourhood increasingly attracted post-socialist migrants and sojourners looking for economic opportunities. Moreover, since the early 2010s, the neighbourhood has also attracted migrants from more distant places, such as sub-Saharan Africa, adding another layer to the population's diversity (see Biehl 2015).

In light of these waves of migration, Brink-Danan (2012) notes that the Istanbul of today cannot be considered as a 'depopulated cosmopolis' as suggested by Komins (2002). The city certainly lost large percentages of Greek, Armenian and Jewish populations; however, later in the twentieth century it became home to many other newcomers, including post-genocide Armenians from rural Anatolia (Björklund 2003). A more adequate label for contemporary Istanbul, I suggest, would be a 'repopulated cosmopolis', where neighbourhoods with non-Muslim architectural heritage are still part of the urban palimpsest and appropriated by newcomers in multiple ways. As the next chapters explore, the city is also still home to Armenians and other non-Muslims. It remains a city rich in 'asymmetrical aesthetics' in which the physical (as in tangible and artistic, and architectural) presence of these populations is not always reflected in their present numbers (Bartu 1999). The next section is centred around a similar concern of reflecting contemporary Kumkapı (and Istanbul) in a context of population movement, a periphery and a centre simultaneously in decline for some and of increasing importance for others.

Peripheral centres

As hinted earlier, there is a part of Kumkapı that attracts nobody besides the residents. Although some of the most important Armenian churches, in addition to the Patriarchate, are located in the neighbourhood, it is mostly only Armenian migrants residing here or nearby who visit the churches on the most important Armenian religious days such as Easter and Christmas. Very few Armenians from other parts of Istanbul come here for religious days, baptism ceremonies or weddings. They prefer churches or community spaces for those purposes in their own neighbourhoods, such as Kurtuluş, Yeşilköy or Kadıköy. As increasingly more Armenians from Istanbul send their children to non-Armenian schools, there is only one Armenian school, the Bezciyan Primary and Secondary School, still in operation in this neighbourhood (but see one exception to this example below). Due to the shrinking numbers of the local Armenian population in Istanbul, this is part of a general trend as other schools located elsewhere in the city have also closed.

Consequently, once a centre for Armenians from Istanbul, Kumkapı is now not an integral part of their lives. It is *in practice* located at the margins of their city, even if it remains *symbolically* important within their heritage narratives. However, for migrants from the Republic of Armenia, Kumkapı is *practically* the centre of their social, economic and everyday affairs, even though it does not have a *symbolic* value for them such as it does for the Armenians from Istanbul. Taşçı (2010) notes that the Armenian Patriarchate in the neighbourhood does not provide migrants 'systematic support in terms of accommodation, rent assistance', or 'any spiritual support particular to the migrants in cases such as marriage, baptisms or funerals' (125). Moreover, at the time of this research, marriage ceremonies of migrant couples were not allowed in the Armenian Apostolic Church on the grounds that civil marriage is a prerequisite of religious marriage in Turkey (ibid.). Hence, undocumented migrants, who cannot have a civil marriage in Turkey in the first place, are precluded from marriage in the Church. This situation is directly related to how the Patriarchate was acknowledged as the only official interlocutor for the Armenian community by Turkish governments in the post-Ottoman period (Özdoğan et al. 2009). Similar to Armenian schools and hospitals, the Church also distanced itself from undocumented migrants for the sake of protecting its interests at the state level (Körükmez 2012: 160).

When asked in a newspaper interview whether migrants sought assistance from the Patriarchate, Patriarch Mesrob II responded that:

> up until two to three years ago, they [the migrants from Armenia] used to approach us for financial aid. We would investigate [their situation] and help them by covering their transportation costs if they were stranded without any money to go back to Armenia. Soon we realized that they were going until Samsun and Trabzon, getting off the bus, and coming back to Istanbul. We decided not to assist them financially anymore.
>
> (5 August 2006, *Hürriyet*; my translation)

Later in the interview the Patriarch was asked about the main motivation for Armenian migrants to settle in Kumkapı. He responded that Kumkapı was one of the cheapest neighbourhoods of Istanbul and the location of the Patriarchate did not play a role (ibid.).

At the time of my research in 2011–12, Kumkapı was still a relatively cheap neighbourhood to live in, but rental prices were increasing. None of my migrant informants stated that the location of the Armenian Patriarchate played a crucial role in their decision to settle in the neighbourhood. Based on interviews among migrants who had lived in the neighbourhood for relatively longer periods of time (as opposed to 'newcomers'), I argue that the initial emergence of the neighbourhood as a suitable place to settle was based on economic reasons. For Armenian migrants from Armenia, the fact that Kumkapı was historically an Armenian neighbourhood with the Patriarchate at its centre did not play a role in their decision. The main parameter for their decision to settle in the neighbourhood lies in the constitution of margins elsewhere in Istanbul, Turkey and the world.

The transformation of a nearby neighbourhood into a hub of transnational trade in Istanbul also reflects a similar situation.

As indicated in the previous section, Laleli, a neighbourhood in walking distance of Kumkapı and Samatya, where the Armenian Patriarchate and the Emniyet bus station are respectively located, emerged as the centre of shuttle-trading in Istanbul. The majority of shops visited by shuttle-traders from Armenia and other parts of the post-socialist world in Istanbul are located here. Deniz Yükseker (2004, 2007), in her work on shuttle-trading between Russia and Istanbul, argues that transnational business networks between producers and traders are formed through particular processes of marginalization in their 'home' settings: Kurds from eastern Turkey (i.e., the producers) and citizens of post-socialist countries (i.e., the traders) responded to political conflict and the collapse of waged labour markets by seeking economic opportunities elsewhere, including in Istanbul (for a similar account on Gagauz migrants from southern Moldova in Istanbul and Moscow, see Bloch 2014; see also the previous chapters). This is how Laleli, a formerly decaying neighbourhood, became a meeting place for migrants and shuttle-traders in Istanbul.

The exodus of the majority of non-Muslims from Istanbul first resulted in the abandonment of particular neighbourhoods located in Istanbul's Old City Peninsula.[3] Neighbourhoods like Kumkapı and Laleli were then occupied by rural migrants, especially those of Kurdish origin, from the 1980s onwards, adding another layer of marginalization of these neighbourhoods in the minds of the urbanized middle class of the city. This is why Laleli's emergence as a business hub and Kumkapı's as a residential migrant neighbourhood have to be understood in relation to these waves of marginalization, depopulation and repopulation.

In Berlin's migrant enclave of Kreuzberg, Ruth Mandel writes about how the neighbourhood simultaneously emerged as a centre and periphery:

> In this new place, by their own actions and decisions, they [migrants from Turkey] are setting new precedents, as they project agency of their own design, reshaping the Kruezbergs of Europe into novel and heterogeneous communities. It is in the recognition of an alternately constructed center that the Turks are able to seek positive identifications. Paradoxically, however, this center is located in a peripheral place vis-à-vis Turkey, the original affective orienting center. Thus, the longer the migrants live in the 'peripheral center,' the greater its prominence and the more of a competing threat it poses to the traditionally central role occupied by Turkey.
>
> (Mandel 1996: 163–4)

Here, Kreuzberg is a 'peripheral centre', a process in which the neighbourhood is increasingly positioned as more significant than what was once a centre, Turkey. However, Kreuzberg is still a periphery, given its physical condition and social marginality in relation to the rest of Berlin. The situation of Kreuzberg in Berlin resembles that of Kumkapı in Istanbul in a number of ways. On the one hand, I take the liberty to define Berlin as another 'repopulated cosmopolis' to stress how the post-Holocaust city went through various waves of labour migration from Turkey and other countries, as well as accommodating German-speaking populations from former socialist countries (see Rapaport 1997; Mandel 2008).[4] It is in this sense that the making of centres and peripheries in the two cities has been historically based on the depletion of particular communities and the arrival of successors in their place. On the other hand, similar to Kreuzberg and probably many other migrant neighbourhoods around the globe, Kumkapı is simultaneously a 'peripheral centre' – a direct result of its demographic transformation and the subsequent deterioration of its physical condition in relation to other neighbourhoods in the city – and a 'central periphery', for its contemporary migrant residents and the politics and the economy they aggregate.

The following ethnographic fragment captures a specific moment in which these centres and peripheries come into existence, and are displayed, through articulations of affiliation with people and particular places.

Meeting Hranoush

The first time I met Hranoush and her friend Hayk was at a café located in the heart of Kumkapı. That evening, the café was busy with customers, all speaking different languages. I heard the waitress approaching most of them in Russian. When she came to our table, she spoke to Hranoush in Turkish and Hayk in Russian. When I asked about her fluency in Russian, she said that her mother was from Turkmenistan and had come to Istanbul after the collapse of the USSR. The waitress's father was Turkish, her parents having met in Istanbul; she was fluent in Russian, Turkmen and Turkish. At the café, I observed that most customers were from different parts of the post-socialist world. I heard Russian, Azeri and Armenian all at our table. Some other customers spoke Kurdish.

Hayk hardly uttered a word during our meeting and did not look like he was in a particularly good mood. Later I learned that he was a famous folk singer in Armenia. He had received the Armenian Music Award for best album in Los Angeles in the early 2000s. Hayk had lived in the United States for a while, and, when he came back to Armenia, he looked for jobs but could not find any. He travelled to different parts of Russia for construction work, but at the same time kept performing music as a source of income. He gave concerts in major cities with Armenian migrants in Georgia, Ukraine and Russia. In the end, he decided to visit his sister, who lived in Istanbul and was best friends with Hranoush. At the time of our meeting, he was still looking for a job in the city.

Unlike Hayk, Hranoush was very talkative. She was in her mid-fifties, single, and had lived in Turkey for over a decade. She was fluent in Turkish and so our entire conversation took place in Turkish. We ordered coffee and a slice of cake for the three of us to share, but none of us wanted to be the first to taste the cake. While the cake sat untouched, Hranoush turned to me and asked why I was interested in meeting her. Without waiting for an answer, she told me she knew why; I wanted to know, she contended, why she had decided to come to Turkey in the first place.

Again without waiting for an answer, Hranoush explained that she came to Turkey because it was her *memleket*, a term that simultaneously refers to a specific place of origin (as in a town or a province) and a wider ancestral homeland (as in a country) in Turkish.[5] She added that she *felt very much at home* in Turkey. Her family was from the villages of the Sassoun Province of the Ottoman Empire, now called Batman and today a predominantly Kurdish area of south-eastern Turkey. She told me that during the Genocide years, half of her family had headed east and ended up in Kars, a city then under Russian control. They later moved from Kars to Armenia. The other half of Hranoush's family ended up in Syria and Lebanon. A handful of other relatives were dispersed around Anatolia; some made their way to Istanbul.

Hranoush was born in the Soviet Republic of Armenia. She was an actress in the state theatre in a provincial town in the west of the country, close to the Turkish border. She told me that, while she objected to much under 'Russian rule', 'the Soviets nevertheless provided Armenia with culture', particularly in terms of arts and literacy. She added that Turkey as a country should not compare itself with Russia as a world power; Turkey, in her opinion, lacked 'the culture' to realize a parallel global status. Then she talked about how she had decided to come to Turkey a decade ago, and how she decided to stay. She told me that after coming to Istanbul she still wanted to act, even for free, but she could not find a single Armenian theatre willing to give her an opportunity. She asked for help from Armenian artists and private theatres, but they all turned her down on the grounds that her Armenian was not good enough: Hranoush speaks Eastern Armenian, as opposed to the Western Armenian spoken by local Armenians in Istanbul that is hegemonic in the city's Armenian cultural scene. She was indignant.

A sudden move by Hranoush abruptly put a halt to our conversation. She turned around and started to shout in Armenian at the couple sitting at the table just behind us. Until that moment, I had not realized that there were others from Armenia in the café. The couple being berated by Hranoush consisted of a woman in her late thirties and a man who looked about a decade younger. Hranoush yelled at the pair, asking them how they dared to talk about sex so explicitly and shamelessly in a public space. The young man replied that they were not in Armenia but in Turkey, and he could not have known whether there were Armenians around or not. He said that it was impossible to check every person every time, and added that Hranoush should mind her own business. Hranoush got even more furious at his response and replied that it didn't matter; whether in Armenia or any other place, people should never talk like that. The young man again insisted that he couldn't have known whether there were Armenians around and pointed his finger at me, asking whether we were all Armenians at our table. Before I had a chance to speak, Hranoush replied that everyone at our table was Armenian.

The fight was over in a few minutes, but it was hard to calm Hranoush. She started speaking to herself in Russian without looking at me or Hayk. This monologue in Russian went on for a few minutes. Then she turned to me and told me how sorry she felt about the situation. She apologized again and again, and told me that I was 'the guest' and it was not nice to have fights in front of guests. She explained to me that it was unacceptable for such a young man to talk about such things with a woman, a woman older than him. For her, the couple's sexualized chatter was evidence not of a love affair but a monetary relationship. The woman, in Hranoush's eyes, could only have been a prostitute. She told me that she didn't understand where these people came from. She believed that they were all ignorant, just like the Turkish and Armenian middle classes in Istanbul, for whom she worked as a cleaner. She continued speaking in a mix of Turkish and Russian:

> They are all *bezkulturny* (in Russian lit. uncultured)… *bezkulturny*… *bezkulturny*… *bezkulturny*… these people behind me and the young people for whom I do cleaning. They have money, but they don't have a single shelf of books. I remember my father, we had three walls full of books: one wall for Russian classics, one for Armenian classics, and one for world classics. He was a true Soviet man. But where do all these people come from? Where? These people cannot be Armenians. I am so sorry for this.

Then she turned to Hayk, and started to speak exclusively in Russian. Hayk hardly replied, only nodding. She told me in Turkish that she needed a cigarette. After a couple of minutes of silence, she apologized once again, not about her own actions, but about what those other people had done. She said once again that it was not nice to have these kinds of situations arise in front of guests. Suddenly it occurred to me that I could perhaps improve her mood by fulfilling my responsibilities as a guest; for this reason, I took a bite from the slice of cake that had remained untouched on the table until that moment. She was very pleased.

I want to analyse the above in terms of three separate modes of encounter involving Hranoush. The first is between Hranoush and me, a Turkish man; the second is between Hranoush and a younger generation of migrants from Armenia; the third involves Hranoush and the middle-class Armenians from Istanbul for whom she works. All three encounters are informed by two interrelated processes. At one level, these encounters show the everyday articulations of imagined centres and more personal peripheries. They also demonstrate how imagined centres and their margins are appropriated on a daily basis. In the next section, I attempt to account for the particular processes in which these centres are defined at their respective margins.

The two imagined centres I would like to discuss in this book can be best described by the totalizing terms of 'community' and 'homeland'.

Fear of the unknown: 'Where do all these people come from?'

There are various differences at play among migrant populations in Kumkapı. Biehl (2015) suggests approaching the neighbourhood as a context of 'superdiversity' – a term that Steven Vertovec (2007) used in order to account for differences of religion, gender, ethnicity, migration history and legal status within and between migrant populations. The term aims to account for the differences not only *between* migrant communities but also *among* their members. Over the course of my research in Kumkapı, I observed how differences in gender and generation among Armenian migrants produced particular outcomes. For instance, in expressing her disappointment with the younger couple behind us, Hranoush asked 'Where do all these people come from?' Her question was not only directed at the particular couple that occupied the table behind us; she was also making a point in relation to the younger generation of migrants in general. The differences between the younger and older migrants should be understood in relation to the transformation of moral frameworks in the post-socialist era (Humphrey and Mandel 2002; Wanner 2005; Bloch 2017), which often reflected itself in episodes of 'moral panics' in Armenia (Shirinian 2016: 25 citing Cohen 2002 [1972]; see also previous chapter). While for many older Armenian migrant women the moral frameworks in which they were raised as Soviet citizens were still intact, younger post-socialist women in Istanbul tended to consider their work and life as 'an escape from the confining socialist structures and gender ideals of the past' (Bloch 2017: 16). Within this moral framework, Hranoush's reaction towards the younger couple was informed by how she situated herself as an Armenian in relation to other Armenians around her. As in many ways morality is a guideline for individuals to express bonds and affiliations, migrant superdiversity in Kumkapı challenged Hranoush to articulate what she and others shared in common.

These differences among migrants resulted in particular urban anxieties that limited Armenians of different ages and social backgrounds from socializing with one another. However, these differences also helped them navigate their roles and positions in a diverse social environment. Susan Pattie (1997), in her detailed account of the development of the post-genocide Cypriot Armenian community in Cyprus and later London, notes that 'fear of the unknown' was a significant emotional aspect of encounters among Armenians (70). This is why, she argued, many Armenian newcomers to Cyprus more readily started friendships with Turks, whom they found more familiar, than with resident Armenians or Greeks. If I follow the emotive framework presented by Sarah Ahmed (2004: 63–6), fear should imply a realization of a direct threat based on the approach of a moving object or a person. I also believe that the feeling should point at the sudden familiarization of the object, not the consolidation of its unknown qualities. In this sense, 'fear of the unknown' implies a moment of rupture from anticipation, or similarly from projection of the self in future settings, by way of transforming an internal epistemological discussion into an ontological one on what is properly in place and what is out of place. This discussion on the social positionings of the self and others is also reflected in the sentiments of my informants in Istanbul, many of whom also expressed that there is much mistrust among Armenians. As reflected in Hranoush's case, there are significant perceptions of difference between older and younger Armenian residents of Kumkapı. The older generation of migrants is usually those who arrived first, while the younger generations are newcomers to the city. However, older migrants often arrived in Istanbul alone, as opposed to the younger generations, whom I observed mostly came with other family members.

Thus, while older generations had to build trust and establish friendships with the wider population of the city, this was less of an immediate imperative for younger generations. Many older migrants informed me that they preferred Turks as friends and business partners over other Armenians. However, this is mostly a rhetorical formulation of the 'fear of the unknown' as put by Pattie (1997).

The generational differences among Armenian migrants also helped me comprehend what kind of migrants they were. None of my informants from Armenia in Kumkapı stated that they came to Turkey as a place to permanently settle. However, the ways they saw their future in Istanbul varied (cf. Grigoryan 2018: 15). For the older generation, Turkey was usually – if not always – the first and only place they went for work following the collapse of the USSR. They first decided to come to Turkey for short periods of time, but when the work proved lucrative, they stayed. They all believed that they would eventually go back to Armenia to unite with their families. In cases where their families were dispersed around the world, they felt that Armenia was the place to wait for them. For younger generations, there were more options in life. They considered leaving Istanbul for Armenia, but they also frequently noted that they could eventually go somewhere else. Similar to the older generation of migrants, the younger generations also had friends and family abroad, but the latter's relative time remaining in life (i.e., younger age) made them think in more flexible terms in naming a final place to settle. In this way, the accounts of the younger generations define a migratory moment of transit; however, I do not conceive of them necessarily as transit migrants waiting for or in search of their next destination.

Earlier in the book, I argued that many Armenians en route to Turkey took mobility for granted as a direct result of the extended networks of dispersion formed by histories of trade expeditions, migration, exile and genocidal processes. While this holds valid for both older and younger generations of migrants in Istanbul, the latter group has a particular capacity to move further away. In this capacity, there is an important element of 'motility' (Leivestad 2016: 133), which puts movement in a temporal perspective and subsequently directs our attention towards understanding mobility as an open-ended process (144). As Salazar (2011) notes, migration is greatly linked to the ability of people and their social networks to imagine other places and lives (577). In the particular case of younger generations of Armenian migrants in Istanbul, those other places and lives are made possible through personal time to invest in mobility that is otherwise taken for granted. However, a recent legal change, described below, has led the younger generation to feel more settled in the city.

Biehl (2015) notes that Kumkapı is a space where migrants are continually reminded of their uncertainties, not only about their future, legal status or livelihood, but also their roles in relation to other migrants (603). One of the primary sources of concern for migrants from Armenia is their children's education and future in Turkey (Körükmez 2012: 158). This is especially the case for younger migrants, many of whom, as opposed to the older generation, brought their children to Turkey. Until 2011, it was not legally possible for migrant children to receive education in Istanbul's local Armenian schools, as the law[6] did not allow foreign nationals to receive education in Armenian, Jewish or Greek schools (6 February 2015, *Agos*). In 2003, an informal primary school was organized for Armenian migrants in the basement of Gedikpaşa Armenian Protestant Church. The school followed the curriculum of schools in Armenia, although it could not provide any transcripts or diplomas to its students. After the assassination of Hrant Dink in 2007, the school was named for him. In September 2011, the Ministry of National Education announced that non-Muslim minority schools were permitted to accept foreign nationals as 'guest students' and passed a new regulation in February 2012 to legalize this decision.[7] With the new regulation, 'guest students', who, as undocumented migrants, were formerly not entitled to official diplomas or transcripts (12 March 2012, *Radikal*), were allowed to register formally in non-Muslim schools and, it was hoped, eventually pursue university education in Turkey (21 March 2012, *Agos*). However, the new regulation did not open up this channel of higher education for 'guest students'. At the moment, undocumented migrant children are only provided with a certificate (in Turkish: *belge*) from the schools they attend, in place of official diplomas or transcripts; the certificate has little weight and does not permit entry to university.

This change in law has, nevertheless, had an impact on Armenian migrants in Istanbul, especially for younger generations. As noted earlier in this chapter, Bezciyan Primary and Secondary School is the only functioning Armenian school in the neighbourhood of Kumkapı. In an interview, one of the vice-principals of the school explained to me how the new regulation came into effect at the same time as the new regulation on visas for foreign nationals. As noted in the previous chapters, in February 2012 Turkey changed its entry requirements for foreign nationals entering the country as tourists, granting Armenian nationals visas on arrival for 30 days, with a limit of staying in the country for 90 days in a 180-day period (see also Chapter 1). These two legislative changes in 2012 produced unexpected results: as the vice-principal at the Bezciyan School noted, because it was now more difficult to go back and forth between Istanbul and Armenia, newer Armenian migrants increasingly brought their children to the city. The restrictions on their mobility forced many into an undocumented status if they wanted to stay in Istanbul, while the new regulation on education simultaneously gave them an incentive to bring their families with them.

In addition to difficulties in terms of employment, undocumented status and education, uncertainties amongst migrants in Kumkapı are also gendered. Many women from former socialist countries in Turkey believe that they are perceived as potential sex partners by Turkish men and fear being forced into sex or prostitution (Bloch 2011; Biehl 2015). However, there is another side of the story in which it is not unusual for post-socialist women to enter romantic relationships with local Turkish or Kurdish men. With almost no prospect of regularizing their status, many post-socialist women 'are keenly aware of how very much their intimate relationships with Turkish men define their experience of mobility' (Bloch 2011: 515). This is also because marriage – whether for love or convenience – has emerged as a popular strategy for residency in Turkey and eventual citizenship (ibid.; see also Biehl 2015: 600). Whether or not sexualized relations lead to marriage and citizenship, the neighbourhood of Kumkapı – along with Laleli, the shuttle-trader hub of Istanbul, and touristic areas such as Sultanahmet – is perceived as a space where such relations are realized in an otherwise conservative society (Biehl 2015: 601; see also Bloch 2017). Hranoush's outrage towards the couple should be understood within this context of uncertainties in Kumkapı. As noted, morality provides individuals with a guideline to express what they share and do not share with the people in their social environment. It also helps them navigate the movements of a diversity of actors by paving the way for a constant reiteration of what is in place and what is out of place (see Creswell 1996: 10 for a nuanced discussion).

Thinking through a community of Armenian migrants

A particular mode of informal economy operates amidst this 'fear of the unknown' (Pattie 1997) in this context of uncertainties. Writing on the relationships between Armenian migrants and Armenians from Istanbul, Taşçı argues that:

> the presence of a certain relationship, even mutual dependency, between these two groups was certain. After all, Armenian migrants were working – not solely but mostly – in the houses of Armenian families [from Istanbul]. The members of an old enclave, the Istanbul Armenians were currently surrounding those of a new one, the Armenians of Armenia. However, *it is not the ethnicity that is the main determinant of this enclosure, but the ethnic community that arises from this shared ethnicity* and the positions of its actors in the social hierarchy.
>
> (Taşçı 2010: 135–6, emphasis mine)

It is particularly the emphasized sentence in the above quotation that I find problematic. Based on the encounters taking place between Armenian migrants and Armenians from Istanbul, the sentence implies that a new ethnic community is in the process of emerging. While I recognize the attempt to account for the business/work relationships among Armenians from Istanbul and Armenian migrants, there are limitations to this approach. On the one hand, the author aims to study community-making without an ethnic lens. On the other hand, her solution does not critically engage with the 'complexities of ethnicity' because the ethnic community she looks for is based on shared ethnicity. In fact, it looks like an impossible task to realize without recognizing ethnicity's vast array of definitions, which I attempt to tackle below. Instead, I argue that rather than a sense of shared community, Armenians from Armenia and Istanbul are acutely aware of (and at pains to demonstrate) the differences between them. Emphasizing what is *not* shared plays a significant role in reproducing both as distinct communities.

In *Cosmopolitan Anxieties*, Ruth Mandel (2008) pointed to the danger of reducing ontogeny to essentialist ontology. She wrote that 'one of the central problems with many ethnicity theories is that an a priori assumption regarding the ontological significance and primacy of ethnicity says little about the particulars of its history or onto[ethno]genesis' (84). Although here I follow the self-ascriptive method, identifying Armenians as individuals who consider themselves Armenians, I nevertheless find it important, following Mandel's lead, to ask what defining 'Armenian migrants' in Istanbul as an 'Armenian migrant community' tells us about the particulars of its history and its onto[ethno]genesis. I suggest that it does not tell us much.

I am particularly critical of the term 'ethnic' in referring to a community of Armenians – whether 'local' or migrant – in contemporary Istanbul. I sense that in Taşçı's work (2010) a group of migrants from Armenia is necessarily understood as forming an ethnic community because they share language, citizenship and country of departure. These similarities also continue in terms of work as many are employed by Armenians from Istanbul. In this view, the community formation is only assumed (and reduced) to take place along ethnic lines (see Mandel 2008: 85). I call for a distinction between the ethnic enclosing of communities (whether by researchers or community members) and the historical processes of ethnic community formation. I argue that the confusion between the two is based on limiting analytical lenses on what people share in terms of origin, instead of looking at the historical narrations of those origins. As I discussed in the previous chapter, ethnicity is productively understood as a 'process of classification' of relating things and people to one another (Comaroff 1992), and 'a domain of cognition' in which knowledge about the self, the other and the difference between the two is constituted (Brubaker 2004). It is in this sense that an ethnic community being defined through shared ethnicity runs the risk of totalizing the former, simply because consensus in the latter by the group members should precisely come after emergence of the former (as in the historical formulations of the myth-symbol narratives argued by Smith 1986, 2009; see also Paksoy 2017: 47 for a similar approach towards ethnicity in the case of Armenian migrants in Istanbul). Perhaps, as the rest of this book depicts, even consensus on the matter is not as much needed.

These views are in line with Pattie's (1997) observations on Armenians in Armenia and the diaspora. Pattie sees Armenians as a long-standing ethnos with shared institutions, people who have invested in creating a modern Armenian nation despite the great deal of disagreement on the relative importance of components of the Smithian myth-symbol complex (29). In this sense, there is a side to ethnicity that should be stressed: in its operation of relating people to one another, and hence as a process, it depends on a tension between 'what is' and 'what should be' shared by group members. The encounter between migrants at the Kumkapı café demonstrates that there is a multiplicity of ways of being Armenian. There is no consensus on what is socially acceptable. However, at the same time, the disagreements about what is and what is not acceptable for Armenians demonstrate that there is a basis for conversation. In fact, the lack of consensus on social norms and values constantly reminds Armenian migrants that they are different from non-Armenians and local Armenians in Istanbul. A similar observation was made by Fran Markowitz in *A Community in Spite of Itself* more than two decades ago. She wrote:

> Community, like language, emerges from dialogue. Indeed, community is made possible only through conversations among people who assume that they are alike, and with other societies and cultures that are viewed as alien and come to be placed along a continuum of difference.
>
> (Markowitz 1993: 5)

Markowitz added that the lack of consensus implied some sort of a 'primordial agreement' on particular issues:

> The postmodern community is a heteroglossic entity derived from talk. Because it is a symbolically constituted, socially constructed arena of debate, argumentation, challenge, enjoyment, and even agreement, it cannot be a place of unitary sameness. It is an entity formed from confrontations with otherness coupled with a historically based idea that some people are more alike than others. Even the groupwide ethnic identity that somehow persists over the centuries does not mandate uniformity, tradition, or unchangingness. Rather it signifies some sort of agreement on origins, hopes, desires, morality, knowledge, sentiment, discussion and doing.
>
> (Markowitz 1993: 260)

As elucidated by Markowitz, debates on norms and values constantly inform migrants like Hranoush about what they simultaneously share and do not share with other Armenians in the context of Istanbul. It is in this sense that 'dispute' can function as a basis for common ground among migrant populations. As observed by other researchers in the field, 'it is precisely the heterogeneity of local groups' that gives their shapes as Armenian communities (Firsov 2006: 76, quoted in Siekierski 2016: 17). It is the debate about those norms and values that challenges straightforward definitions of what identifies an individual as Armenian. Thus, disputes of this nature appear as both a catalyst of and an obstacle against community formation. As I construe the dynamics of everyday relationships among Armenian migrants, the extent to which disputes emerge as a source or obstacle to community formation depends on whether the issue in dispute is understood as a source of anxiety or not (or fear, as Pattie 1997 noted in the context of Cyprus). Biehl (2015) notes that Kumkapı is a context of uncertainties for its migrant residents, as the competition for economic gain and lack of legal status (and subsequently limited access to education, health, justice and security services) make 'trust' a difficult asset to look for in other people (see also Bloch 2017 for how 'intimacy' became a key domain of everyday practices to seek support to eliminate the possible negative effects of those uncertainties). This is why I contend that in this context of uncertainties, the making of a community of Armenian migrants is jeopardized.

I observed that neither Armenians from Turkey nor Armenian migrants constituted distinct communities, which, according to Taşçı's view, were expected to enclose one another and merge one day. In fact, both the former and the latter group were highly divided among themselves. Especially for the latter group, it is possible to argue that a population of atomized Armenian individuals lives in Istanbul, rather than an emergent community of Armenian migrants. However, before concluding this section, it is important to note that there are possible ways to see 'the community' Taşçı (2010) looked for. One way could be to focus on what is obvious – that is, what the migrants in Kumkapı share in common before everything else, a decision to leave their former place of residence. Here, I find Pattie's approach to community helpful.[8] She provided two conceptualizations of community, both of which stress departure from home as a unifying factor in the context of globally dispersed Armenians. Pattie (1997) wrote that the Armenian word for community, *kaghout*, can be understood as a state of living as strangers (or *ghariboutiune*, from Turkish/Arabic *garip*) (28).[9] In 2004, Pattie wrote that the term is believed to derive from the Semitic word for exile, *galut* (121, footnote 8). I believe these are useful conceptualizations that help to reflect on what Armenian migrants share in Istanbul as they consider their own travel histories within larger histories of Armenian diasporization and re-diasporization and tend to locate their mobility within a historical perspective of inevitable mobility (see Chapter 1 on how I identified my informants as people who took mobility for granted). However, such diasporic affiliation does not always presuppose departure from a 'homeland'. As the previous chapters argued, 'the place to return to' could be a place of former exile in history.

It is possible to continue exploring this theme of migration-settings-as-homelands in the words of Hranoush. She started the conversation by saying that she came to Turkey because 'here' was her own country or *memleket*. There were ambiguous aspects to this statement. At the beginning of our conversation, I was curious to find out whether she was talking about contemporary Turkey or Istanbul, Constantinople (that is, Ottoman Istanbul), or Armenian ancestral lands that are part of contemporary Turkey. The word she specifically used was *memleket* in Turkish, which has four related but different meanings. First, the term historically translates as 'country' (Özkan 2012: 22). This is in line with the Arabic root word, which means 'kingdom'. However, this translation sounds old-fashioned in contemporary Turkish, as with the language reform of the early Republican era, a Turkic word, *ülke*, was introduced to replace *memleket* as 'country'. This should not bring us to the conclusion that the word was abandoned; a second primary meaning provided in Turkish dictionaries defines *memleket* as 'a place where someone was born and raised'. Third, the more general sense of the term is 'the place where the family came from'. Finally, in everyday speech in a large-scale immigration context such as Istanbul, it means 'the place where the father was born, and most often where he came from'. In this last meaning, the emphasis is on the father instead of the family as a whole, necessarily implying a gendered component in imagining a place of origin. It is most often the third or the fourth meaning of the term that is used in contemporary Turkish. Hence, it implies a strong sense of migration that is not an individual experience but a collective one experienced as a family.

As this range of definitions suggests, *memleket* is much more nuanced than the totalizing notion of homeland, or its Turkish and Armenian translations, *vatan* or *yurt* and *hairenik* or *yerkir,* respectively. Demir (2012) notes in her study of Kurdish migrants from Turkey in London that the term *memleket* is always relational and positional, never referring to a fixed territory. When somebody says 'I am off to *memleket*' or 'I miss *memleket*' outside the borders of Turkey, the term can refer to Turkey; when in Istanbul, it can refer to a specific region in Turkey, or to a particular city; and in that particular city, it can refer to a smaller town or village that one's family originates from (820). In many ways, for speakers of Turkish, including Kurds and Armenians from Turkey, the term comes to define an imagined place that functions as an 'inverse mirror' (Bennani-Chraïbi 1994) 'signifying everything seen as lacking' in everyday contexts of migration (quoted in Elliot 2012: 80). However, the term often refers to a much more concrete and tangible place of origin, where the possibility of 'going back' is not terminated.

In the Armenian case, the possibility of going back to one's *memleket* – in the sense of an ancestral village – was terminated by the Genocide. Nevertheless, during our conversations, *memleket* was the only word used by my Armenian informants from Istanbul when referring to a place of origin (see Türker 2015 for how this sentiment resonates with Greeks from Istanbul). I never heard *hairenik* (or its Turkish or other Armenian equivalents) a single time when Armenians from Istanbul referred to the specific places their families left behind in various corners of Turkey.[10] Among the younger generations, the number of people who had visited their ancestral lands was very low and they often seemed uninterested; however, they also expressed that they never felt like they lived far away. In Istanbul, local Armenians were very much within the imagined and physical boundaries of their *memleket*. This does not mean that they were in denial of the fact that their bond with their places of origin was an interrupted one. They were rather making a very particular claim to other people around them in the social environment.

I will address the politics behind this claim in the following chapter. For now, I suggest that, in making this claim, by saying that she came to Turkey because it was her *memleket*, Hranoush mirrors the discourse of Armenians from Istanbul and positions herself as *not* an 'outsider' in Turkey. Especially in the first two decades after the collapse of the Ottoman Empire, nation-building processes in Turkey resulted in the remaking of Muslims as 'Turks' and non-Muslims as 'foreigners' (in Turkish: *yabancı*) (Cagaptay 2005).[11] This is why, similar to Armenians from Turkey, Hranoush's elaboration of *memleket* is relational and positional (Demir 2012), not only in terms of the physical distances between places but also regarding the imagined distances between people. For instance, in Hranoush's account, she and I share the same *memleket*. A *memleketli*, someone from the same place of origin, does not need to be Armenian. It is in this sense that the term is different from 'homeland' (and its Turkish and Armenian equivalents), as it works towards establishing affinities and similarities between people from different ethnic backgrounds. In short, *memleket* does not imply ethnic exclusivity in the way that *vatan* or *hairenik* does. In Turkish and Armenian, both equivalents of homeland are understood specifically as 'national(ized) territories' (see Tölölyan 2010; Özkan 2012).

Demir suggests that the difference between *memleket* and homeland reveals itself in the distinction between 'home' and 'house' in the English language, as the term is more deeply ingrained in the emotional component of 'home' than the material component of 'house' (2012). I believe this insight, while important, lacks an adequate explanation of the homely feeling behind *memleket* as a place of origin. *Memleket* indeed accounts for the homely feeling in the house, a familiar landscape with the material and emotional components of a house and a home, respectively. On the other hand, the distinction between *memleket* and homeland corresponds to the distinction between 'home' and 'house' as much as the former defines a personal and intimate site of relationships among inhabitants more than the generic 'house'. Demir's distinction relies on a particular conceptualization of homeland that necessarily feels like home – a claim which is contested by the narratives of my informants in the next chapter.

Chapter 4

FOLLOWING NEW ROADS IN OLD HOMELANDS

I first glimpsed Armenia from the train, early in the morning: greenish-grey rock – not mountains or crags but scree, flat deposits of stone, level fields of stone. A mountain had died, its skeleton had been scattered over the ground. Time had aged the mountain; time had killed the mountain – and here lay the mountain's bones.
(Vasily Grossman, *An Armenian Sketchbook*, 2013 [1998]: 23)

If there is a crack, instead of writing [of it] by pretending that there is not one, it is necessary to settle in it.
(Nurdan Gürbilek, *Second Life*, 2020: 92, my own translation from Turkish)

I was leading a group of Turkish and Armenian photography students in the city of Muş in Eastern Anatolia when the earth shook with a magnitude of 7.1 on the Richter scale on a late October day in 2011. The epicentre of the earthquake was the city of Van, located some 225 kilometres to the east, but before we had even turned on the television in our hotel's lobby for a glimpse of the extent of the destruction and the number of casualties, we were quite certain that it had been one of the major earthquakes that had been shaping the landscape of this mountainous region over the millennia. Not long after we had met our need for cigarettes and caffeine to briefly celebrate our 'survival' after the first shock, the participants from Armenia began receiving phone calls from family members and friends who wanted to confirm their well-being. As we came to the realization that the earthquake had also shaken Yerevan – which, at 210 kilometres, was located even closer to Van than Muş was – the border between these two countries acquired a new, albeit temporary, meaning that was informed by its superimposition as a line that altered daily realities (see Green 2012: 581). As I will revisit the particular reflections of this border demarcation in the following pages, I need to also note that among the participants from Turkey, almost all of whom were from Istanbul, only one received any phone calls at all. For our families and friends, the city of Muş, as is widely the case with the predominantly Kurdish eastern and south-eastern provinces of post-genocide Turkey, was simply impossible to locate on a map. As I will argue in the following pages of this chapter, the disconnectedness of Muş not only points at earlier histories of displacement, dispossession and death but also further shapes a very particular form and mode of travelling in and around the city. I accordingly take the city (and its surroundings) as a medium of historical arguments on space (Creswell 1996: 152) that specifically operate through the practices of movement and 'trail following' (Ingold 2011). In this sense, what is being mediated by the city should be understood in relation to complex and coexisting bits and pieces of knowledge, information and memory that I understand in sum as *an affect* of travel.

On the day of that earthquake, the organizers of the photography tour, who worked with two NGOs from Turkey and Armenia and who had developed a joint arts and oral history project, had originally planned to stay indoors and discuss ideas for a future joint publication by the participants (see Kharatyan et al. 2013 for the final outputs of this project). At that point, we had already been in the city for a week and we had collected enough visual and ethnographic material. However, immediately after the earthquake, the organizers of the trip decided that the students should be taken on an excursion, hoping to somehow minimize the demoralizing effects of the continuing aftershocks. Upon our first arrival in Muş a week ago, I had been given a list of places to visit by the organizers of the trip, and now I came to the bitter realization that all items on my list had already been crossed off. As we had no further suggestions, I approached the organizers again, only to learn that they had been unable to identify any other places of significant Armenian heritage during their 'fact-finding mission' some months ago. With a deep sigh, I helplessly watched local bureaucrats and undercover intelligence agents take over every possible seat in the fake leather chairs scattered throughout this four-star hotel lobby to discuss what to do in that moment of emergency. As I was offered a cigarette with an inviting hand gesture from our minibus driver, Rüstem, from the other side of the sliding door that separated the main street of the city from its only inviting hotel, I asked him what he considered to be the most visit-worthy place in this entire plain and the mountain range surrounding it. He responded that the village of Arak was home to one of the old Armenian churches with the best panorama overlooking the vineyards of the region, which had once produced wine. I approached the organizers once again and asked them whether Rüstem was talking about the famous Surp Arakelots Monastery, which was believed to have been founded by Gregory the Illuminator in the eleventh century and had developed and thrived as one of the most important Armenian seminaries until the Genocide. The organizers replied that they had already visited the monastery during their 'fact-finding mission' and that nothing was left there – implying that it was completely destroyed. I found myself easily persuaded that the village and the church mentioned by our minibus driver must have been a different place, perhaps something of secondary importance. Lacking other options, however, the photography students and I set out on a short journey that would manage to transform our entire understanding of time and place in Turkey.

As our minibus slowly proceeded over the narrow dirt road that divided the village of Arak into two halves, children of various ages first started to wave their hands and run after the vehicle. However, after realizing that our minibus was only passing through, not stopping, they began throwing stones after us and screaming, without actually assuming threatening faces. Looking back now, and having experienced similar attitudes towards 'foreigners' in the various pockets of contemporary Kurdistan, it is clear that those children's thirst for attention was never going to be sufficiently met by people who were only interested in the history of the region. I believe our disconnectedness from them was based on and further re-emerged in relation to what kind of foreigners we were – or at least what kind of an '*outside*' we meant for them as a group of Armenian and Turkish tourists. This outsider situation, I further believe, was informed by the contestedness of the inside, or its everyday political structurings, as a Kurdish village in a predominantly Kurdish region that was politically controlled/ruled/owned by Turks and historically claimed by Armenians.

Following Alice von Bieberstein (2017) and her analysis of the current political and economic tropes of dispossession and marginalization in Muş, I similarly find *Ermenî* (in Kurdish: Armenian) and its wider association with rubble and ruins scattered across Eastern Anatolia to be a signifier of a generic pastness, unspecified in its historicity (177). In this sense, the encounters between Kurds *in* the region and Armenians *of* the region, epitomized in the throwing of stones by the children and the general disinterest of visiting tourists, should be taken as manoeuvres to make sense of an abstracted cycle of death and life, demanding an impossible resolution on what should historically come after the other. As our bus reached the outskirts of the village and stopped to drop us off at the beginning of a steep footpath uphill, we were to contemplate this cycle more through the rest of our journey to a church that was unidentified by any of the passengers – including the local driver, who had suggested going there in the first place. Going upwards for another 45 minutes on foot and slowly leaving the plains behind, we first saw a huge bell tower. Perhaps a hundred metres behind it, there stood what had been the main part of a church, with modern Turkish inscriptions of people's names, like Ali, Sevda and Ahmet, defacing ancient Armenian inscriptions, crosses and other religious ornaments; piles of garbage (mostly cans and bottles); numerous pits of fire and charcoal both inside and outside, revealing the frequency of visitors who had come up here, whether for refuge or for a barbecue; and dozens of holes dug into the ground everywhere by treasure hunters. All of these juxtapositions of life, death and the in-between clearly constituted a context of 'temporal pollution – matter not in its correct temporal place' (Stewart 2017: 135 paraphrasing Douglas 1966). Nevertheless, the buildings and the land around them had not been completely desecrated for their Armenian visitors.

This place was large; it must have been an important religious complex before its destruction in the aftermath of the Genocide. Mesmerized by the dimensions of the tower and the main church building, and by the colourful palette of the autumn vineyards surrounding us, everyone in my group of photography students went their own ways. We were left to our own devices until the silence was broken by some sheep herders, mostly consisting of young boys with the exception of two older men, who slowly approached me and asked with furtive smiles whether we were looking for Armenian gold. Meanwhile, my eyes caught three Armenian participants in three different parts of the ruins: the first one took a candle from her pocket and lit it in one of the still-standing windproof corners of the main building; the second one, following virtually the opposite order of bodily movement, began to fill his pockets with earth from the ground, to later be put into a plastic bag in the hotel and carried all the way back to Armenia; and the third sang a beautiful old hymn in classical Armenian. On that day of the earthquake, all of these people became pilgrims of this unintentional detour and unknown place because of the challenging orderings of meaning in the post-genocide world and their particular actions that temporarily localized their remembrance of loss (cf. Darieva 2006).

Upon our arrival back at our hotel later that day, I found the organizers of the trip in the lobby, which resembled a chaotic newsroom, with many people coming and going and the TV still broadcasting the catastrophic news of the earthquake. When I told them about the spectacular location and the massive dimensions of the buildings, or what was left of them, they were puzzled. They insisted again that they had visited all places significant to Armenian heritage, including the Surp Arakelots Monastery, and had made a full list of places worth visiting. Although it had been one of the most important centres of theology education in the pre-genocide Armenian world, the monastery no longer made the list. The site they had visited was completely destroyed, no ruins remaining, only rubble. Very suspicious due to the resemblance of the names of the village (Arak) and the monastery (Arakelots), I continued to press them, and we finally opened maps and compared old images circulating online with those we had captured. I had indeed visited Arakelots, without having known it. The organizers had previously visited another church, which was now suddenly unknown to them.

If there is an already existing place to discover in contemporary Turkey, what kind of local knowledge should be encountered to make sense of travel and space? In opening this chapter with this long ethnographic vignette, I am inclined to move towards unpacking *belonging* not only as a relationship between physical movement and personal emotive frameworks that both lead to and stem from that movement, but also as a domain of knowledge in its own right. I am particularly interested in the sort of knowledge people acquire and similarly give back en route to somewhere, in the way suggested by Ingold (2011), who construed life as lived along lines – a topic that also requires revisiting a theme from the previous chapters on transgression and regimes of (im)mobility. The present chapter therefore offers a comprehensive analysis of how Armenian 'travellers' (in the widest sense of the term as explained in the previous chapters) located themselves in relation to past and present Armenians and to dispersed, separated and hidden corners of ancestral homelands within the boundaries of what is now Turkey. In presenting Anna's illuminating narrative of belonging below, I also intend to complement that of Hranoush from the previous chapter.

Meeting Anna

Muş, exactly a century ago, with its 299 churches, 94 monasteries, 53 pilgrimage sites and 135 schools, was a major religious and education centre for Armenians of the Ottoman Empire (Kévorkian and Paboudjian 2012). When I visited the province for the first time in 2010, there were only a handful of places remaining to be seen by Armenian homeland tourists from both the diaspora and Armenia.

I met Anna for the first time then, at a panoramic fish restaurant overlooking a historical bridge that was named after the river that it crossed: the Murat in Turkish, or the Aratsani in Armenian, one of the two major branches of the Upper Euphrates. There were groups of people sitting, eating and chatting comfortably in individual gazebos decorated with colourful rugs and huge, firm cushions. Anna was very open to talking from the first moment we met, when we both approached the waiter from the two different sides of this open-air restaurant to request menus. She was then in her late twenties and working as a translator of Russian and English in Yerevan. She was travelling in eastern Turkey with her friends, a mix of young men and women from Armenia, and they had already spent more than ten days visiting different cities in the region. I proposed that we could also visit several places together during their stay in the city. Although her friends were not interested in my offer, Anna and I met twice in the area, once in the city centre to shop together and once to visit a former Armenian village repopulated by Kurds in the decades following the Genocide. In the village we visited just outside the city centre, for untrained eyes, there was almost nothing left to suggest that Armenians had once lived there. However, as we knew what to look for, it did not take us long to notice the ornamented columns, vaults and other architectural elements historically used by Armenians in the construction of village houses and other built structures including stables and roadside walls. Almost everything made from stones bore crosses and Armenian inscriptions. That old material had been defaced and upcycled to form a new village that somehow did not look new, but still old.

Unfortunately, the language barrier between us and the villagers did not allow us to learn about the history of their displacement and relocation to this former Armenian village. I was a native Turkish speaker and Anna was a native Armenian speaker. I spoke the 'official language' of the country and Anna spoke the language that was once widely spoken in the area; most villagers only spoke Kurdish, with the exception of some elderly men and younger generations with primary school education (this was also because whoever could successfully find a job in other larger cities and move away were also those who spoke or had learned Turkish). It was an alienating experience for both of us. I felt like a tourist with distinctively colonizing eyes, whereas for Anna there was still a particular aspect of affinity: she could relate to the landscape. We decided to distance ourselves from the village centre a bit; we passed the buildings and the last remainders of a former church and found ourselves on a muddy road leading to the high mountains far away on the horizon. After a long silent moment, Anna turned to me and told me in English with a thoughtful smile that *it didn't matter that Kurds now lived in this part of Turkey, she felt very much at home.*

Anna did not come from a family of Genocide survivors, nor did her family originate from within the borders of contemporary Turkey. She was born in Armenia, her family having immigrated to Armenia in the early 1980s from their hometown in the Azerbaijani Soviet Socialist Republic. Her father was Armenian and her mother was Jewish, born to a family of Holocaust survivors from Ukraine. Anna had never been to see her family's home in Azerbaijan, as the collapse of the USSR had also brought a still ongoing war between the two neighbours. Both of her parents had passed away a few years previously and she did not have much family in Armenia. She didn't know very much about her mother's family, aside from a couple of cousins scattered throughout the former Soviet republics. None of her paternal cousins knew Armenian and she communicated with them solely in Russian.

As we walked, I asked Anna to elaborate more on what she meant by feeling *very much at home* in this part of Turkey. She responded that the mountains, the rivers and the trees looked the same, even the faces of the people. It just looked like Armenia, she said, and in the end, this was her homeland. Even the rocks scattered all around us just looked the same. Upon hearing this, very directly and almost unexpected of myself, I asked her whether she believed Israel was also her homeland. She responded that she did. However, she was also sure that 'it would not feel like home there' as it was 'a place characterized by a different climate and different landscape'. *A desert possibly looked very different from Muş and Armenia.* Nevertheless, she said that she was very keen to visit Israel, just as much as she had wanted to visit Turkey in the past (and, as we will see in the following pages, some years later she indeed attempted to visit that country).

Sharon Macdonald (2009), in her work on the Nuremberg Nazi Rally Grounds, argues that for many visitors, sites of 'difficult heritage' 'become an occasion for prompting reflection' where 'many people use it as a starting point for contemporary critique', even if such critique was not actively attempted by the site or exhibition (190).[1] For many visitors to one of the most famous landmarks of the Nazi past in Germany, this site often triggers very personal reflections about one's own place in the world and history. It is in this sense that a site of 'difficult heritage' challenges, shocks and often embarrasses its visitors. These sites exert a 'heritage effect' upon their visitors, a sensibility grounded in particular visual and embodied practices prompted by certain kinds of spaces and modes of display (3).[2] As a result, the rendering of particular sites of heritage as 'difficult' is related to the quality of the self-reflection of the visitors that emerges at particular junctures of heritage display and witnessing. However, as in the case of Anna, such 'difficulty' does not need to be grounded in relation to one's ability to process and make sense of information or to go through a moment in which imagined anxieties transform into tangible fears (cf. Ahmed 2004: 63–6). It could also perhaps be defined in relation to one's identification and expression of affinity with a place or a people that are located *on the way from* the widely personalized histories of destruction in Armenia.

However, there are three particular components of Armenian heritage in Muş that remarkably set it apart from Nuremberg, and I wish to discuss them in their relationship to the making of particular roads and routes available for travelling there. First, as the most obvious fact, unlike in Germany, genocide denialism has been the official policy of consecutive Turkish governments. This stance is institutionalized to the extent that the distorted imaginations of victims-as-perpetrators and perpetrators-as-victims have led many Armenians, at least in Turkey, to self-blame for what happened to their ancestors (see Suciyan 2015 for the wider implications of this ongoing impunity for the organization of the state and everyday life in Turkey). Following that, second, this denial constitutes a unique context of heritage display that is not informed by preservation or memory-work but rather works towards redistributing the powers of speech (and silence) to Armenians, Kurds and Turks at different levels. My intention here is not to speculate on the extent to which any tangible remnant of an unrecognized historical crime could possibly perform in a representational capacity simultaneously as a signifier or a signified (cf. Biner 2010; von Bieberstein 2017) but rather to stress its organizational force in making people and everything else move. The third difference between Muş and Nuremberg should come into existence in the ways in which space is demarcated as historically specific place, or, in other words, in relation to the physical and imagined borders that need to be transgressed to reach it. If stigmatization of the Genocide has further stigmatized people (as enemies), things (as fetishes), landscapes (as polluted) and ways of living (as unorthodox), I put forward an argument on the irreversibility of place-making – which, in the absence of preservation projects and open public discussions on loss, should also imply the inevitability of what kind of a place Muş will have become in the future: 'an out-of-the-way place' (Tsing 1993) where political meaning is destabilized (27).

In how many different ways can we come to conceive of the Muş of today precisely in relation to its making in the wake of its marginalization as a place of death for Armenians and life for Kurds? As a representation of a future Muş that is yet to further decay from ruins into rubble? As a direct and lived consequence of a past Muş, where life for Armenians is never possible again? As a city with no real-time presence? As a place polluted by time? I think the confusion does not arise from the destabilizing effects of Muş – both as a heritage site and as a place of pilgrimage – on political subjectivity and belonging. To be more precise, I think the confusion arises from the very political organization of everyday life and space in the aftermath of the Genocide, which is widely understood in relation to Michael Taussig's particular concept of 'public secret' (1999) in Turkish and Armenian studies. In constantly unbecoming a place where either a genocide occurred or did not, I do not find in Muş a concept accounting for the sudden shifts in place that bring about 'an official orthodoxy concerning what is proper as opposed to what is not proper' (Creswell 1996: 10). Instead, we need a concept like 'taboo', something that might guide us through moral frameworks in deciphering everyday justifications of actions and behaviours. We must ask how people's anticipation of what is publicly acceptable and what is behaviourally expected of them (i.e., anticipations of anticipations) constantly inform and shape each other. Otherwise, I do not believe that the silencing of a not-nearly-forgotten past event simply turns it into a publicly shared secret.

Freud (2001 [1913]) notes that taboos refer to sites, issues and rituals that are simultaneously sacred, forbidden and dangerous, with such coexistence implying that the defacement and over-writing of past traces of history should be one of its commonplace qualities. However, he also notes that the term's Polynesian antonym, *noa*, refers to things that are publicly accessible (ibid.). Similarly, for Durkheim (1995 [1912]), taboo 'denotes the institution with which certain things are withdrawn from ordinary use' (304), implying a discontinuity between sacred things and profane beings (303). Taboo defines a site of inaccessibility in which both the individual person and the wider society are protected from the dangers they pose to each other (Steiner 1967 [1957]: 21). In this sense, taboo is an essential component of social organization and the very basis for the diverse structures of rules, laws and regulations observed in all human societies (Bataille 1962; Douglas 1966; Levi-Strauss 1969; Steiner 1967 [1957]). As mentioned above, by specifically identifying what is publicly acceptable and individually expected, taboo has an organizational effect on everyday life, which itself emerges at a particular juncture of politics and morality. In the context of Turkey, Leyla Neyzi (2002) argued that taboo issues are mostly violent events of the past 'that are not easily visible or voiced'; confronting them often comes 'with a high cost for individuals' (142) (also quoted in Brink-Danan 2012: 147). Neyzi's argument follows Freud (2001 [1913]) and Steiner (1967 [1957]), in the sense that not only are such violent histories invisible but bringing visibility to them is often a dangerous enterprise in Turkey. Consequently, as a stigmatizing past event, the Genocide constantly draws lines between people in a way that denotes where they fall into place and where they fall out of place. Expanding on a theme from the last chapter, the next section tackles the drawing of such lines of distance and proximity.

Of homelands that feel like home

As in the narratives of Anahid, Mariam and Hranoush, my informants from the previous three chapters, Anna's understanding of place and space was shaped by her personal mobility. When she made a distinction between eastern Turkey as a 'homeland that felt like home' and Israel as a 'homeland' that she did not 'expect to feel like home', the underlying element of distinction was the familiarity she felt with the landscape of the former. Over the course of our friendship that has spanned more than a decade now, Anna has never articulated Istanbul, a city she visited frequently, as part of her homeland. In fact, she often commented, she was critical of the rigid social compartmentalization along gender, class and community lines prevalent in the city. A point that I will touch upon again later is that, unlike her first initial observations of place in Muş, in Istanbul her criticism specifically targeted the erasing of non-Muslims within the cityscape, the silencing of historically sensitive issues, and everyday practices of boundary-making in the city. As a half-Armenian and half-Jewish woman, she sought new avenues for establishing relationships with local non-Muslim communities, both Jewish and Armenian alike, but she was always disappointed by them. In her understanding, the big city somehow provided a sense of anonymity, at least at the level of the street, but she often noted that she found many doors to community meetings and events 'closed' to her. However, while she never felt welcome by these middle-class urbanites, a feeling that necessarily stressed hindrance and limitation regarding social mobility, she repeatedly referred to our first and only time together in Muş, where she found both the landscape and the people much more 'open'. These metaphors of space that she used most, 'open' and 'closed', defined people, spaces, landscapes and communities and helped her navigate a socially and materially fragmented environment.

In Hranoush's case, portrayed in the previous chapter, we also saw repetitions of specific metaphors of time and space. For Hranoush, these were reflected in her frequent usage of 'here' and 'there'. While 'here' implied all the different and dispersed components of her *memleket*, 'there' denoted the places and time periods that were not incorporated into it. In her account, these metaphors also cut through time zones in their identifications of places as inside or outside of *memleket*; 'here' was elaborated particularly through contexts of the past, while 'there' appeared as a context of the present. For instance, with regards to the expression of a sense of proximity to the past, Sassoun (from which her ancestors had fled), Constantinople (where perhaps the most historically significant Armenian community had once thrived) and Soviet Armenia (where she was born and spent almost half of her life) constituted the distinct components of Hranoush's depiction of *memleket*. Following the traces of her knowledge of place further, Batman (the present-day Kurdish city/province that displaced historical Sassoun for Armenians), Istanbul (not Constantinople) (see also the resemblance to the narrative of Ani presented in Chapter 2), and a landlocked and diminished Republic of Armenia (no longer an integral part of a major world power) were somehow disconnected from what she defined as a place of origin. It seems that this expansive *memleket* was made possible because of Hranoush's particular interpretation of temporality, which was further reflected in the ways she talked about both the distances between these places and the other people who similarly claimed belonging. In doing so, she differentiated among places in relation to their marginalization in the history of Armenians. Similarly, she differentiated among people by following a somewhat straightforward binary between old generations (Ottomans and Soviets) versus new generations (Turks, Russians and Armenians). In this sense, her formulation of a *memleket* indeed emerges as a formulation of homeland, as long as the latter has a capacity to endure against the histories of marginalization. *Memleket*, thus, appears as *a way in and around* to the homeland and its multiple former enactments and modern indoctrinations; it gives meaning to a localization of a place-identity that comes into light through stress on connections with its surroundings.

In contrast, Anna's understanding of a homeland constituted a very physically contiguous and less temporally diffused concept, but her distinction between homely and less homely feeling homelands should also be understood as challenging to the impositions of a totalizing Armenian homeland – and similarly a Jewish one. Taking a detour here, I want to speculate on the making of homely homelands not in relation to the feelings of security and intimacy that 'home' is directly expected to purport but rather by way of critically engaging with the mental and emotive aspects of travelling the roads that lead to them. Kasbarian (2009) noted that the concept of 'return' is at the centre of multiple disciplinary discussions (362) and I do not see added value in the application of that term in this book's narrative of mobility, which clearly refrains from reproducing 'home' as a timeless place to be returned to. However, in my anticipation of temporal and other forms of pollution at and en route to home, I suspect that 'return' can only be a claim, perhaps an intervention, for belonging. It is important to note here that 'return' is usually portrayed as a move towards Armenia on the part of Armenians from the diaspora; it is not widely discussed in the context of travelling from Armenia to Turkey. However, if Armenian diasporic tourism in general raises the question of 'how cultural and political representations of the Armenian loss get transformed in the course of interaction with the new social order and new actors following the break-up of the Soviet Empire' (Darieva 2006: 87), my attempt is similarly to think through how transgression into Turkey, despite the closed border, should redefine the country as a place of origin and an ancestral homeland specifically in the post-socialist era.

Some three decades after its independence, in Armenia, people still make a distinction between internal and external diasporas, the latter only referring to the dispersed communities outside the borders of the former Soviet Union (Pattie 2004: 111). This situation is directly related to the kind of mobility that was once possible in the USSR, where Armenians gained access to other Soviet republics and were denied access to the rest of the world and the diaspora. After independence in 1991, the relationships between the country, the diaspora and the wider world did not stand still; they were transformed and reconfigured (Dudwick 1997; Platz 2000; Pattie 2004; Kasbarian 2009). As this distinction is now very much normalized in contemporary Armenia, there is a need to locate the country in the making of new borders, as in the making of new mobility regimes and zones of accessibility, following the collapse of the USSR. However, it should also be noted that differences in generation, occupation and level of education imply different understandings between the internal and the external (diasporas). For the older generations and people with higher levels of state education, the border-like qualities of the former Soviet Union's border in demarcating an inside versus an outside remain intact. It is essential to keep in mind that for these older generations, those borders indeed remained unchanging for almost seventy years, further consolidating these juxtapositions of access, mobility and navigation. On the contrary, for the younger generations and for people born into and living in the world of the contested and almost constantly changing borders of the post-socialist South Caucasus, and who have friends and family visiting or settling in Paris or Los Angeles, the decoupling of the world has been far less clear-cut. For both groups, however, the relational location of contemporary Turkey constitutes the most ambiguous – but not necessarily abstract – component of an Armenian world (see also Chapter 2).

In the case of Armenians from Turkey, those indexical qualities of the border between the two countries have been increasingly – if not eternally – solidified. As I observed, for instance, the borders of historical Armenia, not as a political entity but as a 'mesh' of past and present ancestral lands, never go beyond the current state borders, which further implies that the Russian expansion (1877–8) and Soviet retreat (1921) do not have any negative or positive effects on the imagining of contemporary Armenia as a physical, cultural and historical continuum of Anatolia and ancestral homelands. Of course, such division between the two Armenias has been reproduced at the levels of artistic and literary representation and everyday knowledge on both sides of the border and beyond. I believe a detailed historical account of this division would be better suited as the focus of a different study. Nevertheless, the multiple reiterations of the Turkish-Armenian border as both a demarcation line and a barrier should be ethnographically recontextualized in light of the travel practices of the researcher and the informants if we want to understand the dynamics of Armenian mobility en route to Turkey and place-making in this former place of origin. It is in this regard that I am not going to redefine the overladen concept of homeland. Instead, I seek to account for the particular processes of travel and/or everyday experiences of marginalization through which sense was made of the concept by my informants.

It is in the double reiteration of the border, first as a demarcation line of survival during and after the Genocide and second as a barrier once between NATO and the USSR and later between two nation-states in conflict about the political future of the South Caucasus and former socialist territories, that there is a constitution of a centre of its own right in Armenia. However, I also sense that there is more to the daily operations of the border in the way it functions as a lens to detect, decipher and define information about place and space. If Muş – and all other places of pre-genocide Armenian dwelling in what is now Turkey – has destabilizing effects on political meaning and belonging with their particular effects of heritage on their Armenian visitors, the border antithetically works towards a stabilization of putting places and people in order. It does so by cutting through, and hence permanently transforming, an otherwise 'world of surfaces' (Ingold 2011) where people and places hang in space. This is not to raise an argument on what the region would have been like had there not been an Armenian Genocide. Rather, this is to think through the direct and indirect effects of genocide denialism on connecting and similarly disconnecting places to/from places, and people to/from people. In Turkey, where genocide denialism requires a legal system to both impose truths and stigmatize anti-denialists, knowledge is primarily 'transmitted' from generation to generation through personal communication and experience (Suciyan 2015: 18). However, the travels and other mobility narratives of my informants in Eastern Anatolia suggest that there are possibly additional ways of being and becoming in the world.

In contemporary Muş, as in all other places in the world, a physical surface is in the making by the forces of nature (e.g., earthquakes), people (e.g., construction) and multiple combinations of the two (e.g., ruination). This surface is the physical dimension in which our daily movement as perceivers and producers of knowledge should take place. However, in empirical social sciences and history, it is also the dimension that is abstracted as reality from the person who perceives it (Tilley 1994; Massey 2005) (see also Ingold 2011: 129–30 for a discussion on the promises of a phenomenological approach). In analogy to Tsing (2000) and Clifford (1989), I believe that this is the primary example of reducing *a series* of locations to a single *moment* of place. In going uphill to reach the Surp Arakelots Monastery, everyone in the photography group followed literal trails to attain the knowledge of this then-unknown place, portraying the most obvious example of growing into knowledge (Ingold 2011: 162; see also the previous chapter). It is important to stress here that as we finally came to know about this place, the so-called Arakelots, perhaps another Armenian monastery located somewhere else, which had been previously visited by the organizers of the art project, became unknown. As I sense a sharp distinction between the signified and the signifier, and hence a unidirectional passing of knowledge from object to person, or from person to person, in the process of 'transmission' I do not see a possibility of its undoing.

For its Armenian visitors from Armenia, Muş is polluted by time more than once. This is because, in Turkey, the varying degrees of Armenian Genocide denialisms, which are reflected in a spectrum of official ideologies onto everyday trivialization by the ruling classes and the local people, respectively, shape the physical surfaces of the city and its surroundings. In Armenia, the wider understandings of the Genocide as a major force giving shape to Eastern Anatolia further give the region its final shape as a place of origin that was once *unpolluted*. It is in this sense that, for Anna, both the Muş of now and the Muş of then do not constitute a 'foreign country': the ongoing ruination and practices of defacement make the crystallization of the past impossible (Gordillo 2014; cf. Lowenthal 1985). On top of that, following the lead of Darieva (2006), rituals like lighting candles or singing hymns momentarily *localize* memories and the loss of ancestral places of origin. In Anna's case, then, a homeland that feels like home, or like a place dearly known, only emerges through the possibility of pollution in which the past and the present are not clearly separated. For her, Israel at the time of our meeting did not offer such internal discussions on belonging that were informed by the destabilizing effects of 'an out-of-the-way-place' (Tsing 1993: 27), which is defined not by its political or any other tangible marginalization but by the level of mental and emotive work it requires to reach it.

A yearning for visibility: 'Where did all these people go?'

In the months and years that followed, Anna and I kept in contact. She visited me several times in Istanbul as she was very eager to know more about the history of the city and the ways its non-Muslim denizens continued – and did not continue – their lives in the wake of different phases of violence, displacement and dispossession. Over the months and years that followed her first visit, I observed that she cultivated an interest in learning about the Jewish heritage of the city. She attempted to make local Jewish friends, but at the end she concluded that theirs was a 'closed' community and her attempts were futile. She also made an attempt to visit Israel. She booked her flights through my personal contacts in Tel Aviv, but her visa application was denied on the grounds that she did not have any documents to prove that she was Jewish. Nevertheless, we continued our neighbourhood and museum visits simultaneously embracing Jewish and Armenian perspectives.

One day we decided to visit the Jewish Museum of Istanbul (officially the Quincentennial Foundation Museum of Turkish Jews), the only Jewish museum in a predominantly Muslim country.³ At the time of research, the museum was located in the defunct Zulfaris Synagogue, on a tiny dead-end street in the neighbourhood of Karaköy.⁴ It was very hard for untrained eyes to spot the museum, a fact that caught Anna's attention. As we attempted to enter through the gate that separated the dead-end street and the synagogue, a security guard asked why we had come, as if he were waiting to hear whether we were lost or actually knew what we were looking for. I responded that we wanted to visit the museum and this time he asked us where we came from. He was a bit surprised that one of us was from Turkey and the other from Armenia, and he asked whether he could see our IDs and keep them until the end of our visit. After our bags and clothing were checked, we were finally allowed inside the building.

When we were alone amongst the exhibited material, Anna asked me whether there was anything unusual about the security measures we had been subjected to. Having visited the museum several times before, I responded that there was nothing unusual on the day of our visit. The security measures had been tight for a long time, and I explained that there had twice been terrorist attacks on Istanbul synagogues, in 1986 and 2003. She reasoned that this explained a lot about the Jewish community and why its members seemingly kept a low profile. Marcy Brink-Danan (2012), in her research on Jews in Istanbul, notes that the curator of the museum once explained that 'he was compelled to create the museum after the 1986 attacks, when the general population in Turkey (as well as the international press) recorded its shock at the revelation that Jews *still lived* in Istanbul' (43, emphasis original). It is in this context that the museum simultaneously serves the local Jewish population as an intimate community space and, as the curator also stressed, 'is *really* intended to "present the face of Judaism to the *outside*"' (43, both emphases mine).

As we came to the end of our tour of the building, I asked Anna whether she had noticed anything particular about the exhibition. She had not, so I pointed out that there was no material exhibited on the Holocaust.[5, 6, 7] Anna said that she wasn't surprised by this; for her, any mention of the Holocaust (in Turkish: *Yahudi Soykırımı*, lit. the Jewish Genocide) would necessarily have echoed the Armenian Genocide (in Turkish: *Ermeni Soykırımı*).⁸ At this point, Anna expressed that she believed everyone lived in 'bubbles' in Istanbul, while she was lucky enough to go beyond her Armenian bubble. She added that the younger generation of students, NGO experts and volunteers from Armenia in Istanbul still did not realize two important things. First, they mistakenly believed that Turkey was changing. In their professional and social circles, the Genocide was not a taboo topic, and they were surrounded by open-minded people. Anna said that the situation among the majority of Turks would have been demoralizing for Armenians. Second, Armenians did not understand that Turkey was 'multicultural' and did not recognize the diversity of the population who had become Turks over the last century. This particular group of people from Armenia, who were employed by civil society organizations in Turkey, she believed, spent most of their time with people who were not different from themselves socially or politically. At the end of our tour of the Jewish Museum, Anna did not seem impressed. For her, the museum did not really give a sense of the history of the Jewish community of Istanbul. She asked: 'Where did all these people go?' I responded in a rather provocative way, suggesting 'Possibly Israel?', but I already knew that she had intended to ask a different kind of question.

Anna had asked me the same question once before, during our visit to the Museum of Innocence, named after Nobel-laureate Orhan Pamuk's novel of the same title. The museum brings life to the protagonists of the novel, mostly members of two Westernized, secular upper and lower middle-class Muslim families from the 1970s, by way of presenting a large body of everyday items such as shaving kits, cigarette butts, dresses and earrings, as well as black-and-white photographs of people in Istanbul from the 1970s and earlier decades. Like the novel, the museum is a work of fiction (23 January 2016, *The Guardian*), and it is hard not to see this tiny museum as largely an act of nostalgic appreciation for an Istanbul that does not exist anymore (29 April 2012, *New York Times*).

Orhan Pamuk, in an earlier book, *Istanbul*, himself wrote of the destruction of Istanbul that still haunted its contemporary denizens:

> For those of us who watched the city's last yalis, mansions and ramshackle wooden houses burn during the 1950s and 1960s, the pleasure we derived had its roots in a spiritual ache different from that of the Ottoman Pashas, who thrilled to them as spectacles; *ours was the guilt, loss and jealousy felt at the sudden destruction of the last traces of a great culture and a great civilization that we were unfit or unprepared to inherit, in our frenzy to turn Istanbul into a pale, poor, second-class imitation of a western city.*
> (Orhan Pamuk, *Istanbul*, 2006: 191, emphasis mine)

When Anna walked the streets of contemporary Istanbul, she did not see life as portrayed in either museum. She observed that Istanbul was diverse; however, as in the Orhan Pamuk quotation above, a feeling of destruction was constantly in narration. For Anna and other Armenians from Istanbul and Armenia alike, this destruction was epitomized by the massive exodus of non-Muslims from the city. As a result, I argue that there is always more than one way to account for and answer Anna's question. As I construe it, her question of 'Where did all these people go?' is a vocalization of the invisibility of the remaining non-Muslims within public life in Istanbul. For the non-Muslims who stayed in the city, more and more invisible but tangible barriers were erected between people from different class, religious and ethnic backgrounds from the 1950s onwards. This situation is reflected in Turkey in two ways: first, through the stigmatization of particular historical issues that went against the official nation-state historiography, and second, through the reorganization of the city in the imagination, in the aftermath of the exodus of non-Muslims and its repopulation by rural migrants.

The invisible but tangible barriers between the denizens of Istanbul can best be understood as an ongoing process through which particular neighbourhoods, sites and institutions (such as schools and places of worship) come to be imagined as more 'different' and 'foreign' than others, and the subsequent making of those spaces as such (see Chapter 7 for more on this). The stories depicted here primarily account for how these borders are made from the inside out. This is perhaps specifically why the Jewish Museum clearly 'departs from the general theme and museum narratives of Jewish museums elsewhere in the world' (Brink-Danan 2012: 43–4). It is possible to understand Anna's reasoning in relation to the wider invisibility of violent and discriminatory events of the past in this setting. At the time of our visit to the museum, there was no mention of the following events that had taken place in Turkey: the 1934 Pogroms (which specifically targeted Jews), the 1941–2 random drafting of non-Muslims into the army (in Turkish: *yirmi kura askerlik*) and forced labour battalions (in Turkish: *amele taburu*), the 1942 Struma Disaster (in which 781 Jewish refugees escaping the Holocaust on a boat from Romania en route to the Mandate of Palestine were denied entry to Turkey; the boat was finally torpedoed by a Soviet submarine off the Turkish coast), the 1942 Wealth Tax (which was levied on non-Muslims only) and the 1955 Pogroms (which targeted all non-Muslims).[9] Talin Suciyan (2015), in her book, argues that denial of these state-sponsored acts of violence and discrimination has been institutionalized through the legal framework that penalized the 'denigration of Turkishness' but not Jewishness, Armenianness or Greekness (83). In other words, when non-Muslims criticized these violent events and discriminatory practices, they were formally charged, not only for going against official historical narratives but also for insulting Turks as a whole.[10] Historical events of violence in general and *soykırım* in particular are taboo in Turkey, not only stigmatized concepts but also stigmatizing for those who publicly attempt to discuss them.

The narrative of belonging portrayed within the permanent exhibition of the Jewish Museum triggered a very particular 'heritage effect' that exposed the double exteriority of Anna in Istanbul, despite being a simultaneously Jewish and Armenian city. I argue that the aforementioned exhibitions in Istanbul, as opposed to the unorganized ruins of the past, tend to have stabilizing effects that communicate political meaning. This is not to suggest that this political meaning should be of an impartial nature (as reflected in the selective narrative of the Jewish Museum) but rather to stress that it can only identify and locate counter-political narratives of belonging always in relation to the mainstream or the publicly available. In other words, Istanbul not only presents itself as a multi-layered urban palimpsest where people, things and discourses are accumulated 'vertically' but also denies any possibility of their individual existence (see also the Introduction and the next chapter). Even if it were possible to practically compartmentalize them – as in the case of the Jewish Museum or any other museum built around a meta-narrative of belonging – they would emerge as introverted islands in a kind of isolation that could only offer a 'mountaintop view' (Clifford 1986b: 22) devoid of any 'noise' (Said 1989: 212–16). As noted earlier, in Muş, however, I find a different organization of space that comes into existence through the 'horizontal' dispersion of Armenian ruins that can be accessed through detours, secondary roads and losing one's way, epitomized in the modern-day possibility of a 'rediscovery' of a monastery and the sudden subsequent tectonic shifts between known and unknown places. If rural and urban landscapes differ in the specific ways they are networked by the roads that both lead to and go through them, I also expect the frequency of travellers as well as the meeting points along these roads to define our knowledge of those landscapes. It is in this sense that I find belonging, depending on its capacity to illuminate relationships between people and places, as epistemology. Consequently, Anna's repeated rejection of Istanbul as part of an Armenian homeland, *not even an unhomely one*, should be discussed in relation to her knowledge of the city – which in her specific case is also informed by her restricted access to many Jewish and Armenian community events and spaces in the city.

Anna observed one of the most direct practices of place-making in non-Muslim Istanbul during our entry to the Jewish Museum. The two of us went through a series of security practices that involved ID checks and a bag and body search. These practices represent a basic element of differentiation in Istanbul, 'the physical border dividing Jewish space from the public Turkish domain' (Brink-Danan 2012: 87). We also found ourselves in a conversation with the security personnel about 'where we came from', a question intended to 'locate a new person, however roughly, on an imagined national map – not with a literal absolute location somewhere in Turkey or in a neighbourhood of Istanbul, but, rather, with an imagined geography that situates a person in some way within the nation, in terms of culture, socioeconomic status, political, or even ethnic identity' (Mills 2010: 1–2). In this sense, it is impossible for a respondent of this question to answer without a historically informed mark of difference. Perhaps, in her rejection of belonging to Istanbul, Anna rejected this mark in a way she did not feel elsewhere.

In the next chapter, I will discuss a particular instance of unmarking such difference in materiality in contemporary Istanbul. Exploring more of the tangible aspects of place-making discussed in this chapter, my ethnographic focus shifts to building homes and naming buildings in an Istanbul neighbourhood. I portray how Armenian responses to state-imposed limitations on belonging further become relevant to the making of national space in Turkey.

Chapter 5

BUILDING HOMES OF UNITY

The secret of Istanbul is that it is unclassified and unorganized. Knowledge about it has not been presented yet, nor comprehended by the people who live in it. Lifestyle here is the crowds' sensing of the historical richness of the city, its multi-layered civilizations without owning them as foreigners do. One of the phrases that I have heard most frequently since I was a child is 'vallahi foreigners know about us better than we do'. In this phrase concerning the visiting tourist with a guidebook, there is more than regret. There is a sarcasm, doubt, and disdain about the person who tries to inform, classify, and understand chaos and puts it in order.

(Orhan Pamuk, *Manzaradan Parçalar: Hayat, Sokaklar Edebiyat* [lit. *Pieces from the View: Life, Streets, Literature*] 2010: 146; my own translation, emphases mine)

Kurtuluş is so busy that it is a miracle not to crash into somebody on the street. On these busy streets *every kind of person is an island*: There are as many headscarved women as those women who do not cover their heads. But no one gives hostile looks to each other; in fact, they all stroll on the streets together. You can come across a Korean street vendor who sells Chinese-made counterfeit stuff, or Africans who mostly live and shop around Dolapdere. Groups of idle teenagers, people who live from work to home, old ladies who cannot do without paying a visit to the hairdresser's, and the rural-looking pious old man are all parts of this mosaic.

(Mehveş Emin, 'Is Kurtuluş the Harlem of Istanbul?', 31 March 2008, *Akşam*; my own translation, emphasis mine)

On New Year's Day of 2013, I woke up very early. I had been invited to a small party to welcome the New Year at a friend's house in the neighbourhood of Kurtuluş. In the morning, my host asked if I was interested in going for breakfast at a local *muhallebici* (lit. pudding shop). I said 'yes', and we were on our way in a matter of a few minutes. When we reached the main shopping street, he told me that it was impossible to believe it was a public holiday. All the shops were open and the streets were full of people. He told me no one in Turkey liked to stay home, because nobody married the ones they loved and instead were all forced into arranged marriages by their families. He reasoned: 'If husbands and wives cannot stand each other, they all prefer to work and shop even on a holiday.'

At the end of his short monologue, he switched to English very briefly on the busy pavement and said: 'This looks like Lonely Planet. Foreigners love this *vibrancy*, but for me sometimes there is too much *diversity*'. And he smiled.

Burak, my host at that New Year's party, was a half-Turkish and half-Armenian man in his mid-thirties. He was an ambitious civil engineer and was working for a widely known international construction company. He had lived and worked in New York for a few years and came back to Istanbul a few months prior to our meeting in the summer of 2012. Apart from the few years he spent in the United States, he lived in Kurtuluş (and in the same house) all of his life. His father was a Muslim man from one of the former Ottoman territories in the Balkans, and his family migrated to Istanbul when he was a small child in the 1940s. They first settled in a remote village on the Bosphorus; as they did very well in their seaside restaurant business, the family moved to the prosperous neighbourhood of Nişantaşı in less than ten years.

Burak's mother was an Armenian woman, born in Istanbul in the same years that his father's family migrated to Istanbul. His maternal grandparents were both Genocide survivors from different parts of Turkey, saved by missionaries and raised in orphanages in Istanbul. They lived their early adult lives as young but hardworking tailors in Kumkapı; however, as they became older and gained experience, they opened their own shop near the Mkhitaryan Armenian School in Osmanbey and moved to nearby Kurtuluş, which was an affordable neighbourhood in which to buy a house at the time. All of his grandfather's family was killed during the Genocide; however, his grandmother managed to reunite with one of her sisters in Istanbul in the early 1920s, who moved first to France and later to Argentina in the 1960s.

Burak's father and mother were raised in neighbourhoods within walking distance of each other; one has been known as a wealthy upper-class neighbourhood and the other as modest and diverse. When his mother and father met and decided to get married in 1971, it came as a great shock to her Armenian family. Considering the time period, they probably constituted one of the very rare examples of Turkish-Armenian mixed marriages. When we once went through the black-and-white wedding photos among his personal archives at his home, it was impossible not to notice the very small number of people who had attended the ceremony. The first big family gathering took place when his sister was born in 1972, and the ice between the families finally melted when he was born in the early 1980s.

When I met him, Burak's grandparents and parents had long since passed away. His sister also lived in Kurtuluş, with her husband, a Turkish man. Burak was not in contact with his paternal first cousins, who lived in different neighbourhoods of Istanbul. The rest of his extended family was dispersed around the globe. On his father's side, he had second and third cousins in the Balkan states of former Yugoslavia. On his mother's side, he had an uncle and first cousins in different cities in Europe, and second and third cousins in South America. Except for his maternal uncle, who was born and raised in Istanbul and who was a native speaker of Turkish (and Armenian), he communicated with his first, second and third cousins all in English on the rare occasions that he met them in person, as he knew neither Bosnian nor Armenian. He was a native speaker of Turkish and was fluent in English.

Burak's family story perfectly portrays Istanbul in a context of migration, in terms of both depopulation and repopulation. His father's family was among the many Muslims who migrated to Turkey from former Ottoman territories in the Balkans, the Caucasus and the Levant. As we will see in this chapter, they were expected to leave their cultural differences behind and become 'Turks' – reflecting the centrality of Islam (more than language) in the making of this category. On his maternal side, the family's story of almost total extinction in Anatolia, reunification in Istanbul and dispersion around the globe portrays different histories of the Turkification of peoples and places in the country. In the transformation from empire to secular nation-state, they were expected to leave their differences behind, but the state would remind them of those differences 'when necessary', especially in times when non-Muslims were perceived as a threat to national security.

Burak's family history hints at what follows in this chapter, which primarily intends to account for Turkification processes at three different levels. First, it looks at the making of the category of the Turk in its widest sense. It is at this level that the chapter triggers a discussion on the diversity of Muslims who were blended in within the category of the Turk. Second, the chapter looks at how non-Muslims found themselves amidst this nation-building process in the country and often swayed between understanding Turkishness as a cultural category and a definition of citizenship. It is at this level that the chapter invites readers to think about popular perceptions of non-Muslims as 'foreigners' in the context of Turkey. Third, the chapter looks at the issue of Turkification through the lens of urban transformation in Istanbul. Through a comparison of the street names (named by the state) and building names (named by the residents), I attempt to account for the more silent and invisible responses against the Turkification processes. For this reason, I explore the direct impacts of Turkification processes led by the state on the spatial organization of people and buildings.

The information collected for the purposes of this chapter was mostly obtained during my lengthy walks in the streets of Istanbul. The chapter takes walking within the wider notion of travelling, which crosscuts the diverse subject matters of this book as a simultaneously theoretical and ethnographic concept.

Walking in the neighbourhood

The neighbourhood in which I welcomed New Year's Day, Kurtuluş, is still diverse, as Burak suggested. However, its urban history reveals how such diversity of people came into being through the uprooting of non-Muslims from the neighbourhood and elsewhere. Armenians, who had started to move into the neighbourhood around the 1940s, became the visible non-Muslim minority after the expulsion of

Greeks from Istanbul en masse in 1964.[1,2] As I went through my fieldwork notes in tandem with the critical accounts of social and political history of early post-Ottoman Istanbul, it appeared that non-Muslims (including Armenians) sought new homes in Kurtuluş in the wake of political and urban developments at two levels. At one level, state-sponsored violence and policies specifically targeting non-Muslims such as random drafting into the army (and annihilation of manpower in forced labour camps) in 1941, the Wealth Tax in 1942 and the Pogroms of 1955 resulted in the transfer of capital and properties from non-Muslims to Muslims and the subsequent economic marginalization of non-Muslims (Aktar 2002; Güven 2006; Suciyan 2015). At another level, the massive urban transformation projects (in the form of the demolishing of old neighbourhoods for construction of big road networks) in the second half of the 1950s resulted in the physical marginalization of historical non-Muslim neighbourhoods in Istanbul's 'historical peninsula' (Keyder 1999; Akpınar 2016). These developments at both the urban and the national level pushed the remaining non-Muslim minorities in Istanbul to seek affordable and available housing in different parts of the city. The neighbourhood at the core of this chapter was in a process of transformation at this historical juncture.

In order to account for these aforementioned transformations in demographics, urban landscape and economic power, I need to describe where I first started. My very first fieldwork notes in the neighbourhood consisted of my new address in a new home, where I started my walks and my first observations. At the very beginning of my fieldwork, I moved into a house in Kurtuluş in central Istanbul with an Armenian friend from Istanbul. For the duration of my fieldwork – with exceptions of the summers on the island of Kınalıada and shorter intervals of research visits to Armenia – I lived at the address below:

Bozkurt Mahallesi
Ergenekon Caddesi
Türkbeyi Sokak
XXXXX Apartmanı #XX
Kurtuluş
Şişli
ISTANBUL

In everyday Turkey, unlike in the UK, addresses inform strangers about a long and very detailed route in the manner that a location is described to people to find their ways as if walking or driving in the city. This is why addresses are based on a hierarchy of neighbourhoods, avenues and boulevards, streets and alleys, and apartment names and numbers. The lack of postcodes or district numbers clearly indicates the ways buildings, neighbourhoods, streets and people are located in relation to each other. Building numbers are also often neglected in the addresses as the great majority of residential buildings have names in Turkey. Also, there could be many streets with the same name in the same city, which is why one should know how to correlate the different components of an address in order to be able to fully describe it. Most people do not know their own postcodes in Istanbul but would have a clear idea of where a street would be in this city of 15 million people, although not *cartographically*, either. The addresses in Istanbul mostly follow the hierarchy below:

Neighbourhood Name – Bozkurt Mahallesi
Avenue Name – Ergenekon Caddesi
Street Name – Türkbeyi Sokak
Building Name and Number – XXXXX Apartmanı #XX
District Name – Kurtuluş
Borough Name – Şişli
City/Province Name –Istanbul

At first sight, one may notice sophisticated distinctions between different dimensions in dwelling and city planning in Turkey. The nuances between avenues and streets or districts, boroughs and neighbourhoods may sound extremely confusing for a native English speaker, but for people living in Istanbul, it is these nuances that enable them to find their way in the city. As mentioned, some streets, avenues or neighbourhoods share the same name in the city and sometimes all around the country. Sometimes a street name in one borough could be a neighbourhood name in another borough, and a district name in another. Contemporary denizens of Istanbul would never look at a map while walking through an unfamiliar district or street, not because they never get lost, but because their way of attaining knowledge of the city would not be reflected in a map (as also suggested in the Orhan Pamuk quote in the opening of this chapter). As suggested before, they would instead navigate within the city by following a particular imagined order of streets of different scales and sizes. The most recent advances in communication technologies seem not to have changed this situation. During my research, I found many times that my informants did not consult Google Maps or WhatsApp locations to find their way around.

Tim Ingold (2000) argues that a denizen of any city may be unable to specify her location in space in terms of any independent system of coordinates, and yet will still insist that she knows where she is (219). This is because, he argues, places have histories (ibid.). When we look at the combinations of street and other place names in Turkey and their distribution across the country, we see the history of nation-building. A closer look at my home address in Istanbul adds another dimension in understanding the extent of such practices in Turkey:

| Neighbourhood Name – Bozkurt: | Mythical grey wolf that is believed to show the way in times of turmoil. Widely considered as a national symbol in Turkey. Several far-right-wing political associations are named after it. Place name of many localities across Turkey. |

Avenue Name – Ergenekon:	Originally a Mongolian creation myth, later adapted by Turkish nationalists as the Turkish creation myth. Along with the mythical *bozkurt*, widely promoted by state authorities since the early Republican days. Also a name recently given to an alleged clandestine ultranationalist terrorist organization.
Street Name – Türkbeyi:	Literally means 'the Turkish Chieftain'.
Building Name and Number:	(Irrelevant.)
District Name – Kurtuluş:	Literally means 'release' or 'getting rid of things' and 'salvation' in Turkish. The period of war between 1918 and 1922 following the First World War is also referred to by this name. This is why it is widely understood in Turkish and translated into English as 'independence' and 'liberation' as well. Numerous localities are named after this notion in Turkey.
Borough Name – Şişli:	(Irrelevant; however, the borough is widely understood as a historically non-Muslim and middle- and upper-class place of residence.)
Province Name – Istanbul:	Although not directly related to the foundation myths of the Turkish Republic – which are further based on Central Asian legends, tales, heroes, etc. – the name of the city is part of the Turkification process of Turkey. Up until 1930, the city did not have an official name and was generally named differently in the different languages of its residents. In the Ottoman language (i.e., Ottoman Turkish), different names were used, but primarily *Konstantiniyye*, derived from Constantinople. Although the name Istanbul also derives from a Greek root, *eis tin poli*, εισ την πόλι (which means 'inside the city/city walls'), Turkish authorities managed to erase the emphasis on Constantine (i.e., Constantine the Great, Roman Emperor between 306 and 337 AD, who accepted Christianity as the official religion) and replace it with the less Greek, less Christian and less 'foreign' sounding Istanbul (see the following pages for the production of foreignness in Turkey). Many people in Turkey have produced a folk etymology, believing that the name derives from what could

have been *Islambol* in Turkish (which literally means 'plenty of Islam', not Constantinople), demonstrating the extent of Turkification of place names – and its internalization by Turkish citizens – in the country.

In the early days of my fieldwork, I walked in the streets of the neighbourhood, and over the course of my research I was struck by some of the street names that clearly indicated that name change was a pattern for most parts of the neighbourhood. In a series of maps entitled *Plan Cadastral d'Assurances* produced in the 1920s by Jacques Pervititch (1927), it is seen that the name of the street I lived on – Türkbeyi, or the Turkish Chieftain – used to be Rousso (i.e., Rousseau). These historical maps reveal that street names that had non-Muslim connotations were all changed. Such street names included Constantine, Ayazma (from Greek αγίασμα; sacred fountain), Ermeni Kilise (in Turkish: Armenian Church), Rum Kilise (in Turkish: Greek Church), Gürcü Kilise (in Turkish: Georgian Church) and Tatavla (from Greek στάβλος; horse stable) – after which the neighbourhood was also named.

Jongerden (2009) argues that such name changes have always been essential components of the nation-building process in Turkey and governments have been deliberately involved in this process by direct intervention. Öktem (2008) refers to these interventions in space as 'toponymic engineering', which he finds one of the essential components of nation-building along with 'demographic engineering'. In a newspaper article Ayşe Hür notes that from the earliest days of the Republic until the late 1970s, some 28,000 place names were changed in Turkey (31 March 2009, *Radikal*).[3] In Istanbul, however, this process started and was finalized during the first decade of the Turkish Republic. All street names without Turkish origins or roots in Istanbul were changed by 1927 (ibid.). In Kurtuluş, where the street names had already been changed, this process of Turkification of place names was finalized with the name change of the neighbourhood itself in 1929. Therefore, the name 'Kurtuluş' is also a new one, and similar to the street names, the name change of the neighbourhood was in direct relation to Turkification processes in Istanbul and the country. Various Turkish dictionaries indicate that Kurtuluş means 'salvation', 'release' and 'emancipation' as well as 'liberation'. This is why the term is heavily laden with the idea of 'national independence' in Turkey. For instance, the Turkish terminology for the Turkish War of Independence – as it is widely referred to in English – would be more accurately translated as the Turkish War of Liberation.

The above image is a copy of a newspaper article from 1929, which informs its readers about the name change of the neighbourhood. A translation of the article clearly shows why it is no wonder that many Armenians from the neighbourhood found that the name change resonated with not only the Turkish War of Independence but also 'getting rid of' non-Muslim minorities:

Figure 5 *Akşam* Newspaper (24 March 1929).

The Municipality Decided to Change the Name Tatavla
From now on, Tatavla High Street will be named Kurtuluş High Street

After the recent fire of Tatavla, Greek[4] newspaper publications referred to Tatavla as the symbol of the Byzantine Empire in Istanbul.

Such newspaper publications generated very bad effects on Turkish public opinion.

Moreover, the name Tatavla resonates with thieves and murderers. In this respect, Tatavla also reflects bad connotations.

As we are informed, the city municipality has taken these views into consideration and decided to change the name of Tatavla Street to Kurtuluş Street, and also informed the city governorship about it.

Once the governorship finalizes the formalities, the name of Tatavla will be 'Kurtuluş'.

Tatavla, which was once upon a time a place where murderers and evildoers like Hristos sought refuge, is now a clean place where many Turkish families live. In this respect, it is a success to replace the old ugly name with Kurtuluş.

Similar to Jongerden (2009), Öktem (2008) suggests that Turkification in Turkey has been realized at two different levels: first, through undermining the old status quo of the Empire and replacing names of old and historical places, and second, through a creation of a national system of taxonomy by introducing new place names in Turkish. Of course, this would not have been possible without the extermination and forced migration of non-Muslim citizens of the country. This is how and why changes in place names have always been in tandem with state-sponsored violence against these groups in Turkey. It is in this context that I find one of the very last sentences of the newspaper article from 1929 especially worth noting: '*Tatavla... is now a clean* [in Turkish: *temiz*] *place* where many Turkish families live.'[5]

In his discussion of Douglas (1966), Creswell (1996) finds dirt 'a mismatch of meanings that are erroneously positioned in relation to other things' (38). In his understanding, only things that transgress into a place where they do not belong can appear as dirt (39). I similarly sense that identifying non-Muslims as a source of dirt necessarily reflects their situatedness in a wrong place, their non-belonging. This is how I suggest that giving a specifically Turkish name with a specific meaning subsequent to the Great Fire of Tatavla (1929) has been co-constitutive in the demographic Turkification of the neighbourhood. Although the main cause of the fire has never been fully identified, it transformed the physical and social components of the neighbourhood to the degree that its old residents were clearly not welcome anymore. Similar to several historical and more contemporary examples of city fires and urban regeneration/gentrification projects, such direct interventions into the material spaces of dwelling necessarily bring about often fundamental changes in the social ordering of these spaces in return (see Amygdalou 2014 for a comparative analysis of Izmir and Thessaloniki fires). During my walks in the streets and participant observations in people's homes in the buildings, as well as research into the municipality's master plan, I noticed two essential components of such post-fire transformation of physical space in the neighbourhood. First, the material qualities of buildings changed. As the former wooden buildings in the neighbourhood burned down, they were reconstructed in concrete, further enabling larger houses with multiple storeys to be built. Thus, the post-fire reconstruction of the neighbourhood resulted in surplus housing, which provided the physical setting for the increase of the non-Muslim population in the following three decades. Second, during my research, I observed that contemporary Kurtuluş had very ambiguous borders that did not necessarily correspond to the borders of historical Tatavla. In recent memoirs and other publications on Tatavla (Türker 1998; Marmara 2001; Irmak 2003), it appears that the historical neighbourhood refers to a particular zone within contemporary Kurtuluş that centred around the Aya Tanaş (Agios Athanasios), Aya Dimitri (Agios Dimitrios) and Aya Lefter (Agios Eleftherios) Greek churches and the Greek cemetery.

It appears that contemporary Kurtuluş was formed through a merger of three former Istanbul neighbourhoods that were home to different ethnolinguistic populations. In the above aerial photo from 1970, we can see that the neighbourhood is separated from other neighbourhoods by two valleys located to the west and

118 *Mobility and Armenian Belonging*

Figure 6 Aerial Photo of Kurtuluş (1970), with two superimposed lines to stress its peninsula-like quality.

the east. It resembles a peninsula on land. Kurtuluş Street roughly runs about a kilometre between the Latin Catholic Cemetery located in the north and the Aya Dimitri Greek church located in the south and cuts the neighbourhood into two. To the west of Kurtuluş Street is located historical Feriköy, which historically emerged as an Armenian neighbourhood with its Surp Vartanants Armenian Apostolic Church and Armenian primary school. To the east of Kurtuluş Street is located historical Pangaltı, named after the Italian Pancaldi family, where the Catholic Cemetery was once located before its relocation to the northern tip of Kurtuluş Street. This neighbourhood was once home to Italian immigrants and Catholic Levantines (Marmara 2001). In the aerial photo we can see the differences between urban compositions of streets. As opposed to the grid-like structure of the streets that are parallel and perpendicular to Kurtuluş Street, the area in the southernmost part of the contemporary neighbourhood is a maze of narrow streets. Tatavla, the lower-class Greek neighbourhood of Constantinople, was located here, at the southern end of today's Kurtuluş Street.

As I went through the previously mentioned (pre-fire) 1925 maps of Istanbul by Pervititch (1927), I noticed that large pieces of land between these three neighbourhoods located to the west, east and south of Kurtuluş Street were not inhabited at that time. While the fire transformed wooden houses into larger concrete buildings in historical Tatavla, it must have been in the following decades that the gaps between these three neighbourhoods were narrowed and vanished through construction of buildings in increasing numbers. However, for the contemporary residents of the neighbourhood, Tatavla is Kurtuluş and Kurtuluş is Tatavla. For instance, two images from the northern part of today's Kurtuluş Street show how places that were not formerly part of historical Tatavla are constantly being imagined as such. The photograph on the left was taken in 2015, during a public commemoration of Armenian journalist Hrant Dink, who was murdered by Turkish nationalists in 2007. The commemorators emplaced 'alternative' street signs to replace the current ones, and in the picture on the left we see how Ergenekon Street was thus changed to Hrant Dink Street by the people. The second image, on the right, clearly shows what it stands for, as the name Kurtuluş is spray-painted over and changed to Tatavla.

Similar forms of urban critiques against the name-changing policies of the early Kemalist nation-state were commonplace in the streets of Kurtuluş. Many building walls were spray-painted in Turkish and Armenian by anonymous people who brought protests into the level of everyday life. There are many such wall paintings/writings that question the death of Sevag Balıkçı, who was murdered in 2011 by fellow soldiers during his compulsory military service on 24 April, the day that marked the beginning of the Armenian Genocide with the order of the Ottoman government to arrest Armenian intellectuals, artists and politicians in 1915. As demonstrated in the two images below, on the centenary of the Genocide, two particular buildings within 50 metres from my home in Kurtuluş were spray-painted 'Krikor Zohrab Buradaydı' (in Turkish: Krikor Zohrab was here) and 'Zabel Yesayan Buradaydı' (in Turkish: Zabel Yesayan was here), commemorating two of the most important Ottoman Armenian authors from Istanbul.[6]

Figure 7 A Pirate Street Sign Commemorating Hrant Dink.

While such forms of protest/critique were in practice in the neighbourhood, during my walks, a particular building struck my attention. It was a recently constructed building with a large name plate, displaying TATAVLA APARTMENTS in capital letters, visible from the street. I managed to contact and meet the contractor in a few days through friends in the neighbourhood. At the time of research, he was a Turkish migrant in Germany, who after saving a considerable amount of money decided to invest in construction in Istanbul. He owned several other buildings in the area. He explained to me that there was an older building on the site of Tatavla Apartments, which did not have a name, as opposed to most buildings in the area. I asked him why he named the new building after deciding to demolish the old one. He explained that after living in Germany for so many years, he had cultivated a 'new eye' for looking at things in Turkey. He considered himself a leftist. After learning about the history of the neighbourhood from his local friends based in Kurtuluş, he came up with the idea of honouring the memory (in Turkish: *anısını yaşatmak*) of the place where he got involved in the construction business.

I also asked him about the other buildings he demolished and reconstructed. Sometimes he kept the previous names of buildings, and when the old buildings

Figure 8 Spraying the Street Signs in Kurtuluş.

did not have names, he did not name them all. However, there was another particular building for which he changed the name. The old name of the building was Eleftherios, clearly a Greek name, and after he demolished it, he named the new building Babylon. He told me that he wanted to honour the memories of all the different languages that were widely spoken in Constantinople, which reminded him of the Tower of Babylon, where the legend says that all languages originated from.

In many ways, the contractor's involvement in recent urban transformation (through demolishing old buildings and constructing new ones) reveals two different sides of contemporary politics of naming in Kurtuluş. In an era in which memory is increasingly equated with recognition of 'historical' facts and social justice, 'workers of memory' such as artists, activists and protesters define alternative sites of memory (Hoelscher 2008: 26). In the context of Turkey, denial and impunity of crimes against non-Muslims 'have remained taboo subjects for decades, only to be recently thematised, but not yet acknowledged and condemned as racist state policies or considered a cause for reparations' (Suciyan 2015: 83). This is why even during a short walk in the streets of Kurtuluş one may

Figure 9 Commemorating Krikor Zohrab in Kurtuluş (civil.net).

come across 'pirate' street signs or writings on buildings walls that commemorate Armenian intellectuals who are regarded as victims of the Genocide, or journalist Hrant Dink and soldier Sevag Balıkçı, who were murdered by Turkish nationalists in 2007 and 2011, respectively.

However, it seems that 'memory work' also bears the possibility of silencing *other* memories. When the contractor demolished an old building in order to construct a new one, he not only changed the name of his building from Eleftherios to Babylon but also erased a distinctively Greek component of the urban landscape and rendered it more generic and 'acceptable' – although he did not change the name directly into Turkish, either. As Ruth Mandel wrote in relation to post-Holocaust Berlin, 'these forms of manipulation of the visible landscape point to an ambivalent desire to expunge, transform, or to neutralize uncomfortable elements of the past' (2008: 116). As portrayed in the Introduction, such interventions necessarily 'create a new meaning about the past that is usable toward present claims' (Brink-Danan 2012: 73). However, as portrayed in the previous chapter, such post-intervention meanings exert destabilizing effects on visitors to Muş, where the organization of space appears more 'horizontal' than 'vertical'. In Istanbul, I find all the signs that point at a physical appropriation of place one way or another 'to be endowed with the essentialized or reified property of historicity' (Parmentier 1987: 12). Similarly, in the transformation of Tatavla into Kurtuluş and back again to Tatavla in the form of critique/protest against Turkification of the neighbourhood, the imagined boundaries of the historical Greek neighbourhood are enlarged to the extent of masking other histories of Turkification in the Armenian Feriköy and the Catholic/Levantine Pangaltı. In a present-day context in which contemporary Kurtuluş covers the area of all three

Figure 10 Commemorating Zabel Yesayan in Kurtuluş.

neighbourhoods, what is left of the history of Tatavla if the former is bluntly equated with the latter? It seems this is a matter of historicity-in-the-making.

Amy Mills (2010) in her analysis of the similarly multi-ethnic neighbourhood of Kuzguncuk in Istanbul argues that the exodus of non-Muslim minorities left behind a contested urban landscape. As she notes, the mental maps of contemporary residents in such neighbourhoods simultaneously acknowledge the historical diversity of the place and deny responsibility for confiscated and redistributed non-Muslim properties. In the context of Kuzguncuk, one particular example provided by Mills is a confiscated public garden that the state wanted to demolish for the construction of buildings, whereas activists and protesters wanted to keep it as a green space for the neighbourhood community and an elderly Greek woman who claimed ownership demanded the return of the piece of land to her family. The striking aspect of this combination of actors is that the activists/protesters claiming the land for the community were amongst the people who were critical of the Turkification of the neighbourhood and the exodus of non-Muslims following the 1955 Pogroms. In this context, it seems, there is a limit to which violent histories of confiscation and looting of non-Muslims properties are being unsilenced in Turkey.

In addition to properties that were confiscated, the massive amount of abandoned non-Muslim properties such as houses, lands and a variety of institutions such as schools, hospitals and orphanages entailed a new set of legal regulations and practices by the state that are often complex and contradictory. This is why in similar neighbourhoods there are properties whose ownership is claimed by a variety of actors, which could include a Turkish individual in Istanbul, second – or third-generation non-Muslim family members abroad, ministries and several other state institutions. Over the course of my fieldwork such properties with contested ownership status were constantly making the headlines in the Turkish media. These included properties on massive scales such as the Çankaya Presidential Residence complex in Ankara, Diyarbakır Airport and Zeytinburnu Stadium in Istanbul, which have been claimed by Armenian families abroad or Armenian foundations in Turkey.

Mills (2010) argues that such contested property ownership is related to Turkification processes in various forms and indicative of one's relationships to the Turkish nation-state, which are based on the hierarchies among Turkish citizens. While people with Sunni Muslim Turkish backgrounds are at the top, the rest – Muslim immigrants from former Ottoman territories who did not speak Turkish at the time of their arrival to Turkey, Kurds and Arabs, Alevis and non-Muslims – are situated at different levels of this hierarchy. For this reason, in the following section, I will portray how these hierarchies were formulated through the imposition of Turkishness as the officially acceptable ethnic category and the base definition of citizenship in the first decades of the nation-state.

Concentric zones of Turkishness

Soner Cagaptay (2005) argues that the institutions and ideology of modern Turkey were firmly established in the 1930s, during a decade of authoritarian nationalism. It was in this era that a specific understanding of what *still* constitutes Turkishness was defined, was incorporated into the constitution as a principle of the Turkish state and became legally enforced and publicly accepted (2–3). In order to understand the different levels and scales of the distances between non-Muslim citizens and the state in Turkey, it is essential to understand the official definitions and operations of Turkishness, which Cagaptay argues are composed of three concentric zones defined by the state: an outer civic zone for non-Muslims (based on shared territory), a middle religious one reserved for non-Turkish Muslims (based on a particular definition of shared culture) and an inner ethno-linguistic one reserved for Turks (based on a particular definition of shared race) (160). Hence, these three zones of Turkishness depended on three different articulations of the term under the nation-state ideology. This is why the category of 'Turk' should be understood in context-specific terms, and not always in ontological opposition to non-Muslims (such as Greeks, Armenians and Jews) in the country. Moreover, it should imply that for non-Muslim minorities there are obvious limits to their inclusion in the Turkish polity (Bora 1998; Neyzi 2002; İçduygu and Soner 2006; Keyman and Kancı 2011; Ekmekçioğlu 2016).

The zonal constitution of Turkishness in the nation-state era should be understood in relation to the mindset inherited from the citizenship practices of the Ottoman state and a particular approach to community-state politics that is still based on them for benefits and security (Barkey and Gavrilis 2016: 34). The former Ottoman system divided its diverse population into strict compartments of communities based on faith, called millets. Although the term, borrowed from Arabic, translates as 'nation' in contemporary Turkish, it had a very different connotation before the emergence of Turkey as a nation-state. The system was pragmatic in its elaboration of the different millets of the empire (Belge 1995; Barkey 2008). According to this system that categorized the Ottoman population, there were initially Muslim, Jewish, Armenian (Apostolic), Greek (Orthodox) and later on Catholic and Protestant millets with the supremacy of the Muslim millet, which consisted of Turks, Kurds, Arabs and various Balkan and Caucasian Muslims as well as Greek- or Armenian-speaking Muslims. This is also why Turkish-speaking Armenian Christians were considered as part of the Armenian millet and Turkish-speaking Greek Orthodox Christians were considered as part of the Greek millet. The religious communities under the millet system were not homogeneous in terms of language; however, for centuries, the system merged various diverse ethnic populations into religious ones, making the religious identity dominant among many Ottoman subjects (Cagaptay 2005).

In an attempt to centralize its power over its vast array of diverse populations, the late Ottoman state introduced equal citizenship for Muslims and non-Muslims alike through secularization – hence holding individuals accountable directly to the state, not to their faith communities (Ahmad 1991; Zürcher 2004). However, this centralization through secularization resulted in an ironic consequence in which millets achieved a degree of formal institutionalization they never had in the classical Ottoman period that catalysed secessionist movements led by their lay elites (Zürcher 2010: 62). This is how the system that emerged as a matter of Islamic law and the bureaucratic pragmatics of the Ottoman state, centred around faith in the first place, subsequently laid the basis of articulations of collective/communal identities in the late-Ottoman period.

Feroz Ahmad (1991) stresses that the terms *millet* (lit. nation) and *milli* (lit. national) evolved in the 100-year-long period between the mid-nineteenth century and mid-twentieth century and so the terms should be understood from a historical perspective (6; also cited in Zürcher 2010: 226). He argues that both terms had more Islamic connotations than Turkish even in the 1919–22 period, in which the 'national struggle' was seen as a religious struggle, a jihad against Western powers by the Muslim millet for its very survival, thus *milli mücadele* (lit. national struggle) (Ahmad 1991: 6). It is in the aftermath of the emergence of the nation-state of Turkey that the term increasingly became devoid of a Muslim connotation and acquired a Turkish connotation, as the founders of the state modelled Turkey through continuation of secularization processes launched by the Ottomans (Zürcher 2010: 149).

However, in the decade roughly between the start of the First World War in 1914 and the emergence of the nation-state of Turkey in 1923, the Muslims transformed into a nation of Turks while non-Muslim millets transformed into minorities. As Rodrigue (2013) notes, the new terminology adopted in the Lausanne Treaty in

1923 – the foundation treaty of Turkey – not only recognized Greeks, Armenians and Jews officially as minorities but also emphasized their fundamental difference from Turks and implied that they were never to become true Turks (40–4; also cited in Barkey and Gavrilis 2015: 34). On the other hand, the prioritization of Turkishness as the major determinant of the new country's official identity posited a fundamental problem where 30 per cent of the population did not have Turkish as their mother tongue (Zürcher 2010: 149). Cagaptay argues (2005) that this situation was closely related to the constant migration of diverse Muslim masses to Turkey from former Ottoman territories.

Leyla Neyzi (2002) wrote that the term 'Turk' 'disguises the diversity of the linguistic, ethnic *and* religious origins of Turkey's "majority" population' (141, emphasis original). As I construe this particular history of nation-building, it appears that an 'outside' should have been articulated first, as there was no homogenized 'inside' within the concentric zones of Turkishness. As Cagaptay (2005) notes, first of all, in the 1924 constitution, all people living within the borders of Turkey were recognized simultaneously as Turks and Turkish citizens, including Jews, Armenians and Greeks, making shared territory the least important criterion in the articulation of Turkishness. Second, through the 1930s, the definition of Turkishness in state documents recognized culture (in Turkish: *hars*) with an emphasis primarily on shared religion (and shared history to a much lesser extent), bringing Muslims closer to the centre of Turkishness than non-Muslims. Bernard Lewis (1968) once wrote that 'one may speak of Christian Arabs – but a Christian Turk is an absurdity and a contradiction in terms… a non-Muslim in Turkey may be called a Turkish citizen, but never a Turk' (15; also quoted in İçduygu and Soner 2006: 454). Third, as evident in the 1934 laws on resettlement of migrants from different countries, the definition of Turkishness this time took into consideration bloodline (in Turkish documents: *soy*), which 'did not necessarily denote immutable biological characteristics, passed down genetically' and instead meant 'ethnicity-through-language' (Cagaptay 2005). Non-Muslim Turkish speakers were prevented from moving towards the centre of Turkishness (Kirişçi 2000). By the same logic, Muslims were able to be considered Turks in the case that they learned Turkish and abandoned their ancestral languages, and they could move towards the centre of Turkishness (Cagaptay 2005; see also Bora 1998). In the decades that followed, this 'internal hierarchy' continued to be instrumentalized in the wake of the different migration waves from former Ottoman territories into the country (Danış and Parla 2009).

In the following section, I attempt to understand how these differentiated zones of Turkishness are reflected and remade in the urban material landscape of Kurtuluş, where direct state intervention pushed non-Muslim minorities to leave and introduced a new Turkish landscape by changing the names of streets and the neighbourhood. However, this should be only one aspect of these Turkification processes that were reflected in the ways urban landscapes transformed in the neighbourhood. Another aspect that should be taken into consideration is the remaining people's responses to these nation-building processes. Here, my enquiry is based on understanding whether these people adapted to these processes, silenced or internalized them, or, to the contrary, employed critiques and tactics against them. A third option is that they possibly came up with their own hybrid formulas instead of either rejecting or accepting them.

A state of unity and a taxonomy of apartment names in Kurtuluş

I suggest that the making of three zones of Turkishness has materially translated into the spatial organization of buildings in contemporary Kurtuluş. This is why an ethnographic focus to test the links between wider state policies of nation-building and the ways ordinary people named their homes and their children is needed. As Bodenhorn and vom Bruck (2006) noted, names 'serve as a means of structuring social relations as well as a powerful medium in which to talk about those relations' (26). During my lengthy walks around the twenty-four city blocks (in Turkish: *konut adası*, lit. island of dwelling), I noticed patterns in building names, which I could roughly group into seven categories. The first group of buildings comprises buildings without any names. These buildings have only building numbers. The total number of these buildings is very small and there are no more than two or three such buildings on each street. The second group includes buildings that were named after the street they were located on; for instance, there are two Türkbey (i) apartments on Türkbeyi Street and again two Bilezikçi apartments on Bilezikçi Street. The third group includes flower names such as Gül (lit. rose), Nilüfer (lit. lily), Leylak (lit. lilac) or Sümbül (lit. hyacinth). The fourth group comprises different place names from Turkey and neighbouring post-Ottoman countries with building names such as Midilli (Lesvos), Teselya (Thessaly) or Şumnu (Shumen) in contemporary Greece and Bulgaria and Erbil or Halep (Aleppo) in contemporary Iraq and Syria, all clearly indicating immigration to Istanbul from different corners of the post-Ottoman world.

There is a further pattern among names from Turkey as well. On the one hand, there are building names from towns around Bithynia and Thrace, the nearby coastal areas around the Sea of Marmara and Istanbul, such as Bilecik, Bursa, Iznik or Tekirdağ. On the other hand, there are building names from eastern and south-eastern Anatolia, such as Bingöl, Bitlis, Diyarbakır and Harput – cities with considerable Armenian populations before the Genocide and the subsequent Turkification processes. In many ways, such names demonstrate immigration to Istanbul from the city's hinterland as well as the empire's more distant Armenian-populated provinces. It is interesting that hardly any place is mentioned in between these eastern Anatolian towns and the smaller towns around Istanbul. One exception to this situation is Ankara – the capital of the new Republic – and Çankaya – the neighbourhood of Ankara where the presidential palace is located and for which it is named.

A fifth group of building names corresponds to people's names: some Turkish, some specifically Armenian (such as Sevan and Ani, which are also place names) and some others clearly non-Muslim but not necessarily Armenian (such as Viktorya, Kristin and Elizabet). The buildings with non-Muslim names make up the smallest group – the number of such buildings is less than twenty in total among the hundreds of buildings I listed in Kurtuluş. The buildings of the sixth group are named after their contractor's family or company names, such as Öger and Yenilmez apartments scattered around the neighbourhood. The seventh and last group of buildings has names based on abstract concepts, such as Huzur (lit. peace or peace of mind), Işık (lit. light, also a unisex name in Turkish), Arzu (lit. desire, also a female name in Turkish) or Rüya (lit. dream, also a female name in Turkish). There is another particular building name that belongs to this last group, Birlik (lit. unity, state of union or oneness), which is the most frequent name among the last group of buildings.

For a person raised in Turkey, *birlik* resonates with the unity of the nation. For instance, on the website of the Atatürk Research Centre of the Atatürk Culture, Language, and History Institute under the direct authority of the Turkish prime minister, national unity (in Turkish: *birlik*) and togetherness (in Turkish: *beraberlik*, but *birlik* also translates as union) are elaborated by bullet points as follows:

> 'National unity and togetherness' is one of the fundamental principles of the Turkish Revolution [referring to the Six Principles of Kemalism]. It is closely related to nationalism, national sovereignty, and national independence.
>
> Atatürk's unifying and integrating, fusing idea of nationalism is expressed through national unity and togetherness.
>
> National unity and togetherness implies unity as a nation, co-existence, and completeness. National unity and togetherness firmly ties the individuals of the nation who live together. Unity as a nation means unity in the components of the nation, union, and completeness.
>
> [...]
>
> National unity and union is also the means for the realization of the nation state.
>
> National unity and union mean unity and union primarily among the components of the nation (atam.gov.tr).

In many ways, in contemporary Turkey, *birlik* is very laden with Turkification processes and their violent history. Over the almost 100 years of the Turkish Republic, politicians, state officials, mayors and other bureaucrats constantly repeated that Turkey needed 'national unity and togetherness'. Although there was no direct reference to the principle of national unity in the 1924 constitution of the Republic of Turkey, 1937 amendments introduced the Six Principles of Kemalism – republicanism, nationalism, populism, statism, secularism and reformism – and enshrined these as the basic qualities of the state (as referred to on the website of the Ministry of Foreign Affairs of Turkey). Hence, national unity within the framework of what would later be coined in the 1982 constitution as 'Atatürk's nationalism' (in Turkish: *Atatürk milliyetçiliği*) sought unity among the concentric zones of Turkishness.

In the preamble of the 1961 constitution, it was clearly stated that:

the Turkish nation, prompted and inspired by the spirit of Turkish nationalism, which unites all individuals, be it in fate, pride or distress, in common bond as an indivisible whole around national consciousness and aspirations, and which has as its aim always to exalt our nation in a spirit of national unity as a respected member of the community of the world of nations enjoying equal rights and privileges... enacts and proclaims this constitution.

(translation of Balkan, Uysal and Karpat 1961, anayasa.gen.tr)

Article 3 of the 1961 constitution also stated:

The Turkish State is an indivisible whole comprising its territory and people.

(ibid.)

Some twenty years later the notions of national unity and indivisibility of the country (with its people and territory) were repeated in the preamble of the 1982 constitution:

(As amended on 23 July 1995) Affirming the eternal existence of the Turkish Motherland and Nation and the indivisible unity of the Sublime Turkish State, this Constitution, in line with the concept of nationalism introduced by the founder of the Republic of Turkey, Atatürk, the immortal leader and the unrivalled hero, and his reforms and principles [...] (As amended on 3 October 2001) has been entrusted by the TURKISH NATION to the democracy-loving Turkish sons' and daughters' love for the motherland and nation.

(global.tbmm.gov.tr)

Several constitutional articles (including article 3 on the duties and responsibilities of the state, article 26 on the freedom of expression and dissemination of thought and article 58 on the protection of the youth) repeated that the state aims to 'safeguard the indivisible integrity of the state with its territory and nation.'[7] It becomes apparent in these official texts that national unity and the indivisible integrity of the state are fundamental issues in the legal constitution of the relationships between the state and its citizens. I consider these repetitive notions of national unity (*milli birlik*) – along with national togetherness (*milli beraberlik*) and national integrity (*milli bütünlük*) – in these aforementioned official texts as indicators of the state's unceasing and abiding anxieties about the fate of nation-building processes in the country. As suggested earlier in this chapter, ideologists of Turkishness specifically for this reason articulated three zones of Turkishness through their own defined frameworks of territory, culture and race and *enclosed* all the diverse populations of the country within the category of 'Turk'. Hence, unity – or national unity – in Turkey should imply unity within the category of the Turk, which has been formulated in terms of citizenship (i.e., Turkishness-through-territory), religion (i.e., Turkishness-through-culture) and bloodline (Turkishness-through-race).

Figure 11 A Collage of Birlik Apartments in and around Kurtuluş.

As argued in the previous section, articulations of distance and proximity vis-à-vis the concentric zones of Turkishness have been constantly kept in place by the state and the people who lived within its borders. It was in this context of the production of the category of the Turk and Turkification processes that I noticed and recognized the pattern of Birlik apartments within Istanbul's urban landscape:

In the archives of the construction master plan of the municipality of Şişli, where Kurtuluş is located, I found that apartments with the name Birlik mushroomed in the neighbourhood after the 1955 Pogroms. During my walks around the twenty-four city blocks in the neighbourhood (or the 'island of dwelling' as understood in Turkish), I identified eleven buildings with this name, and in the municipality archives I found that nine of these buildings were built after the 1955 Pogroms in the neighbourhood, one was built in 1955, and the last one was built before that, in the early 1950s. My research in the archives also revealed that the small number of buildings with non-Muslim names were all constructed before 1955. As we will also see in the following two chapters, for the great majority of my informants from Istanbul, including the ones who were not born at the time, the Pogroms of 1955, or *6–7 Eylül Olayları* (lit. the Events of 6–7 September), constitute the most violent episode in the history of Turkey, resulting in organized murder and rape of non-Muslims and the looting of their properties. At one level, it is impossible to deny that the Pogroms mark a moment in the history of the neighbourhood, cutting across two time periods with different patterns of building naming. Moreover, Kaymak (2016) notes that on those two days in 1955 many non-Muslim families in Istanbul sought protection by hanging Turkish flags in their windows (89) (see also Güven 2006 and Bali 2012 for a longer discussion on the background of the Pogroms). During my research in Kurtuluş, I repeatedly observed how my Armenian neighbours and friends (or their family members) paid special attention to hanging their Turkish flags in their windows, balconies or building entrances during national holidays – sometimes after ironing them. This is also how, at another level, I find it important to suggest that the Pogroms also marked a moment in which non-Muslims in Turkey defined on which levels and to what extent they would expose their differences to the 'outside', which in this chapter I tackle only in relation to the street level.

Welcome to *Birlik Apartmanı*

I was supposed to meet Hakan in his family's home in an apartment building named Birlik in Kurtuluş. He had lived on the third floor of this multi-storey building with his family up until his marriage a few years ago. Recently he had moved to another apartment nearby, less than 5 minutes walking distance. I was previously told that the elders of his extended family, mostly his uncles and their wives, lived on other floors. While the unmarried children of the family kept living with their parents in this building, those who got married, similar to Hakan, all lived a short walking distance from the family building.

When Hakan called me, I thought he would direct me to the Birlik apartment where he had once lived with his parents as a single man. Instead, he instructed me to find my way to another building with a different name, *Manolya*, where his sister lived. I rang the doorbell at the entrance of the building and through the intercom Hakan told me to come to the top floor. As he let me in, I came to understand that he had a very large family. That evening there were a dozen family members scattered around a dinner table with lots of food in a very small room. He introduced me to his aunts, siblings and nephews and nieces. The room was so small that some of the family members were sitting on the floor cross-legged or standing up while eating at the same time. I similarly attempted to sit on the floor, which caused a temporary family crisis among siblings on whether or not to let the guest sit on the floor. When I finally took my seat on a chair (confiscated from one of the children) next to Hakan's sister, she told me I was welcome to the Birlik Apartment (in Turkish: *Birlik apartmanına hoşgeldiniz!*). They were obviously very well informed about my research topic. As if I did not understand her, I responded that this building had a different name. She laughed aloud, pointed at the crowd of people and told me that it was the crowd that was the *birlik* (in Turkish: *Birlik budur!*).

It was Hakan's sister who lived here with her husband and their new-born baby. They explained to me that they met at a family member's house and had dinner together every weekend. That night in the room, there was a complete mix of people from different and distant parts of Turkey, from predominantly Kurdish- and Turkish-speaking families. In recent years, the family had expanded through new members who were Armenian, Kurdish or Turkish. Hakan himself had married a woman from Turkey's tiny Azeri community from a town located on the Armenian border. This was one of the reasons why there were family members with names in Armenian, Kurdish, Turkish and Kurdish/Turkish (i.e., names that exist in both languages but not in Armenian).

Hakan's Turkish name did not give outsiders any clue that he was Armenian. Before I met him, I thought he came from a family of Armenian converts to Islam, but this was not the case. His family was from the present-day province of Batman (Sassoun in the Ottoman period), which had a large Armenian population and still has a large Kurdish population. Unlike other Armenians who survived the Genocide from their village of origin, they did not immigrate for another six decades and lived among the Kurdish Muslims who replaced the victims. I was told that they always identified themselves as Armenians, albeit not publicly.

In the specific context of Turkey, naming practices of people are historically interwoven with the wider political context of nation-building (Spencer 1961; Bulliet 1978; Mardin 2002). This is how the migration history of Hakan's family was reflected in the ways they named their children and grandchildren. The first post-genocide generation of men and women who were born and raised in the village had Kurdish/Turkish/Muslim names. It was only after their immigration to Istanbul that they gave some of their daughters Armenian names. However, the sons, who were in contact with the outside world more often than the women through business, continued to be given Kurdish/Turkish/Muslim names. Finally, for the third generation, born in the late 1990s and 2000s, some boys – but not the majority – were also given Armenian names. The girls all had Armenian names. However, in opposition to earlier generations, none of the third-generation boys had names with Islamic or Turkic connotations. In cases where they did not have an Armenian name, they had secular Turkish or Kurdish names that did not originate from the Quran, Islamic terminology or Arabic. For instance, there were men in the older generations with names such as Ahmet or Sadullah, but the third generation had names such as Kıvanç or Erman from Turkish and Sidar or Reyas from Kurdish.

It was Hakan's oldest uncle who initiated the immigration of the family to Istanbul in 1981, right after the coup that escalated the violence in predominantly Kurdish south-eastern Turkey. However, in the first decade after their immigration they continued visiting their village of origin in the summers. In the first half of the 1990s they finally abandoned their summer visits to their village when a commander in the Turkish Army summoned everyone to the village square and 'warned' them against enemies inside and outside. The villagers were advised not to cooperate with PKK supporters or Armenians in the village, or else they would face the consequences. The fight between the Kurdish guerrillas and the Turkish Army finally revealed the family's Armenian background to their fellow villagers.

After some tea, Hakan asked me whether I was ready to go to the Birlik apartment that I had been interested in visiting since the first time I met him. We left the family and in less than two minutes arrived in front of a building that I was sure I had never noticed before. At first, I thought I had probably missed the building during my walks in the neighbourhood, as I had walked that street many times. However, I could not see any label or nameplate on the building indicating its name. When I asked about this, Hakan responded that the name plate had recently broken and they would probably replace it soon. Therefore, this particular building constituted the twelfth and final Birlik apartment on my list.

It was Hakan's paternal family who lived in the building, where his father and his five siblings had their own apartments located on six floors. Nazife was Hakan's oldest uncle's wife. She was the eldest in the family, and this was why Hakan believed that I should talk to her. She told me that she was born in Batman, but unlike her husband's family, she moved to Istanbul at the age of six when her father took the entire family. When she was a teenager, her father decided to arrange a marriage for her with an Armenian boy, who was Hakan's uncle, from his ancestral village in Batman. Hakan's uncle married and took Nazife back to Batman and they lived there until their migration to Istanbul in 1981. When they arrived in Istanbul, they bought an old apartment building that had belonged to a Greek family who had left Istanbul for Greece in 1964, on the same site where the current Birlik apartment is now located. They lived on different floors of the old building for sixteen years. In 1997 they demolished the building and rebuilt it with more floors and space that would be enough for the expanding family.

When I asked Nazife about the origins of the building's name, she told me that she, her husband's brothers and their wives decided on the name together once they demolished the old building and rebuilt it. She said, 'we brought the foundation of our entire family here, in this building where it stands, and this is why we named it "unity"' (in Turkish: *Ailemizin bütün temelini buraya, bu binanın olduğu yere getirmişiz, işte bu yüzden de adına 'Birlik' demişiz*). She repeated what Hakan had told me previously, that they had lived together in this building up until now, and those who left due to marriage all moved into apartments *centring* around it (in Turkish: *yeni evlenenler de hep bu binayı merkez alarak etrafında yaşarlar*). She explained to me that all of the family members lived within walking distance. While speaking, she rotated her hand in a specific way that stressed that the building was the centre for everyone in the family.

Towards the end of our conversation, one of her sons – thus, one of Hakan's first cousins – entered the house. He was a single man who lived with Nazife and he looked tired as he had just come back from work. As he saw that Hakan was in the living room, he approached him and asked how life was in the 'other' apartment (in Turkish: *öteki apartmanda hayat nasıl?*), which was also on the same street. Hakan replied that everything was fine and his sister was very happy to live there. He added that his brother rented the shop at the entrance of the same apartment building. When Nazife's son asked whether they considered buying more apartments in the building, Hakan responded that it was certainly on their agenda. One of his younger brothers was about to marry. While Hakan and his cousin were talking, Nazife turned to me at that specific moment, smiled and told me that it was probably the right time to build a (second) new 'Birlik' apartment (in Turkish: *şimdi belki de yeni bir Birlik apartmanı yapmanın tam vaktidir*).

There is a very particular aspect of what I presented earlier in this book that resonates with what I came to observe during my research in Istanbul. Similar to how 'the expanding outside' (as opposed to 'the shrinking inside') accounted for the material readjustments following political and economic change in post-socialist Armenia (Platz 2000), I suggest that we can understand *birlik* as a rearticulation of social distances in twentieth-century Turkey. For both the state and individuals in Kurtuluş, the term defines zones of accessibility, intimacy and connectedness, although in different ways. For the state, the term translates as the unity of the indivisible Turkish nation. For citizens, it sets a goal that is almost never possible to reach, as it sets distances between those who are fit and unfit for becoming Turks. I suspect that the 'intentional vagueness' in defining Turkishness by the state (Ekmekçioğlu 2016: 105) has been fundamental in persuading citizens to struggle for such an impossible task.

I argue that *birlik* has been articulated by what it does not literally stand for, an emphasis on immutable differences between who the state recognized as Turks and as *only* Turkish citizens. The term appears not only as a state-imposed category of national unity but also as a popular imaginary unit of distance measuring the differences between cores and margins of Turkishness with direct implications on the material space of apartment buildings in Istanbul. At one level, the frequency and the construction dates of the Birlik apartments suggest that their non-Muslim owners responded to Turkification processes in an accommodating way. However, at another level, in the accounts of Nazife, Hakan and other members of their family, the notion of unity and the apartment name of Birlik do not resonate with the national unity defined by the ideologists of early Kemalism. On the contrary, their notion is based on a deliberate counter-articulation of the term that is critical of the form of unity imposed by the state. This poses a direct answer to what Kabir Tambar (2013) asked: 'In what ways are hegemonic formations of national

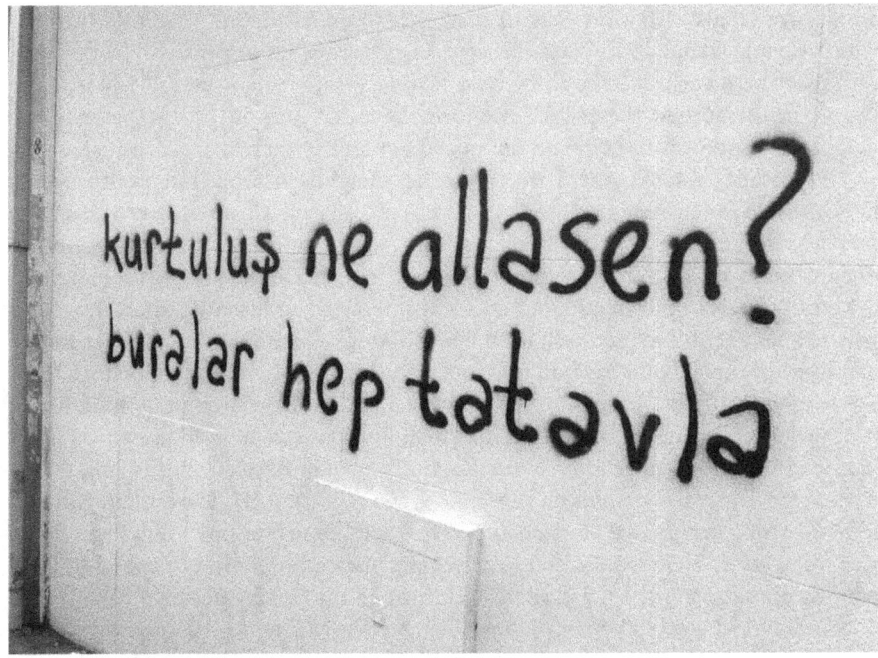

Figure 12 Spray Painting on a Kurtuluş Wall.

citizenship confirmed, troubled, or remade in acts of historical critique?' (121). For Nazife and Hakan, unity is understood as the unity of their dispersed and enlarging family across different towns, languages and countries.

I believe the polysemy of 'Birlik' matches the polysemy of Tatavla in contemporary Kurtuluş in many ways. In December 2015, I delivered a public speech in Istanbul entitled *Turkification in Kurtuluş: Urban Transformation and Dwelling Biographies*. Upon listening to my speech, someone from the audience raised her hand and expressed her confusion over the historical location of Tatavla. She was a documentary filmmaker in the process of finalizing video shootings in the area, which she identified as historical Tatavla. However, she was very surprised to hear that contemporary Kurtuluş had come into being through the merger of three historical neighbourhoods. She concluded by asking whether she had shot her documentary in the 'wrong' location. Many other people in the audience also wanted to know about the 'exact location' of Tatavla. I responded that there was probably no one to decide on that. Tatavla could have been a historical neighbourhood with more or less publicly acknowledged borders before the 1929 fire and its merger with two other Istanbul neighbourhoods. However, as I explained to the audience, what the name Tatavla has come to represent for the residents of contemporary Kurtuluş should be understood in less rigid terms. I added that, as an anthropologist, my duty was to shed light onto historical processes through which people understood certain things in certain ways at present. Therefore, I said that there was no such thing as a 'wrong location'. However, I felt that the people in the audience expected me to make a decision on how to refer to the neighbourhood: was I personally supposed to name it Tatavla or Kurtuluş?

Historically, Tatavla was a much smaller neighbourhood, but politically its name has acquired new meanings in addition to its physical expansion over the past five decades. Just before my speech, I had received an email from another documentary filmmaker working on the neighbourhood. She had read about my upcoming speech in a newspaper and was interested in learning about how and why I came to conduct research on the neighbourhood. She wrote that her family had lived in the neighbourhood for three generations. She attached a photo from the neighbourhood (see Figure 12). However, she did not write anything about it. It stood on its own at the end of the email, the camera focused on words spray painted on a wall that read 'What is Kurtuluş, for God's sake? Here is all/always Tatavla' (in Turkish: *Kurtuluş ne allasen? Buralar hep Tatavla*). The director wanted to figure out my personal relationship to the neighbourhood by asking whether I was from there. She also wanted to check my stance in relation to the politics of naming operating in the neighbourhood through the image she sent.

Similar to what Marcy Brink-Danan (2012) observed on Jewish naming politics in contemporary Istanbul, the wide range of naming processes in Kurtuluş allows us to explore present-day ontologies as historically informed and context-dependent (28). These ontologies, as Brink-Danan suggests, can be best understood as 'ideas about what things exist or can be said to exist, and how such things should be grouped according to similarities and differences' (ibid.). This is precisely why this chapter explored the ways in which the production of the category of Turk was translated into place-making in an Istanbul neighbourhood. In the aftermath of the collapse of the Ottoman Empire, distances to Turkishness defined the differences and the similarities between people, languages and religions. It is for this reason that in this chapter I first demonstrated how 'places' (i.e., cities, districts, streets) were the first targets of Turkification-through-naming. Second, I identified building names as another essential component of place-making, which was reflected in ordinary people's responses to the particular ways space has been imagined and crafted by the state in Turkey. I introduced a taxonomy of building names in Kurtuluş and argued that *birlik* had a very specific connotation of the 'unity of nation' in contemporary Turkey. This is why, later, this chapter briefly focused on the articulations of *birlik* in Turkish constitutions from 1960 to 1982. Lastly, as presented in the accounts of Nazife and Hakan, I portrayed how my informants articulated a counter-definition of unity/union within their own 'islands of dwelling' informed by the dispersion of their family by the violence of the Turkish state.

The next two chapters continue exploring the tangible aspects of articulations of distances against the concentric zones of Turkishness, this time in the context of a physical island off Istanbul. In the next chapter, my ethnographic focus on boat journeys en route to the mainland attempts to uncover articulations of belonging to this particular island and its wider community that includes Armenians and non-Armenians. In many ways, I approach the actual everyday practices of travel on the sea as a mode of passage between the nation's imagined centres and peripheries. In the chapter following that, my ethnographic focus shifts to everyday life on the island, where I detect that the political tensions in the larger national context of Turkey are being constantly translated into historically informed divisions between Armenians and others at the local level of the island.

Chapter 6

TAKING THE SLOW BOAT TO ISTANBUL

It is not easy to be Istanbul. *It is such a city that is not quite clear whether it joins or separates two continents, whether it separates or joins two seas.* The answer to these questions does not lie with nature but with humans. That is why Istanbul is different to every eye which looks upon it [...] Between the two [continents of Asia and Europe], the waters are enchanted. The enchantment of water stems from the tension between parting and bringing together. The almost touching of these two continents is like the fingers about to touch in Michelangelo's 'The Creation of Adam'. *It is this touch, or anticipation of touch, that gives Istanbul life.*
(Mehmet Zaman Saçlıoğlu, 'Winter', 2013: 17–18, emphases mine)

There is an 'Armenian island' off Istanbul (Kaymak 2016), one of the nine islands constituting the Prince Islands Archipelago (also widely referred to as the Princes' Islands Archipelago). On a hot summer's day in Istanbul in 2012, Nadia, an Armenian friend from Istanbul in her mid-thirties, and I attempted to travel to this 'Armenian island', the island of Kınalı (henceforth Kınalıada, lit. the island of Kınalı). Nadia spent the summers with the rest of her family in a modest mid-century apartment building, where each of the three floors were occupied by close relatives. Our boat was delayed for 15 minutes, as the seemingly overgrown crowd of passengers required an 'additional service' (in Turkish: *ek sefer*), implying that a second boat was called into the port to finally transport the remaining passengers who wanted to have a glimpse of holidays on various public and more exclusive beaches scattered across the islands. We finally found ourselves squeezed into a hot corner of the vessel, surrounded by a wall of humans blocking any ventilation. The boat was full of commotion, people talking loudly and some others making music. At that moment, Nadia told me that for all these day-trippers (in Turkish: *günübirlikçiler*), the people who lived on the islands were like souvenirs (in Turkish: *turistik eşya*): mainlanders came to see their lives on display. For her, these visitors never respected the islands, bringing litter, noise and disorder. She added that they just never 'shut up' (Turkish: *seslerini kesmiyorlar*) on the boats as well as on the streets of the island and continued disturbing people who needed to rest before running errands in Istanbul or after work, especially those who had a 'real life' (Turkish: *gerçek hayat*) on this and the neighbouring islands.

In the winter that followed, I was once again on the same pier where I had met Nadia, to make it onto a 7:40 pm boat from Istanbul to the island. There were many others running to catch the same boat after me; however, as I passed through the turnstiles, the officer told the people behind me that no more passengers were allowed in. The boarding was completed. A woman behind me started repeatedly shouting: *hayatımdan üç saat çaldınız!* (lit. you stole three hours of my life!). She was protesting that she had to wait – perhaps sitting at the pier – for the next boat. As I left that woman behind, I came to realize that there was a temporal aspect in claiming a relationship to the island. Especially in the winter, when boats are distinctively less frequent than in summer, the service schedules were perceived to be discriminatory by the people who lived on the island during both the summer and the winter, in that they could leave one stranded for long hours. However, if time discriminated, it also united. On the one hand, islanders (in Turkish: *adalılar*), regardless of class, were affected by and had to learn to accommodate this time constraint on their movements (see Reed 2004 on this organizational effect of time). On the other hand, the ways each group of islanders learned to accommodate time made them different kinds of islanders. In other words, if time spent on the island – for some hours, for some a summer, or both summer and winter alike – defined people as particular kinds of islanders, the time spent travelling to and from the island also operated in the same fashion. This is how, for instance, we can think here about how the word *hayat* (in Turkish: life) was used by the woman at the turnstiles and by Nadia vis-à-vis the island (as opposed to 'real life'). When the woman screamed *hayatımdan üç saat çaldınız!* (lit. you stole three hours from my life!) at the turnstiles, she was making a statement about the centrality of the island – her permanent home – in her life. Nadia's comment was similar in the sense that she was making a statement about the island in her life. While on a packed boat to Istanbul, she suggested a difference between how she and the day-trippers perceived the island, a difference signalled when she referred to her life on the island as *gerçek hayat* (lit. real life), as opposed to a life on display, or souvenir-like. What was the temporal element that prompted Nadia to emphasize 'realness' vis-à-vis life on the island? It appears that, for Nadia, regardless of the fact that she only spends a few summer months of the year living on the island, Kınalıada is a permanent fixture in her life and in how she imagines herself.

In this chapter, I suggest that there is a primary level of distinction between the islanders that is discerned in the time spent waiting for and travelling on the boats. I take this distinction, which is simply based on a person's capacity to move, as both defining and reproducing the various differences between Armenians and non-Armenian Turks in contemporary Istanbul. I believe a diversity of urban modes and forms of daily commute and travel constitute a dynamic social context in which one of the many aspects of ethnic demarcation may be observed. For this reason, I explore speed and slowness in multiple ways, first in relation to the overall enterprise of going to the island, which can be time-consuming, and second in relation to the relative speeds of different types of boats that operate between the island and Istanbul. I argue that boat schedules, waiting, unexpected delays and time spent aboard create a multiplicity of temporalities through which islanders claim particular relationships to the island. This chapter attempts to locate Armenians in contemporary Istanbul in relation to a number of non-human actors and consequently discusses the current tropes of Armenian belonging – and identity – as a matter of urban mobility.

The protagonists: Boats and winds

Boat travel between the island and Istanbul proper involves several human and non-human protagonists. The human protagonists include boat crews, passengers and other people who make a living on those boats (such as music performers, beggars and vendors), but the passengers constitute the most diverse group vis-à-vis their relationships to the islands. There are the various types of *adalılar* (lit. islanders) who own houses on the islands and live there either permanently or temporarily; *günübirlikçiler* (lit. day-trippers), which only refers to Turks (from the perspective of the non-Muslim islanders); and *turistler*, tourists who come from 'foreign countries'.

There are two primary modes of sea travel: slow boats, or *vapur* in Turkish (from French *vapeur* for steam; see the similarity with Venetian *vaporetto*), and fast boats, or *deniz otobüsü*, translated as seabus.[1] As opposed to what their names literally imply, the vapurs have not run on steam for several decades and seabuses are nothing like a bus. The former are landmarks of Istanbul's renowned skyline, with their distinctive funnels and masts, in addition to the city's less mobile domes, minarets and towers. Operated since 1954 by City Lines (in Turkish: *Şehir Hatları*),[2] a state-owned company and now part of the Istanbul Metropolitan Municipality (henceforth IMM), the vapurs run all year round with timetables changing every summer and autumn. The seabuses were only introduced in 1987, again by the IMM, and in 2011 this line was privatized. An average journey from Kınalıada direct to Istanbul's Kabataş pier takes 50 minutes on a vapur and 25 minutes on a seabus. Although faster, seabuses only run during the summer. Unlike the vapurs, which are mono-hulled boats, the fast boats have catamaran-like double-hulled bottoms and are hence very vulnerable in harsh winter conditions. In the summer of 2015, the seabus cost twice as much as the vapur, and in the summer of 2016 there was a further increase in seabus tickets although the price of vapurs did not change.[3]

In contrast to orientalist imaginations about Istanbul's warm and steady climate, for most denizens of the city the weather is unpredictable, both in summer and in winter. This brings our second set of protagonists into the story: two distinct types of wind, the poyraz from the north-east (from the ancient Greek god Βορεάς, or 'north' in modern Greek) and the lodos from the south-west (from the ancient Greek god Νότος, or 'south' in modern Greek). Referred to here directly by their Turkish names, these two winds, one blowing in from the cooler Black Sea and the other from the warmer Mediterranean, bring cold and fresh, and hot and dusty air, respectively, into Istanbul. They shape the everyday life of the average Istanbulite

Figure 13 Satellite Image of the Istanbul Seas (demonstrating sea currents).

and even the public mood. The poyraz is a strong wind, and as a fisherman once noted in a newspaper interview, 'it shivers your insides' (15 October 2009, *Hürriyet Daily News*). Kai Strittmatter (2013) writes that the poyraz is a 'welcome visitor', as it 'brings longed-for coolness to Istanbulites in the oppressive summer, blows the veil away from their eyes, *lets the continents slide closer together*' (85, emphasis mine). It is the lodos that makes the continents separate once again, as this wind has a distinct effect on the water currents of the Istanbul seas and often makes them unnavigable. It is within this climatic regime that once, walking on the shores of the island, an informant, without having read Fernand Braudel's *The Mediterranean* (1972), said that she felt Istanbul was the only place where water seemed to connect people instead of separating them, although 'with the exception of the days when the lodos blows!'

There are days when Istanbulites feel like distances between the shores of the city decrease and others when they feel like these distances increase as the water is less passable. As noted in the opening quote of this chapter by Mehmet Zaman Saçlıoğlu (2013), Istanbul is situated between two large bodies of water and landmasses: the Black Sea and the Mediterranean, and the Anatolian and Balkan peninsulas. This brings a unique climate regime, which gives its character to the city. Istanbul is at the centre of constantly changing pressure and temperature zones. Şeref Kayaboğazı (1942), a local geographer/historian of the city, wrote in his book on Istanbul's geography that Istanbul's neighbourhoods and surroundings bore diverse climatic characteristics different from each other. He noted that different neighbourhoods could experience different seasons in the city, as the winds from the colder north and the warmer south were both strong and the differences of temperature between land and sea, as well as between the Black Sea in the north and the smaller Sea of Marmara in the south, were considerable.

The poyraz is the dominant wind reigning in Istanbul, blowing 126 days a year, and the lodos, its major rival, is the second most common, blowing 75 days a year (mgm.gov.tr). Although both the poyraz and lodos are strong winds, it is hardly the case for any Istanbulite travelling by boat to complain about the poyraz in relation to transportation. Most boats to and from the islands are cancelled when the lodos blows, a situation related to the different sea levels in the Sea of Marmara, the Bosphorus and the Black Sea. The Black Sea is 40 cm above the sea levels of the Sea of Marmara and the Mediterranean. It resembles a lake as three great rivers of Europe, the Danube, the Dnieper and the Don, flow into the Black Sea, while it empties into the Mediterranean through the Bosphorus and the Dardanelles via the Sea of Marmara. Consequently, the water current from north to the south, from the Black Sea into the Sea of Marmara, is very strong. This is why every time the lodos blows from the south against the strong currents of the Bosphorus, the sea heaves and transportation becomes challenging in different ways for vapurs and seabuses. In a moderate lodos most seabuses cannot operate; their double-hulled bottoms and fiberglass structures cannot cope with the lodos shaking the waters of the Sea of Marmara and the Bosphorus upstream. Vapurs, with their heavy and often steel structures, are more durable against the harsh sea conditions in Istanbul.

Apart from obstacles regarding transportation on the seas of Istanbul, the wind has effects on the public mood and is often understood as a reason for headaches and migraines. Accuweather.com warns its users of the risk of severe migraines only when the lodos blows. It is commonplace in Istanbul to hear of people suffering from headaches caused by this south-westerly wind. 'Lodos-struck' (in Turkish: *lodos çarpması*) is a context-specific popular notion that defines the condition of suffering from rising levels of clumsiness, dizziness and even grumpiness. 'This wind is a moody intruder which brings rain and mist and leaves behind melancholy and sadness' (Strittmatter 2013: 86). The lodos, as Nobel laureate Giorgos Seferis (1995) once expressed in his *Mythistorema*, is the kind of wind that drives people mad and strips bones of flesh (10). There is another Turkish saying, *lodosun gözü yaşlıdır* (lit. the lodos has wet eyes), which stresses that the southern wind is not only expected to bring heavy rain but additionally make psychologically fragile people become upset or cry. Notable Turkish poet Necip Fazıl Kısakürek also defined the lodos as a cage around a madhouse (1969 [1939]: 161). There is an interesting matter of culture to note here: people in Turkey might name their children Poyraz, but never Lodos (Strittmatter 2013).

Istanbul is a physical context in which these non-human protagonists (boats and winds) speed up and slow down, advancing and retreating, all simultaneously determining the accessibility as well as the isolation of the islands from the mainland. In the following pages of this chapter, my enquiry is based on understanding the social contexts that depend on this physical context, which I argue has substantial influence on the making of places – and subsequently of people – primarily as different and 'foreign'. It is in this physical context of Istanbul that the public space of a boat can be considered as a *passage* at two levels. At one level, this mode of boat transportation is situated in relation to physical distances between Kınalıada and the mainland. As noted, sometimes these distances are impassable due to weather conditions that shake up the sea (or a municipal lack of organization that operates boats at over-capacity). I argue in the following pages that the people who live on the island only during the summer months have come to accommodate these often sudden shifts in the distances between the island and the mainland rather differently than the mostly working-class permanent residents of the island who live there all year long. In addition to that, the islands of this archipelago are believed to be the only place in Turkey where the distribution of the country's Muslim majority and non-Muslim populations is not in favour of Muslims, although their demographic composition is never officially verified as census data are limited.[4] For instance, Brink-Danan (2012) notes that islands within the Prince Islands Archipelago are often imagined as a 'foreign country' within popular Turkish imagery due to the particular concentration of non-Muslim majority residents here. This is why, at a second level, boat travel en route to the island can also be construed as a passage to somewhere populated by the 'leftovers' from the violently homogenizing nation-building processes in the country (see previous chapter). In relation to this second particular passage, I suggest that the central locus of this chapter should not be viewed as a study of Armenians from Turkey who only have a common relationship to the island, but rather as a study of the common practice of going to the island that always comes in Turkish with a specific terminology: *adaya çıkmak* (lit. going up to or exiting to the island), implying a different type of distancing than simply *adaya gitmek* (lit. going to the island).

'Let's find a nice seat'

The physical atmospheres of the vapur and the seabus differ. On busy summer days many people find themselves without a seat on the vapur, especially on the weekends, whereas each passenger always has a seat on the seabus, as standing up is not permitted on this fast-moving vessel. For most young professional commuters from Kınalıada, a seat (in Turkish: *yer*) is a component of their daily voyage between the city and the island. A primary distinction among people on and en route to the island is made between those who can afford the seabus and those who cannot. People with summer houses on the island (i.e., middle- and upper-class Armenians) can usually afford to pay for this journey, while the tourists, day-trippers and people who live permanently on the island usually take the slower and cheaper vapur. As a result, the seabus has a less diverse spectrum of passengers in relation to the vapur. Thus, in its comparably silent and thus sensorially sterile, and demographically more homogeneous atmosphere, the seabus is a physical setting where Armenian and non-Muslim difference is exposed in a different way than on the vapur. The instance I note below sheds light onto this situation on the seabuses.

One morning in July, I was waiting at the Kınalıada seabus terminal to board the 8:20 seabus. It was delayed, and when it finally arrived, the crew quickly moored and opened the gates of the vessel. People rushed to the gates to grab seats. There was nothing extraordinary about this situation as all through my research I observed how people in Istanbul in general, and boat passengers in particular (both vapur and seabus passengers alike), were always anxious to find seats. I took note of how people talked about seats (*yer* in Turkish): *güzel bir yer kapalım* (let's find/occupy a nice seat/place), *yerimizden olmayalım* (let's not lose our seats/places) or *ya yerimizden olursak* (what if we are kicked out of our seats/places). It was apparent that *yer bulamamak* (not being able to find a seat/place) was a serious matter for boat passengers between the island and Istanbul proper. As a side note, while a concern to find seats should be common among the denizens of metropolitan areas around the world, during boat journeys I often found myself wondering if this concern with seats reflected long histories of dispersion, expulsion and forced migration in Turkey – at least metaphorically.

Everything appeared normal as we hustled through the turnstiles. However, once on the boat, the crew made an announcement that the electronic turnstiles were not working properly. There was a system failure and the turnstiles had not been able to count down the number of people as they swiped travel cards or inserted coins to enter the boat. As part of boat regulations, all passengers on the seabus must be seated, and, as a result, the announcement made it clear that those without seats now had to disembark. When the last seat was taken (in Turkish: *son yer de kapıldı*, which can be translated as 'the last remaining place has been occupied'), the crew attempted to remove the people left standing. Already delayed, and having missed the slower vapur by 5 minutes, those without seats began to protest. Passengers and crew were yelling at each other, until one member of the crew shouted *sizin kafanızı kesmek lazım!* (lit. It is necessary to *cut off* your heads!). This pronouncement shocked the passengers, myself included. Everything went quiet, the jostling ceased and people seemed almost paralysed as the words cut through the air. Finally, the crew was able to escort all the standing passengers off the boat, and the fast boat eventually arrived at the same time as the slower vapur, although it was scheduled to arrive some 25 minutes earlier.

In the days that followed, I observed how news of this event circulated among Armenians from Kınalıada. In WhatsApp groups people told each other about who had already sent e-mails of complaint, and who still planned to. Facebook was full of the issue, which became a subject of discussion even amongst those who had not come to the island for a long time. There were calls to boycott the seabus in favour of the vapur. Scuffles between boat crews, bus drivers or airline stewards and passengers normally do not receive such public attention in Turkey, but this time both the content of the fight and the public were different. *Kesmek*, the Turkish verb used by the member of the crew that translates as 'to cut' in English, resonates in many ways with the massacres of the Armenian Genocide. As Talin Suciyan (2015) has suggested, Turkey is a 'denialist habitus' in which denial of the Genocide defines the taboos and the firm line between what is and is not socially and historically acceptable, and constantly reminds citizens how they are expected to read history. This situation has significant consequences for my informants, as they cannot publicly talk about the Genocide. This is why words such as *kesim* (i.e., the cutting off) made their way with very particular meanings into the daily lexicon of Armenians.

The incident of 'cutting heads' also denotes a moment in which metaphors of past violence break free into everyday circulation. For Rapaport (1997), these violent sentiments and their particular vocalizations as such set the tones of relationships between genocide survivors and the wider social universes around them. In the particular case of Armenians from the island, receiving these sentiments and their own perceived inability to respond to them constantly repositioned them as survivors of an unpunished crime. Moreover, at a very crucial level, receiving these sentiments also reproduced what kind of islanders they were in relation to Greek and Jewish residents of the other islands within the archipelago – necessarily signalling to my informants that *theirs* was not a community as much as those of *others*.[5] Especially positioning themselves as opposed to local Jews in Istanbul, Armenians widely believed that they could not manage to *birlik olmak* (lit. to be unified or to become unified). In this regard, Jews are usually praised for their ability to help each other, maintain solidarity as a closed community and keep the welfare of the community members at an optimum level. This stereotype explains why, when faced with personal difficulties or a lack of help from friends and acquaintances, I often heard my Armenian informants say in Turkish *Yahudiler olsaydı böyle yapmazdı* (lit. Jews would not have behaved this way). Jews are also believed to be pragmatic, opportunistic and efficient workers, skilled at solving community-related problems immediately.[6]

One of the most explicit and direct everyday articulations of this Armenian difference from this other non-Muslim community is constantly made through comparing Kınalıada to its neighbouring Burgazada, with their imagined Armenian and Jewish majorities, respectively. In order to expand more on this observation, I want to share the following discussion which took place around a dinner table on an early summer's evening at a friend's house on the island. A couple of people at the table had felt unable to go to mainland Istanbul earlier that day, as the island was again packed with day-trippers; the boats – vapur and seabus alike – were full. Someone else from the table told us that she had called the municipality in order to report her complaints, but, just like in previous summers, it was of no use. The boat schedules were always a favoured topic among my informants, especially for those who commuted to Istanbul every weekday. For them, there was a need for more frequent boats. Moreover, the boat journeys were not comfortable, as the boats were full of tourists, often making it impossible to get a seat (in Turkish: *yer*). Another friend responded that this was never the case with Burgazada – the neighbouring island with a significant Jewish population, a kosher restaurant, a Jewish social club and a still operating synagogue. She believed that on such weekends, the islanders of Burgazada simply did not let the boats approach and moor at their piers.

I was puzzled, as no resident of any island would have the power to keep scheduled boats from disembarking. While her observation was actually based on the weekend cruise boats that transported day-trippers from mainland piers that were not otherwise served by vapurs or seabuses, there was a rare instance of consensus among my friends around the table. As my friend continued elaborating on the difference of this neighbouring island, she noted that the islanders there made a claim to their place (in Turkish: *yerlerine sahip çıkıyorlar*, which could be translated in multiple ways including 'taking ownership of place' or 'taking care of place'). In her understanding, islanders on Burgazada similarly did not want tourists, and, unlike the islanders of Kınalıada, 'they could manage to do it'. While everybody else at our table was nodding and affirming what she had said, I asked what set Kınalıada apart from Burgazada. As if there was already a consensus among them, a couple of people responded that it was the Jews. Armenians did not know how to get together, make their voices heard and protest. They did not know how to defend their interests. They did not know about their interests at all, as there was no unity (in Turkish: *birlik*) among them. But Jews were different. They were united. For the people around the dinner table, the neighbouring island was a place of tranquillity (in Turkish: *huzur*). The islanders of Burgazada acted as a single unit (in Turkish: *tek bir insanmışçasına davranıyorlar*), and they loved their island. This love for the place also apparently explained why Jews lived on Burgazada all year long, in stark contrast to Kınalıada, which my informants believed was abandoned by Armenians in the winter. In their view, the houses of Burgazada were well maintained, similar to its streets. It was much more beautiful than Kınalıada in every sense; it was green and had far better restaurants. At the end of their praise for the island, I asked them why they didn't consider moving there. Everybody laughed in response to this suggestion. One of them responded sarcastically: 'We shall spend the summers on Kınalıada and the winters on Burgazada then'. Everybody laughed again. My proposition was not even an option. No one was interested in leaving Kınalıada for Burgazada. The case was closed.

The discourse that circulated around the dinner table that night should be understood as operating in three ways. Initially, it depicts how the two islands are idealized as the embodiments of the two communities. While the success of Burgazada is attributed to the success of its Jewish population, the failure of Kınalıada is attributed to the failure of the Armenians living there. Such failure is understood not in terms of the financial situation of Armenians, but lack of solidarity and cooperation. Moreover, the expression of failure shows how the temporal experiences of the respective residents of each island affected the ways they established bonds with their island, and how each community was believed to have distinct ways of collective action and mobility. The lack of unity among Armenians was partly reflected in the fact that they only lived on Kınalıada during the summer and abandoned it in the winter, thus not giving it the value it might have actually been worth. The lack of unity among Armenians was believed to reflect the lack of unity between people and their places, in this case their land, their *yer*.

Why was the case closed at the dinner table? My informants all seemed to be very fond of Burgazada, its physical setting, the lack of tourists and the level of privacy it offered its residents. The island was seen as a place that offered a touch of fresh air from the crowding of Istanbul, a feeling impossible to have a sense of on Kınalıada. However, as they made clear, they rejected any idea of moving to the neighbouring island. Despite its shortcomings, Kınalıada continued to attract Armenians from Istanbul. This is primarily because comparison based on the difference of the island from other islands defines a community, albeit through over-iteration of feelings of individualism that otherwise stress personal interest rather than community service. As we will see in more detail in the following chapter, apart from holding a physical space for a place- and time-specific Armenian community in Istanbul, the island provides my informants with a performative site of social intimacy to redefine their community borders. As I have suggested in this chapter, one of those daily practices of demarcation entails making sense of the physical distances between the island and the mainland. As such, I take everyday urban travel en route to the island as an ethnographic context to observe those articulations of distance and proximity not only in relation to the time spent on boats but also specifically through the diversity of Armenian, Jewish or Turkish human actors it brings together.

Just as Fabian (1983) argued that discourses of time are made to otherize, I similarly argue that ethnic demarcation between Armenians and non-Armenians (and Muslims in general) is also a process of temporalization in the context of the island; everyday conceptualizations of belonging to the island – and to Turkey – are deeply embedded in the making and covering of distances en route to Istanbul proper. Over the course of my research, many people told me that the boat schedules for both the vapurs and seabuses were intentionally organized contrary to the islanders' needs. A local newspaper from the islands published articles on the issue and argued that the schedules were intended to isolate the islands (in Turkish: *kendi haline bırakmak*) and punish (in Turkish: *cezalandırmak*) the islanders (15–31 October 2007, *Adalı*). Many believed that the state did not want Armenians and other non-Muslims to enjoy the islands. There were reasonable grounds for such thinking. There were few boats in the wintertime and 'too many' in the summer, privileging day-trippers instead of residents. In winter the last vapurs from Istanbul to the island were scheduled for 7:40 pm and 11 pm; hence, if one was just a bit late in arriving at the pier after a day at work in the city, she needed to wait at the terminal for almost three and a half hours. This lack of evening boats was felt acutely as the seabus did not operate in winter due to the unpredictability of the lodos and the limited number of passengers at that time of year. In the summertime, boats (both vapurs and seabuses) were scheduled frequently, with extra boats on the weekends in order to accommodate the large number of visitors from the mainland and foreign tourists. However, on summer weekends, it was unlikely for islanders to find seats on a vapur, given the amount of competition. Because of the excess of passengers, many Armenians living on the island chose not to leave the island on the weekends, and if they had to, they took the seabus instead of the vapur. The seabus, which cost almost double the price of the vapur at the time of research, not only provided a seat for everyone, but also thanks to air-conditioning provided a more comfortable mode of transport on hot summer days.

In attempting to show how travelling on slow or fast boats informed my informants of their own relationships to Kınalıada, I would like to close this chapter with a story that highlights an emotive aspect of slow travelling en route to Istanbul. On a beautiful summer's day, Garo, an Armenian man from the island who was in his mid-sixties, expressed his perfect confidence that he would make it to Istanbul on the slower vapur before I did on the seabus. He simply loved the vapur and would never take the seabus where he could not sit outside. He belonged to a time period when an *Istanbullu*, as Orhan Pamuk put it in his memoir *Istanbul* (2006), could identify various boats while they were still on the horizon. At present *Istanbullu* and Istanbulite no longer refer to the same thing and they are no longer terms fit for direct translation between Turkish and English. Garo was specifically a proud *Istanbullu*, with a family history going back generations in the city, as opposed to millions of others who had lived in the same city for only a generation or so – namely, the Istanbulites. As he was looking at the horizon, he told me that the *Fahri Korutürk* – the largest and fastest vapur on the Istanbul seas, named after the sixth Turkish president – was on its way to Kınalıada. He firmly believed that the boat could make it directly to Istanbul in less than 40 minutes, and as he anticipated that the seabus would be delayed again, he believed that he would arrive in Istanbul before me.

The seabus arrived on time, however, and I reached Istanbul some 15 minutes before him. On that day Garo could be slow, whereas I was hurrying to arrive at a meeting on time – and, more importantly, prioritized getting ready by going over my notes in full concentration within the silence of the seabus. He was eager to wait in any case, take his time and enjoy the lively atmosphere of the vapur. For me, there was no time to socialize.

Chapter 7

AN ISLAND THAT IS NO MORE

Also, that an island is deserted must appear *philosophically* normal to us. Humans cannot live, nor live in security, unless they assume that the active struggle between earth and water is over, or at least contained. People like to call these two elements mother and father, assigning them gender roles according to the whim of their fancy. They must somehow persuade themselves that a struggle of this kind does not exist, or that it has somehow ended. In one way or another, the very existence of islands is the negation of this point of view, of this effort, this conviction. That England is populated will always come as a surprise; humans can live on an island only by forgetting what an island represents. Islands are either from before or for after humankind.

(Gilles Deleuze, *Desert Islands*, 2004: 9, emphasis original)

In the two previous chapters of this book, my ethnographic lens focused on looking at an inside from the outside. On the streets of Kurtuluş and on the boats en route to Kınalıada, my research captured moments of demarcation in which a sense of unity (in Turkish: *birlik*) was defined by my informants. In the concrete Istanbul neighbourhood consisting of apartment blocks, I portrayed that, at least for one Armenian family from south-eastern Turkey, unity came to mean the unity of their dispersed family. On the Istanbul seas that separate the mainland from the Prince Islands Archipelago, where my travel companions imagined each island as having a concentration of a different ethnically defined community (of Greeks, Jews, Muslims and Armenians), I also portrayed that it was this time the lack of unity – and the very particular ways unity was yearned for – that informed a community of Armenian islanders on Kınalıada (see also Chapter 3 on the potential influence of conflict and lack of consensus on community-making).

I pursue the argument that one of the ways to account for the making of unity is to further decipher its everyday relationship to Turkishness, which emerges not only as a state-imposed category of political and cultural belonging but also in relation to its particular appropriations by people, including Armenians. Although *birlik* was primarily defined by the state in order to impose homogeneity among the different zones of Turkishness, for Armenians it described another zone where they negotiated their proximity to each other instead of proximity to the innermost zones of Turkishness. In this context, the terminology of Turkish nationalism was reproduced by Armenians to critique such a situation.

This chapter takes the issue of articulating distance and proximity to the innermost centres of Turkishness to a new level, through a different ethnographic and theoretical framework. In addition to my indirect observations provided in the following pages, two fragments of research enable me to sketch out processes in which ethnic difference is articulated in contemporary Turkey. Here I focus on the everyday articulations of difference in the context of life on Kınalıada, travels to which were at the centre of the research presented in the previous chapter. As noted then, this 'Armenian island' off Istanbul (Kaymak 2016) was a place where most of my Armenian friends and informants had inherited summer houses from their families. They were not necessarily wealthy, but all had university degrees and worked for large companies or ran their own businesses in which they employed other people. Having a house on the island, they considered themselves different from the several other thousands of Armenians in Istanbul who did not. They were first and foremost *adalı* (lit. islander) vis-à-vis other Armenians; however, they considered themselves as *Istanbullu* among Istanbulites, implying a difference from people who were *from* Istanbul and who only *lived* in Istanbul, respectively. These terms should not be understood as direct translations of each other, as *Istanbullu* defines not only a place of origin but also a very particular urbanized and mostly – if not entirely – middle- and upper-class group of people in a city of 15 million. It is in this sense that the distinctions between *Istanbullu* and Istanbulite (cf. Öncü 1999) point at the transformation of the city into a 'repopulated cosmopolis' (see Chapter 3). As for Armenians in Istanbul, there is great diversity regarding family histories in the city. In this context of depopulation and repopulation, owning a house on the island provided my informants with a social and physical base to claim longer histories in Istanbul both in relation to the massive migrant population of the city, which included Muslim Turks, and to other Armenians.

The island also came with stigmas that took their source in the Turkish nation-building project. The non-Muslim majority population of the islands off Istanbul, a situation in contrast to the rest of the country, resulted in wider popular imaginings about the island as a 'foreign country' (in Turkish: *yabancı ülke*) (Brink-Danan 2012), where non-Muslims are denied becoming 'natives' (in Turkish: *yerli*) of Turkey. The following pages primarily aim to understand how such 'differences' are articulated by my informants in their own terms, and how these are imposed in the wake of ongoing nation-building processes, within the 'public life' (Navaro-Yashin 2002) of the island(s).

An island without strangers

Marcy Brink-Danan in *Jewish Life in Twenty-First-Century Turkey* asks:

> how does public discourse, the patterned and crafted statements that display regularity and consensus (Foucault 1972: 38), intersect with the smaller, more intimate conversations, silences, and secrets that are the sites of everyday contestations about the way things are, were, and should be?
>
> (Brink-Danan 2012: 27)

In the summer of 2013, I closely observed how wider discourses that separated strangers from insiders were reflected at an everyday level when a Turkish family moved to Kınalıada. Most of my friends had summer houses there and in the first half of the 2010s I spent three consecutive summers with them. As this chapter will unpack, the island is widely understood as a 'meeting point' for Armenians in Istanbul or abroad – or as a 'centre of gravity', in Sari Hanafi's term (2003).

The Turkish family who moved to the island consisted of a mother and a father – both high-income, white-collar professionals – and their two-year-old daughter. Although there were always some other middle-class Turkish families who had summer houses on the island, the arrival of this family came as a surprise to my Armenian informants. For them, the decision of a new Turkish family to spend the summer on Kınalıada, without any former friends or connections on the island, did not make any sense. They believed that all other Turkish families had bought houses on the island through former personal connections with the Armenian residents. As we were having a late Sunday brunch around a big table in a friend's garden in 2013, we started to talk about the new arrivals. One of my friends, Nora, asked 'Why on earth would someone who doesn't know anyone on the island move here?' She continued by saying that 'they don't seem to have any *adalı* (lit. islander) friends here. They could have easily rented a house on the other [neighbouring] islands where Turks also live'. Following her, Alen, Nora's husband, added that there must have been another motivation for them to move to the island: 'No one comes to this island unless you have friends here; it's not like the other islands'. Another friend at the table nodded in agreement and added: 'It's bizarre to come to this island to make friends'. Alen replied that the island was often thought of as a *sıçrama tahtası* (lit. a springboard) by many emergent middle-class Turkish families. He believed that for most middle-class Turks, having non-Muslim minority friends was a good investment in the social capital that they usually lacked.

As the summer proceeded, the confusion and accompanying suspicion doubled for my informants when the mother of the Turkish family brought her child to the Sunday liturgy at the Armenian church of the island a couple of times. While unconcerned by the initial visit, the following Sunday visits to the church bothered many: this was no longer a touristic visit by a culture-curious Turkish mother. For my Armenian friends, there had to be something else – some other motivation – behind this untypical situation. Despite growing curiosity, however, they never approached this family to talk to them. In many ways they had 'fears of the unknown' on a tiny island where everyone is supposed to know about everyone else. Here, I am particularly interested in the community-making aspect of this particular emotive framework, which is based on an everyday relationship of proximity that reproduces difference and stereotypes (Ahmed 2004: 63; see also Pattie 1997 and Chapter 3).

Instead of talking to this new family, my friends came up with answers themselves. First, they believed that these people might have been individuals with Armenian grandparents; at least one of their ancestors could have been Armenian. Second, they believed that the Turkish couple could have been descendants of Armenian converts to Islam, crypto-Armenians or the *dönme* (a pejorative word that translates as one who converted/returned/transformed), as my informants put it. From the perspective of my informants, the underlying difference between the first and the second possibility also implied the level of assimilation to 'Turkishness' and whether it took place on a 'voluntary' basis. Often, a person with an Armenian grandparent is understood as a descendent of the Genocide, a victim whether identifying herself as Turkish (and Muslim) or not. The nuance here is that Armenians in contemporary Istanbul perceive a difference between Armenians who were forced to convert to Islam, often as individual orphans, and the families who 'deliberately' converted in order to survive (see also the beginning of Chapter 2). This is not to suggest that the latter group was not subjected to the violence of the Genocide, but rather to reflect how Armenians in contemporary Istanbul sense that the crypto-Armenians survived through self-initiated assimilation.

The new Turkish family on the island did not fit into these two categories. As one of my friends explained, their appearance, class, level of education and the way they spoke Turkish were not similar to Islamicized Armenians, who most often came from provincial towns in Anatolia. In any case, my informants believed that people without Armenian origin would not have come to the island. Alen believed that, if an Armenian family history was really at play, the main motivation for these people to move to the island was a matter of *vicdan azabı*, guilt felt strongly in one's conscience. For him, they were the descendants of people who had rejected their own origins in order to have an easier life in the post-genocide context of Turkey and now it was time for them to confront the decision of their parents or grandparents.

In the end, nothing was revealed about this family who remained complete strangers to us. None of my Armenian friends from the island initiated conversations or even attempted to exchange greetings with them. At the end of the summer, the couple left the island and never came back. The purpose of this chapter is not to identify who the Turkish couple was. Instead, the discussion about this family reveals wider and deeper everyday discussions about ethnic or cultural distance and proximity at three levels. First, it displays the mental as well as the physical location of the island vis-à-vis other Armenians and stranger Turks (i.e., those not known by Armenians from Istanbul in person) in their immediate environment. Second, following the discussions in the previous chapters, this discussion points to my informants' articulations of distance to various zones of Turkishness, which is, I argue, always further informative of how they perceive other Armenians and others around them. Following that, third, the discussion among my informants depicts a hierarchy of different ways of being Armenian. This depends on mixing with Turks or Muslims and conversion to Islam, based on a similar zonal imagination of ethnic identity, this time not directly by the state but by the individuals who are located in the outermost zone of Turkishness.

Brink-Danan (2012) argues that members of the Jewish community in Istanbul (which, unlike my understanding of Armenians in Istanbul, she comfortably calls a community) have developed a knowledge of their difference from Turks by 'comparing their lives to the ways Jews outside of Turkey live and to the ways Jews have lived in the past, yet they perform and disavow this difference at different times and on different stages' (1). I can speculate here that it should be the zonal constitution of Turkishness that pushed 'Turkish Jews [to] perform a doubled identity in light of demands for Turkish integration and out of fear of being marked as non-Turks, that is "different" or "foreign"' (86). It should be noted that Brink-Danan's account of Jews is primarily based on understanding their relationships to the wider category of Turks. All throughout this book, I am tackling the ways of being Armenian in Istanbul vis-à-vis the others around them, investigating an ethnic zone surrounded not only by their significant others, the Turks, but also by *other Armenians*, as well as Greeks, Jews and Kurds. For instance, Alen's comments about the *dönme* (i.e., Islamicized Armenians) suggested that there were a variety of *ways* of being Armenian for Armenians, accepted within a hierarchy. This is not to say that he necessarily placed himself at the top of this hierarchy of being Armenian by comparing himself to present and past Armenians. On several occasions he 'confessed' (he used *itiraf etmek* in Turkish, which translates as 'to confess') that the primary reason for his present wealth was the Armenians who died during the Genocide. He believed that Turkey's tiny remaining Armenian population shared a fortune that was disproportionately large for its numbers.[1]

At the time I met Alen, he was in his early forties. He ran his own export-import company, which he had founded several years earlier with capital he inherited from his parents, who came to Istanbul in the late 1960s from Malatya in eastern Turkey. His family, along with a couple of other Armenian families, lived in the city as, in his words, 'Armenians who did not convert to Islam'. Although having never studied in an Armenian school, he was proud of his level of competence in the language. From time to time, he put people around him up to Armenian vocabulary contests, in which I scored better than most of his *Istanbullu* friends. Often his Armenian friends on the island made fun of him for being 'a little too Armenian', as his Anatolian family was among the relatively latest Armenian migrants to Istanbul. In many ways, he was proud to be not from Istanbul as his friends were, and he often organized charitable projects for poor Armenian families in the city or the current Muslim residents of his village of origin in Malatya. The reason for him to be taken as 'a little too Armenian' was not limited to the fact that he cared for lower-class Armenians or maintained relationships with his family's place of origin. Alen also loved to talk and 'advise' openly about polarizing issues in the context of Turkey, including what stance to take on Genocide recognition and commemoration in the country, how to understand the ongoing Kurdish political movement, how to vote in general and municipal elections, and whether to take Armenian return converts to Christianity as a 'conspiracy'. Concerning the last item on this list, he firmly believed that these people had made a pragmatic decision to survive whereas his family had not, and they could have easily been part of a hidden Islamicization project of the state.

Alen's feelings of guilt are perhaps experienced by many other survivors in post-genocide contexts (see Miller and Miller 1993 for a collection of oral history interviews with the survivors of the Armenian Genocide). This feeling is usually (if not always) discussed in terms of survival as opposed to death, not in terms of wealth accumulated in the aftermath of genocide. My intention is not to analyse these feelings extensively here, as I believe that should be the subject matter of an individual book on this particular issue. What I am interested in is understanding how these feelings of guilt further inform us about the various distinctions among Armenians themselves as well as between Armenians and Turks. In her book on Jews in Germany after the Holocaust, Lynn Rapaport (1997) writes that the *metaphor* of the Holocaust is the lens through which Jews perceive and interpret everyday life in Germany, the tool they use to construct Jewish ethnic identity, and the idiom that affects the tone of Jewish-German relationships (12). Here, such a metaphor could exactly serve the task of understanding the distances between Armenians in Istanbul and elsewhere. In *Margins of Philosophy*, Derrida (1982) argues that metaphor reflects the ways we engage with the differences between things, instead of the similarities between those things. It exerts a power, the power of relating one thing with another and thus the power of establishing and projecting differences and forcing meaning to change social positions (cited in Saybaşılı 2011: 15). As a result, the metaphor of the Genocide for informants such as Alen cannot be expected to have one rigid meaning, reduced to the history of this catastrophic event and its subsequent traumatic influence on its survivors and following generations. Drawing on Rapaport (1997), the metaphor should rather be understood as a tool and an idiom that indicates the tone of Armenian relationships to many others around them at an everyday level.

Unlike in the case of Jews in Germany, the Genocide is still a disputed issue among Armenians from Turkey (though this is not to suggest that there are no Holocaust denialists in Germany). As opposed to the public consensus in Armenia and the diaspora, I observed a panoply of approaches and definitions regarding what happened in 1915. This is not to suggest that my informants from Turkey denied the extent of the violence and extermination that their families experienced. Nevertheless, there was no univocality among them in naming what it was. A similar observation was made by Ayşe Gül Altınay and Fethiye Çetin (2014), who, in their book, *Grandchildren*, wrote that survivors of the Genocide and following generations had a multiplicity of concepts to define it: 'convoy, relocation, expulsion, migration, exile, slaughter, massacre, genocide or just "those days"' (xiii).

Such diversity in the everyday terminology of past violence can be expected in a political setting where 'the Armenian issue' has been publicly and individually silenced for a century. As noted earlier, a fundamental aspect of being Armenian in Turkey comes to the surface regarding the lack of public spaces for the exchange and circulation of narratives on the century-long history of violence that targeted non-Muslims in the country. This is why, for Armenians from Turkey, knowledge of the Genocide is highly personalized in that it is transmitted from one generation to the next through personal communication (Suciyan 2015: 18).

In her comparative study of the Jews and Armenians in post-war France, Maud Mandel (2003) argues that there has been a link between how the Jewish population remained remarkably visible in the decades following the Second World War and how this visibility transformed the community's public face to reflect a growing ethnic consciousness among them (161). Here I want to question whether the impossibility of such public visibility for Armenians in Turkey, which is based on the denial of the Genocide and the very particular construction of Turkishness, further determines the extent of differences between Armenians and the people around them. Following Mandel, in the next section I explore how public visibility has been an important element in the articulations of such difference.

Where Turks talk and Armenians listen

In the context of the island, lines of difference were constantly made, unmade and remade between Armenians and Muslims (i.e. Turks), between Armenians and other non-Muslims, and among Armenians and Muslims. For my informants from the island, ethnic demarcation was a fundamental source of information for public behaviour. In other words, they knew how to read and make use of signs that were not necessarily based on a rigid definition of ethnicity, which for them referred to an ongoing process of classification as suggested by John Comaroff (1992). In other words, my informants were informed by the diversity of others surrounding them. As argued above, they were also informed by their own diversities as Armenian people and people with Armenian origins. The zonal constitution of Turkishness has been fundamental in defining both Armenians and Muslims as diverse. The following paragraphs depict a context in which difference is articulated by Armenians and reflected through particular forms of public behaviour. By focusing on discourses in the public sphere and the public visibility of politically sensitive matters, I aim to understand how the Genocide and other forms of state-sponsored violence targeting non-Muslims in its aftermath can be viewed as metaphors in marking Armenian difference in contemporary Turkey.

After the two-week-long public occupation of Gezi Park and countrywide protests against the ruling government in the early summer of 2013, environmentalist politics took a new form in Turkey. All through that summer, in most parks of major cities, 'park forums' mushroomed, where protesters, environmentalists, activists and people who were merely curious met weekly or fortnightly. As the park forums scattered all around Istanbul, people on each of the Prince Islands started to organize their own forums, as well. On Kınalıada, where the majority of summer residents were Armenians from Turkey, a forum was organized in a similar way. First, posters appeared on trees and walls, and the Facebook page of *Adalar Postası*, literally 'the Islands' Mail', announced that people willing to participate were welcome to join the discussion in Hrant Dink Park, the first public space named after the famous Turkish Armenian journalist who was murdered by ultranationalists in 2007. The Facebook page named after the forum, *Kınalıada Forumu*, where people from the island discuss issues related to life on the island, is still in use.

The first *Kınalıada Forumu* gathered at the end of June 2013 and attracted some twenty people. In the first forum only the rules of discussion were decided on, about listening, talking and moderating, and a schedule for further meetings was made. Thus, in the first forum there was hardly any political discussion. It was decided that the forum would meet on Sunday evenings every fortnight. The second forum attracted a larger crowd of forty to fifty people. Most seemed to be individual participants without any prior knowledge of each other. It seemed, even on the tiny island, that there were people who did not know each other. Over the course of conversation, it was revealed that almost all had summer houses on the island and spent the summer there. However, I noticed that there was limited participation from the people who lived on the island throughout the year. Lastly, I noticed participation by other people, such as activists from the mainland, who had no connection to the island but whom I knew from other park forums in mainland Istanbul.

People gathered around in a circle on the grass and the discussion started. The forum was being 'observed' by others, as well. Some twenty undercover policemen from mainland Istanbul (i.e., not the local police of the island) remained standing around the sitting crowd. The policemen did not bother to hide their identities. Their walkie-talkies and the constant sound of beeps clearly showed us who they were. As the discussion went on, they walked around the circle of participants, took photos of people (including me) and constantly talked to their supervisors on their cell phones. None of the participants seemed disturbed, or at least for a while we pretended that was the case. When someone from the group asked the police whether it was enough, the hidden tension and anxiety revealed itself. Others started shouting loudly and expressed their anger. Although the police and the anxiety remained, the discussion continued and covered political topics, centring on two issues: the social and environmental problems of the island, and how to engage with the mass demonstrations that were going on in the rest of Turkey.

In this second forum, one instance made me realize that it was only Turks of Muslim background who did the talking. On this 'Armenian island' (Kaymak 2016), where Armenians believed (in the absence of official population numbers) that they constituted the majority, their participation was overshadowed by politically engaged Muslim Turks. Near the end of the debate, one young Turkish woman raised her hand for permission from the moderator to talk and asked everyone about how to show solidarity with the political protests going on in the rest of Turkey. She suggested that the people of the island should get involved in these protests around the country, like the people in mainland Istanbul. Many people nodded, and several other speakers expressed that they shared the same feelings of solidarity with the rest of Turkey. After the last speaker finished his sentence, the moderator asked whether it was time to end this second forum. A moment of silence was broken when the moderator saw a woman in her mid-fifties, silent but raising one hand in the air, murmuring something that the rest could not hear. The moderator announced that the floor was hers and told her to speak up.

I understood that she was Armenian from her accent and the content of her speech. She was holding her neck delicately with her one hand, while still having one hand raised in the air, making slow moves to accompany her explanations. She told the crowd that it was not possible for her to take part in the suggested solidarity protests in any form; she simply could not do it. Her family's *yer* (meaning not only place but also home, location, ground and even earth in Turkish) was known by the *adalılar*, the islanders. She was afraid that her house could easily become a target of mob-driven violence if she participated in protests. At that point, other Armenian women of similar age joined her, nodding their heads. One of the women said that while coming to the forum she had walked through the *kahvehane*, the traditional coffee shop, passing through the gaze of *adanın yerlisi* (lit. natives of the island). *Yerimizi biliyorlar* she whispered, meaning they knew the location of her house. Another woman uttered *biz 6-7 Eylül'ü yaşadık*, meaning that she had lived through the Pogroms of September 1955. This group of Armenian women, having now physically gotten closer to each other and standing up behind the circle of people seated on the ground, started murmuring again and telling everyone around them that they knew what happened when you attracted the attention of a mob in Turkey.

The forum ended with clear opposition between Armenians and Muslim Turks, with different histories and memories, political and social engagements, and agendas. The Turkish majority at the forum respected these anxieties and kept silent while I saw in their faces that they did not know how to respond. At that point it seemed to me that they did not deny what had happened in 1955. They knew that non-Muslims were assaulted, murdered and raped in the two-day-long Pogroms, and that their businesses and properties were looted by crowds mobilized by state officers (Güven 2006; Bali 2012). At this point, it became evident that the forum of Kınalıada could no longer show signs of solidarity with the other park forums and protests that continued for the rest of the summer. Nevertheless, the forum kept meeting every fortnight, focusing on issues that mattered only to the island, which were local and concerned only the locals.

Biz 6-7 Eylül'ü yaşadık was the phrase I heard most during my research in Istanbul. It was an answer several times in response to my questioning of why my informants had moved from one Istanbul neighbourhood to another neighbourhood in the decades before I conducted my research. It was a warning by my Armenian neighbour upstairs in my Kurtuluş apartment when he learned that I did not lock the building door every evening after 9 pm. It was an explanation when a young Armenian woman from Istanbul told me about her reasons for moving to Paris in 2005 (fifty years after the Pogroms). And in the forum described above, it was a call to show respect and recognize the extent of the violence experienced by Armenians (and other non-Muslims).

Over the course of my fieldwork, I observed that for most Armenians from Turkey, the Pogroms of September 1955 were a more significant trope than the 1915 Genocide. Conversation between Armenians and Turks often revealed that most people from the latter group did not understand why it was necessary to keep a low profile in Turkey. The second meeting of the forum of Kınalıada developed in such an environment, where Turks attempted to persuade Armenians to take action and join in solidarity with those who were protesting. Eventually, over the course of the summer, the islanders – both Armenians and Muslim Turks alike – organized several events to clean the streets of the island, found volunteers to clean the seabed and protested against the increasing number of irresponsible cyclists, never making explicit criticisms against the central government. In stark contrast to other forums held in other Istanbul neighbourhoods, where the prime minister and his cabinet were severely criticized and held responsible for the brutal police violence meted out against protesters, on Kınalıada only environmental issues of the island were on the agenda. The hot political discussions of other park forums of Istanbul did not make their way to the island's forum.

Here, I argue that the rationale put forth by the middle-aged Armenian women about keeping a low profile in light of a long history of violence is indicative of different conditions of public visibility. Before checking the validity of this argument, we need to go over the terminologies of difference and distance used by the Armenian women during the island forum. As noted, *yer* in Turkish can refer to different but interrelated concepts: it can denote place, ground, home or location. It is related to where one physically is, although it can also refer to a distant place such as where someone is from. I suggest that *yer* is an articulation of a bond between where one lived and lives, a powerful metaphor in Turkish to denote belonging and place-making. The woman's comment, *yerimizi biliyorlar* (with a triple meaning of 'they know our place', 'they know where we are' and 'they know where our houses are located'), demonstrates a self-articulation of difference at various levels. Moreover, the most important aspect of the word echoes in the term *yerli*, simultaneously meaning 'the local' and 'the native' with -*li* being a suffix denoting ownership and place of origin in Turkish (Delaney 1991: 204; Mills 2010: 1; Brink-Danan 2012: 8). The suffix is crucial for understanding the link between belonging and ownership in Turkish.

The meaning of *adalı* (with *ada* meaning island and -*lı* again the suffix denoting ownership and belonging), a person from the island, changed according to context. It was often a hot discussion topic among Armenians with houses on the island to decide who was *gerçek adalı* (lit. real islander), *yeni adalı* (lit. new islander), *eski adalı* (lit. old islander) and *adanın yerlisi* (lit. native of the island). For Armenians with summer houses on the island, *gerçek adalı* exclusively referred to Armenians who had owned houses on the island for at least three generations. *Yeni adalı* and *eski adalı* could refer to both Armenians and non-Armenians, including the small number of Greeks and Muslim Turks with summer houses on the island. The latter term does not, however, refer to Assyrians who moved to the island and Istanbul increasingly after the 1980s. *Adanın yerlisi* had a more nuanced meaning, referring to the people who lived on the island all year long, which also denoted that they could not afford to have a second house in Istanbul (see also previous chapter). These people were Muslim Turks and Kurds who owned shops or ran other businesses in the service sector, implying a deep class difference from the middle- and upper-class Armenians who came to the island only during summer. However, the term does not refer to the teachers, firemen or police who live on the island all year long. Nor does it refer to the increasing population of Assyrians or the handful of Greeks. It specifically refers to the working class of the island.

Although the minority status of Armenians on the mainland was reversed on the island, the terms *yer*, *yerli* and *adanın yerlisi*, with references to social roles as natives and locals on the island, drew on several overlapping articulations of Armenian difference. Articulating who was local or native to the island also indicated who was a *yabancı*, at least according to my Armenian informants. That term, with its double meaning as 'stranger to somewhere' and 'a person who comes from another country', has emerged as a burdensome stigma for non-Muslims in Turkey. Their distances to the purposefully imagined and crafted centres of Turkishness denied them becoming *yerli* in Turkey, their place of origin. This is why the islands have often been imagined as a 'foreign country' (in Turkish: *yabancı ülke*) by the Turkish Muslim majority of the country, due to the fact that they have considerable Greek, Armenian and Jewish populations (Brink-Danan 2012). The previous chapter demonstrated that these populations have long been imagined as foreigners in Turkey, as they were pushed to the outermost zone of Turkishness. It is in this sense that I find similarities between the local category of *yerli* on the island and the state-imposed category of the Turk as both projected and managed distances between the diverse populations of the island and the country, respectively.

It is always 'outside' on the inhabited island

Rapaport (1997) argues that Jews in post-Holocaust Germany live in invisible ghettos, which prevent free access for other Germans unless Jews permit their entry. She writes that 'it is invisible because there are no physical barriers such as ghetto gates or walls to effectively block their contact with the city or to impede them from developing social relationships with Germans' (4). The ghetto does not refer to the physical dimensions of a neighbourhood in an urban setting; it refers to networks of communication, daily practices of life and a shared memory of past violence that sets Jews apart from non-Jews. As a result, the invisible ghetto appears as more of a voluntary zone of intimacy that Jews build from inside.

There are a number of ways to think about the island context in Istanbul as forming an invisible ghetto. Unlike the invisible ghetto, the island's isolation has a material dimension. It is physically surrounded by the sea and generally inaccessible to the wider public besides the limited number of people allowed by the passenger capacity of boats per day. However, the island is also a nodal point within a network of communication that goes beyond its natural borders, daily practices of life and metaphors of difference that set apart Armenians from other Armenians, and Armenians from Turks. Raised in different Istanbul neighbourhoods with considerable Armenian populations such as Yeşilköy, Kadıköy or Kurtuluş, for my informants the island became a space where they came to know other Armenians from other parts of the city. As one of my informants put it, the island was a 'meeting point' (in Turkish: *buluşma noktası*). A group of friends in their mid-thirties epitomized this situation. They were all from different parts of the city, with different levels of language competence in Armenian. Most were children of mixed marriages (involving members of the Armenian Gregorian and Armenian Catholic or Greek Orthodox Church, but rarely Muslims), who studied in different schools and pursued different careers but had spent the summers together since childhood. Apart from sharing personal histories of going to the island (in Turkish: *adaya çıkmak*) every year, they were all of the upper middle class. They had inherited houses from their families not only on the island but also in Istanbul proper. They all had university degrees and either worked for large international companies or ran their own businesses with capital they had received from their families. Most did not speak Armenian as fluently as a foreign language like English or French, which they had learned in Istanbul's prestigious private schools, if they did not study at an Armenian high school. They were all well-travelled, especially in Europe, but not in Turkey, with the few exceptions of holiday hubs in the Mediterranean, and they took certain pride in having Greek or Jewish friends they came to know from the other islands within the Prince Islands Archipelago and Muslim Turkish friends from school and professional life. One of the most recurrent themes in our conversations was that they all wanted to raise their children as *dünya vatandaşı* (lit. world citizen) as opposed to their own families or other Armenians in Istanbul.

This group maintained their friendship by spending intensive time together every summer. Furthermore, all of them stated that the island was the first place where they had met other Armenians, both from Istanbul and around the world. For them, the 1990s, when they were teenagers, marked a period of time when 'the island was like the diaspora', as many Armenian families who had left Istanbul for other countries in earlier decades started to bring their children to the island. Their sentiment did not refer to a diasporization of Istanbul vis-à-vis an imagined homeland, but emphasized how the island became a transnational space where many languages including English, French and Spanish were spoken and heard, and many Armenians from the island had an opportunity to not only meet distant family but also get acquainted with international friends. In this sense, the 1990s marked a historical moment for Istanbul in which the island became a 'centre of gravity' (Hanafi 2003), in which the networks of the diaspora stretched to Istanbul and repositioned the city as a nodal point within the transnational networks of globally dispersed Armenians.[2]

When I interviewed recently married couples from this circle of friends about their children's future education in Turkey, it emerged that they all primarily relied on their connection to the island as a vital source of Armenian language education for their children. Despite important differences in their thinking on whether to send children to Armenian schools, mixed schools, colleges or abroad, they were all united in making their children spend summers on the island. This was why the island was seen as a guarantee among these couples in providing a link between Armenian individuals and their imagined community of Armenians (see also Kaymak 2016: 377). One couple I interviewed comprised a mother and father who had studied in a mixed Turkish school and an Armenian school, respectively. Both were fluent in Armenian and they wanted their children to learn the language as well. The mother wanted their children to be open to the world and learn English or German properly at school, while the father believed that the children should learn Armenian first. It was in this context that the father explained to me that 'Armenians from Istanbul don't have the historical neighbourhoods such as Samatya, Kumkapı, or Kurtuluş anymore; they only have the island'. That was precisely why the family had a summer house there, no matter what they finally decided regarding their children's education. In the end, the couple decided to send their children to an Armenian primary school and a mixed high school so that they could learn how to read and write in Armenian (in addition to speaking the language), while in the later stages of their education they could get to know the wider social universe in Turkey and be prepared for becoming 'world citizens' through learning a foreign language.

While being a meeting place for Armenians from Istanbul and abroad, the island also informed islanders about their differences from other Armenians and Turks who did not have houses there. In fact, most Armenian families from Istanbul most probably do not have houses on the island. Several lower-class Armenian families instead rented summer houses in apartment blocks in Çınarcık, on the southern coast of the Sea of Marmara. Wealthier families abandoned their houses on the island for villas in Bodrum and Çeşme, Turkey's major holiday hubs (see also Kaymak 2016: 318). This is how having a house on the island implies class differences among Armenians. The contemporary residents of the island are of the (upper) middle class with high levels of education and can afford to send their children to private schools and universities and go for holidays in Europe or North America once a year, but nevertheless cannot buy houses on the Mediterranean coast as wealthier Armenians do. As noted earlier in this chapter, most of them inherited their island houses from their families and in some cases their family homes were demolished to construct apartments to provide flats for each member of the family. In many cases, those families also acquired an extra one or two flats to rent to other Armenians (or Assyrians) on an annual basis.

Apart from the class differences that are at play between Armenians who have summer houses on the island and those who have summer houses elsewhere or who do not have summer houses at all, the stigmatization of the island as a 'foreign country' and non-Muslims in general as 'foreigners' in Turkey demarcates the lines along which my informants knew to emphasize or hide their relationships to the island. For instance, Brink-Danan (2012) writes that Turkish Jews know not only about different ways of being, but also the *contexts* in which one should perform difference (25). I observed similar situations in which my Armenian informants kept the fact that they owned houses on the island a secret from strangers in various encounters in Istanbul proper and on some occasions from me during our first meetings – indicating that having a house on the island implied a blurred family genealogy vis-à-vis Turkishness. In one case, I would not find out that a woman I had met at an Armenian friend's birthday party in central Istanbul had a family house on the island for three generations until we ran across each other randomly on the streets of the island. She was going home with grocery bags on a weekend morning, and when I greeted her and said that I didn't know that she spent the summers on the island, she responded that I probably didn't remember clearly. When I insisted that I remembered what she talked to me about in our first meeting, she told me that she did not feel comfortable letting strangers in Istanbul know that she was a non-Muslim.

Her revelation would not have happened had our paths not crossed on the island. It seems that the cartographic lines separating the island and the mainland correspond to many other imagined, constructed and crafted divisions between Armenians and Turks. As the opening quote revealed, Deleuze, in *Desert Islands* (2004), writes that human beings can only live on an island if they can forget what it represents; otherwise, the island would stay deserted (cited in Saybaşılı 2011: 178). In this view, the island is a materialization of a criticism against the unity of the state and its absolutist impositions of belonging (179). I cannot discuss here whether this holds valid as an anthropological argument for all islands. Nevertheless, it is still relevant to note that in the political context of Turkey, where non-Muslims are imagined as 'foreigners', Kınalıada and the other nearby islands of the archipelago are often imagined in a way that validates Deleuze's suggestion. As indicated, with their disproportionately high numbers of non-Muslim inhabitants in comparison to the rest of Turkey, the islands are imagined as a zone beyond the unity represented by the nation-state and thus as a 'foreign land'.

For the Muslim audience in the country, direct links with the island expose the relative distance of non-Muslims to the zones of Turkishness. It is in this sense that the island is also 'a stigmatizing island' and widely understood as an 'outside' for my informants. This is not to refute that the island constitutes an 'inside' where Armenians from different parts of the city (and the world) know that they will meet other Armenians. However, in a political context where distances between inner and outer zones of Turkishness mark Armenians (and other non-Muslims) as outsiders (as lesser Turks and foreigners), exposing one's connection to the island turns this inside permanently out. This is how, on the island, the distinctions between public and private spheres, where differences would be hidden and exposed, respectively, collapse. The island is where everyone's 'place' (in Turkish: *yer*) is known to everyone else.

I believe the collapse of privacy on the island is precisely related to the fact that Kınalıada is a space that is stigmatized and marked as different (in the sense that it is imagined as a foreign territory). In places with different histories in relation to the making of 'Turks' and 'foreigners' in Turkey, we could expect different outcomes depending on their dynamics. For instance, Saybaşılı (2008) notes that Esra Ersen, a Turkish video artist, in *Brothers and Sisters* (2003) brings our attention to the places where African migrants feel comfortable within the urban fabric of Istanbul. She notes that these migrants only feel at ease in places that could be found in any city, like night clubs, shopping malls, parks, hotels and McDonald's (Saybaşılı 2008: 158). It appears that it is in these places of anonymity that migrants feel racially unmarked and safe – which might be further indicative of their articulations of an inside that we cannot test here. Saybaşılı observes the same situation in her own research in a Kurdish migrant neighbourhood in central Istanbul, which provides a basis for further discussion in relation to my Armenian informants from Istanbul:

> The narrow and maze-like streets of Tarlabasi, which do not lead to any common square but fall back upon themselves, can be considered as 'non-places' and

indefinite spaces. These streets can only impose isolation rather than any form of communication, interaction or participation. They prevent the chance encounter between diverse population and the city dweller. The public space of the inhabitants of Tarlabasi, if there is any, is where they chat in front of their doors that open onto the corridor-like streets. A young Kurd, sitting on the stairs in front of his house, complained that the police always asked for his ID whenever he went to sell mussels on Istiklal Street, only one boulevard away. In the 1990s, while the political geography of sovereignty focused on border wars against Kurds, the urban geography focused on a visual purity that produced continuity between being Kurdish and being a PKK-terrorist. This Kurdish man is reminded that he does not belong there.

(Saybaşılı 2008: 173–4)

Spatial practices are key factors in the constitution of citizenship (Işın 2002: 35) and the making of foreigners as opposed to citizens (Nyers 2003: 1089). The above quotation depicts a particular moment in the history of Istanbul where the public spaces of the city are no longer accessible to the politically marked bodies of Kurds, unless they can hide their differences or leave them behind. The only places where they can hide their difference are the various *other* spaces within the city where the number of circulating people brings anonymity. Kınalıada is no such place for my informants. In the case of the island, the number of circulating people does not lead to a situation where Armenians can *unperform* their difference from the Muslim *adanın yerlisi* (lit. native of the island).

If the physical organization of urban space is an expression of citizenship regimes (Işın 2002: 35; also cited in Nyers 2003: 1079–80), what spatial arrangements and configurations materialize the spatial expressions of the foreigner (1080)? One may think that the island is a natural formation enclosed by the sea, yet the island is also a political landscape that is 'imagined' and 'crafted' (see Navaro-Yashin 2012) as different. This is why, over the course of my research and the process of writing this chapter, I approached various articulations of insides and outsides as everyday articulations of these differences that imagined Turks as natives/locals (in Turkish: *yerli*) and non-Muslims as foreigners (in Turkish: *yabancı*).

I believe, at least in the case of my Armenian informants from the island, that it is in the centrality of the notion of one's own place (*yer*) and through its various articulations and manifestations that non-Muslim difference is played out in the constitution of insides and outsides, and vice versa. As this chapter reveals, one's own place relates not only to places of origin or dwelling but is also defined in relation to one's distances to the innermost zone of Turkishness. In this context, *yerli* should be understood not as where one has *yer* – a place or a point of origin – but as where others think that one is *yerli*. As a result, articulations of *yerli* cut through various insides and outsides without necessarily following articulations of bonds with, belonging to, or historical anteriority on the island: *yer* can be either an inside or an outside, and sometimes both. However, the island is a context where Armenians can never be *yerli*.

I suggest that Armenians on the island do not feel themselves to be insiders in a place that they imagine as a meeting point for Armenians in Turkey and abroad. This is because, despite being a zone of accessibility, intimacy and connectedness between Armenians, the island has a panopticon-like quality in such a way that my informants cannot hide or leave behind their differences (in relation to the category of the Turk) from the gaze of the *adanın yerlisi* (lit. native of the island) and the state. As shown in this chapter, Armenians on the island are keenly aware of their exteriority vis-à-vis zones of Turkishness, as well as the Turkish public imagination of the islands as a foreign country. This situation is reflected in the constant reproduction of the dichotomy between *yerli* (lit. local or native) and *yabancı* (lit. foreigner) in Turkish.

It is in this context that the island is not an island anymore – as much as perhaps a landlocked country like Armenia, a migrant neighbourhood like Kumkapı, a minority museum like the Jewish Museum or blocks of apartments in Kurtuluş simultaneously are and are not islands depending on their extended relationships with the wider world, epitomized in the particular modes of travel to reach them. In the case of Kınalıada, although the island is still off the coast as an independent physical entity surrounded by a body of water, it is not a place where its inhabitants could easily forget what it represents. As much as it is surrounded by water, it is enclosed by the discourse and practices of nation-building in contemporary Turkey. Its proximity to the practices of state power makes it impossible to think about it as an autonomous entity. As Deleuze (2004) imagined, the island may only be an island as long as it is deserted, cut off from any links to the mainland (and the state).

CONCLUSION

Figure 14 A Collage by Aikaterini Gegisian (2015). From left to right: Yerevan, Athens, Istanbul (Original in colour)

Texts produced at different stages of my former doctoral work are subsumed into a particular narrative of dwelling and travelling within this book. As Marilyn Strathern noted in *Partial Connections* (1991), the sense of flow within written discourse is based on a kind of experiential unity inherent to the exercise, although it is at the same time made up of internal discontinuities and jumps over gaps (xxiii). This is what she calls 'the well-known paradox of contacts between surfaces' (ibid.), in which the gaps-in-between are represented as containing nothing by those who focus on distinctions (what things in themselves are), but are not at all empty in the view of those who focus on connections and interrelations (Green 2005: 88). Hence, there are various possible ways of reading between textual landscapes, which should consider the subject position of the reader central to the experiential unity invoked by Strathern (1991). In the case of ethnographic research, where anthropologists are also expected to 'read' the cultural stuff enclosed by those surfaces and gaps (as proposed by Barth 1959), there is a decision to make, as suggested above by Green: whether to focus on what things in themselves are, or to account for connections and interrelations between them. Following that, in this book, I have invested some scholarly time in highlighting the nuances in the ways we investigate gaps that either denote or similarly deny difference. These are gaps with such authority, or such baggage, that they do not allow us to relocate people and places easily.

I opened this book with one image and I close it with another. In the image above, Aikaterini Gegisian presents a collage of images that collapses certain cartographic gaps between Greece, Turkey and Armenia while reintroducing others. The collage intends to introduce a continuous landscape, yet at the same recognizes that there is a 'deceptive' aspect to it. In Gegisian's own words, 'communicating and cooperating, images find their perfect match, as if "everything is in play and in place"' (gegisian.com). At one level, I believe, we should seek answers by looking at the histories of these three nation-states, where 'population exchange' and genocidal processes aimed at mass homogenization in language and religion. Consequently, behind the harmony presented in the above collage (and her other collages), there is a historical context in which the differences between these nation-states are firmly established, both cartographically and in terms of culture. It is in this sense that the collage allows its audience to rethink these divisions between Greece, Turkey and Armenia. At another level, there is something inherent to every textual and visual narrative that makes holes, absences and contradictions inevitable no matter how elegant or seemingly total they look (see Saybaşılı 2008: 83, footnote 3). In one of our meetings in Istanbul, Gegisian explained that the contours between the selected images were deliberately left uneven, so that 'the gaps become autonomous and the images fall into the crack to express new thought' (personal communication on 8 September 2015). This is also how I find my ethnographic writing in this book to form a collage, which exposes interrupted relationships, histories of disconnection and practices of compartmentalization. In my understanding of my own work, different components of meaning and representation are not treated as being in opposition or negation, though not in a perfect harmonious set of relationships, either. It is from this perspective that I invite my readers to once again have a look at the cover image of this book, captured by the author and intentionally printed in colour, and subsequently compare it to the particular visual representations put into place by almost every other book written on Armenians in contemporary Turkey.

In many ways, the narrative presented in this book is necessarily a collage that is descriptive of situations I came across during my fieldwork and the particular epistemological regime that I studied in relation to physical dispersion and the semantics of 'signs in history' – or those objects that are frequently considered to be concrete embodiments or repositories of the past they record (Parmentier 1987). However, it also recognizes its own limitations, inconsistencies and gaps within the narrative of dwelling and travelling portrayed in the post-genocide context of Turkey and Armenia. Issues of access (to fieldwork sites and informants) and subsequent 'offshoots in research' (such as the emergence of bus and boat journeys as fieldwork sites) provided this book with a narrative of 'getting there' in the way suggested by Clifford (1997). Consequently, the gaps located within textual, visual and ethnographic landscapes presented in the works of Strathern (1991) and Gegisian (2015) respectively point at a 'direction' from which to approach different modes of cultural representation. As I construe such effort of redirecting points of entry specifically in relation to my own ethnographic material, this book did not aim to define ethnic communities either from inside or outside. Instead, it has aimed to recognize a 'negative space' where a union of diverse human and non-human actors gave shape to the ethnographic research context. Following this sentiment, what interested me most in this book was to understand and unpack those negative spaces, which I have widely referred to as the imaginary and physical spaces surrounding the metaphorical and the literal islands presented in each chapter of this book, as constitutive of anthropological (and thus political and cultural) subjects, and to identify their places within a larger system of ethnographic representation.

James Clifford (1986a) hints at two possible claims to the representative quality of ethnographic data: as personal truths that are 'examples of typical phenomena' or are 'exceptions to collective patterns' (109). In a book based on direct one-to-one physical and personal contact with informants, there are expectedly limitations in the capacity of personal truths (of myself, the researcher) to represent or even to identify particular narratives as 'Armenian'. However, similar to what an identification like 'Armenian' implies, various other notions analysed in the different chapters of this book could at best account for their own everyday makings in circulation – instead of claiming one-to-one representations of either 'typical phenomena' or 'exceptions to collective patterns' as put by Clifford (1986a). As a result, the epistemological regime portrayed in this book is of a kind that draws a line in identifying what is Armenian and what is not from two specific vantage points: my informants and myself. As the previous pages of this book have noted, the former encompasses a very diverse group of people, without consensus on what it takes to be an Armenian. However, the discussion based on this lack of consensus provides them with common ground for identifying themselves as part of an ancient and globally dispersed community of Armenians. The latter, an anthropologist concerned with the ways everyday epistemologies are studied, deconstructed and reconstructed by our discipline, is a person identified with one of the groups defined by nation-building processes in Turkey. This is not to imply that I have conceived a conflict or an opposition between the two vantage points. Instead, I have construed it as a generative force in the various steps of conducting and writing down this research.

As noted in the Introduction, the epistemological regime, as I construe it, primarily concerns production of truths and facts as direct consequences of power relations (Foucault 1980). As much as this book is invested in exploring the constitution of such a regime of knowledge in the contexts of 'travelling' and 'dwelling' in Turkey, it is also concerned with the anthropological production of knowledge. This is the epistemology of anthropology, which is based on a historically informed way of engaging with research and representation (Rabinow 1986). As Clifford (1986a) wrote himself, for the greater part of its history, anthropology tended to marginalize the intersubjective foundations of fieldwork and relocated/redistributed them to other writing genres or forms of textual representation (109). It is because of this ongoing trend in anthropology that Strathern (1985) called to create a relation with informants and 'search for a medium of expression which will offer mutual interpretation, perhaps visualised as a common text' (17) (also quoted in Rabinow 1986: 255). However, the ways we, as researchers, (attempt to) establish relationships with prospective informants are defined by the political context(s) of the research site. As in the case of my research, the compartmentalization of the researcher and the people in focus into different categorical identities is epistemologically constituted and sustained. In such ethnographic contexts, how would it be possible for the researcher and the informant to produce a common text?

This question brings our attention to the creative field of representation that should find ways to go beyond the divergences and disagreements between researchers and informants. Following research shaped and oriented by issues of access on the part of both the researcher and the informants, hinting at their differences in terms of the extent to which they could and could not move and perhaps encounter each other, I come to the conclusion that the epistemology of anthropology is inevitably embedded with the epistemologies of the research context. Although this observation is not a novelty in the field of anthropology, it is still ignored in the context of Turkey. If the danger of anthropological endeavours is to reproduce hierarchies, divisions and exploitations (among humans, animals and things), its power is to account for their emergence and circulation. Looking back on the very first days of my research, one instance clearly sheds light onto this situation.

In the first month of my research in Istanbul, I attempted to contact various Armenian journalists, academics and researchers for help. Not many people were interested; I received only one response. In the only email I received, from one of the editors of *Agos*, one of the three Armenian newspapers published in Istanbul, I was kindly reminded that my research topic on Armenians was based on social constructions that did not exist. In other words, according to the person I contacted for help, I was pursuing a goal that was proven to be futile:

> As an Armenian who has made it into his mid-20s, I can assure you there is no such thing as 'Armenianness' [in Turkish: *Ermenilik*, which would be understood by a Turkish speaker as 'the state of being Armenian'] in this world. Similarly, there is no such thing as Yugoslavness [*Yugoslavlık*], Italianness [*İtalyanlık*], or Uruguayanness [*Uruguaylılık*].

The editor continued his email with the following words, where he reminded me that there was also a particular political context – and historical baggage – in how this term (and others) resonated in Turkey:

> Don't be concerned by this [Armenianness], as such a thing only exists in our country with Article 301 [of the Turkish Penal Code against the denigration of Turkishness], which protects the concept of 'Turkishness' [*Türklük*]. All these concepts look strange to me and I do not believe that they will be approved of or accepted on an international platform.

Receiving this e-mail, I observed the critical stance of its author against the fixation on relationships between people and identities. However, his critical engagement went beyond a simple social-constructivist concern. As he noted in his email, the infamous 'Article 301 of the Turkish Penal Code against the denigration of Turkishness' reflected the protectionist (in Turkish: *korumacı*) policy of a state-imposed definition of ethnicity. Moreover, one of the most famous victims of the article was Hrant Dink, who himself was the former editor-in-chief of *Agos*. He was murdered in 2007 by a young Turkish nationalist after having been prosecuted three times under this particular article. Dink had been made a target of hate-speech in the media for publicly speculating on the ethnic origins of Sabiha Gökçen, one of the eight adopted children of Atatürk and the world's first female fighter pilot (and thus a proud member of the Turkish Army), whom he claimed could have been one of the converted orphans of the Armenian Genocide. When the news first broke in the Turkish media, the General Staff of the Turkish Army released a public statement which included the following lines:

> ... the Turkish media is expected to be more sensitive about [...] the foundational principles and values of the Republic of Turkey, the unity [in Turkish: *birlik*] and the togetherness [in Turkish: *beraberlik*] of the Turkish nation, and to reconsider its publication policies in light of these views.
>
> (23 February 2004, *bianet*, my own translation)

This speculation on the ethnic origins of Atatürk's adopted daughter and a former prominent member of the Turkish Army was thus widely understood as a threat to the 'unity' (in Turkish: *birlik*) of the nation. It is in this context that, I believe, it should also not come as a surprise that hundreds of thousands of people (the majority of whom were Muslim Turks) chanted 'We are all Armenians' in Turkish (*Hepimiz Ermeniyiz*) and Armenian (*Polors Hay Enk*) at Dink's funeral. It was a historical moment of protest in which the funeral attenders wanted to criticize how a public discussion on Sabiha Gökçen's origins could have been perceived as a 'denigration of Turkishness', ultimately leading to Dink's murder.

There is a core element left to explore in the editor's email, where he also argued that there was no such thing as *Ermenilik* (lit. 'the state of being Armenian'). As this book has focused on understanding the multiple possible ways of unpacking Turkishness (in Turkish: *Türklük*) vis-à-vis the wider popular views or particular state ideologies that identify Armenians and other non-Muslims as 'foreigners' in Turkey, we cannot expect *Ermenilik* to stand as only a hegemonic term that is primarily informed by its ontological difference from Turkishness or what it widely implies in terms of a commonality of identity, belonging or memory among Armenians. This is why, where I recognized the editor's remark that called our attention to how *Türklük* was a hegemonic category of affiliation protected by the state, I approached his social-constructivist sentiment on *Ermenilik* with caution, as I believe his comment should be replied to with another question: what does the non-existence of *Ermenilik* in reality imply for people who identify themselves as Armenians?

The ways in which this book has addressed this question should be understood in light of its author's deliberate attempt to critique particular representations of Armenians and Turks – as well as *Ermenilik* and *Türklük* – in mutually exclusive and homogeneous terms. As I construe them, both terms inform each other, and in a very similar way the book has invested in understanding how 'native' (in Turkish: *yerli*) and 'foreigner' (in Turkish: *yabancı*) and 'dwelling' and 'travelling' or 'stasis' and 'mobility' were co-constituted. If we think about the popular definitions of 'native' as a dweller of her place of origin, as opposed to a 'foreigner' travelling over distances (see Kristeva 1991), the narratives of my informants go beyond such binary oppositions in multiple ways. This is also why each and every chapter of this book has portrayed particular ethnographic contexts in which people, places and time were juxtaposed in ways such that the antagonisms between these established notions of mobility and stasis collapsed, were inverted or met halfway.

Similar to the ways in which many of the narratives of mobility presented in this book involve interruptions, detours and pauses, this book is nowhere near complete. However, a final discussion needs to be put forward in order to provide a departure point for future research. In relation to community-making, I have portrayed accounts of individuals who either discussed ways of being Armenian or who drew lines between what separated Armenians from others around them. In Kumkapı, the 'context of anxieties' (Biehl 2015) and 'fear of the unknown' (Pattie 1997) emerge as the underlying factors in shaping the ways Armenian migrants approached other migrants: Kurds from Turkey, women from all different corners of the post-socialist world including Armenians, and most recently people from sub-Saharan Africa. On Kınalıada, the lines were drawn in the wake of the Turkish nation-building process and necessarily the Genocide. In Istanbul, what I first found was atomized groupings of people who were cognizant of the extent of their diversity as Armenians. Dispersion across a massive urban ocean like Istanbul, differences in mother tongue and religion (in addition to divergences from religious practices), and perhaps most importantly of all family histories of migration and urbanization (as in becoming *Istanbullu*) posed latent challenges in the formation of a monolithic community of Armenians. However, for a particular group within these groups, the islanders, their imagined community of Armenians (and the ways they imagined other communities of Greeks, Jews and Muslims) has a physical basis. The island itself became an enclosure of territory that corresponded to an enclosure of a community of Armenians.

As I have construed in this book, communities do not come into formation through consensus on the defining terms of membership. There are also political and personal agendas that make people look ahead, which buttress feelings of affiliation to a larger imagined group. Although I have not explicitly vocalized those agendas in this book, I would like to share some of my observations for setting the ground for future research. These ideas may be found provocative or lacking a firm base. Nevertheless, I hope they will be taken as suggestions by other researchers in the field. Over the course of my fieldwork in the two countries, and during transitory moments on buses or in Georgia, I observed that Armenians from Armenia sought 'recognition' (i) of the fact that they were the first Christian 'nation' in the world, (ii) that they actively participated in and contributed to the making of a 'human civilization' through their own dispersion to the urban diasporic centres where such 'civilization' was historically cultivated and (iii) of the Genocide. With each and every Armenian I met en route to Turkey, there was a moment in which I was 'reminded' of these facts. There should be more than one way to interpret the frequency of these themes; however, I specifically urge us to think about them from the perspective of place-making, a way of establishing relationships with an Armenian world that is incomparably larger than Armenia now. In this sense, the transformation of Armenia into a post-socialist nation-state with impermeable borders sets the physical context in which these narratives are based – if not originated.

In Turkey, the agenda is less clearly defined for Armenians as they find themselves trying to make sense of their post-genocide atomization and simultaneously to define a community through citizenship. In this sense, their endeavour promises to provide us with a critical perspective to comprehend contemporary Turkishness in all its diversity. In so doing, I hope that they will increase the country's prospects of becoming a truly participatory democracy, in which all citizens are equal and free.

EPILOGUE: CROSSING BACK TO GEORGIA IN A CHANGING WORLD

There are many possible ways to bring an end to a written narrative. The Conclusion aimed to highlight the central themes of place-making that have been portrayed in the pages of this book. However, it should be noted that over the course of the five years I spent writing this book, the world did not stand still; in both Armenia and Turkey, there have been important political changes. While Turkey became increasingly more authoritarian under the rule of Prime Minister and later President Recep Tayyip Erdoğan, especially following the Gezi protests, which I touched upon in Chapter 7, and the coup attempt of 2016, in Armenia nobody was expecting political change. However, following more than ten days of popular protests in April 2018, Serzh Sargsyan, who, similar to Erdoğan, had served as both president and Prime Minister, was finally forced to step down after a decade in power. In this respect, there have been moments in which my friends and wider cohort of informants in Turkey and Armenia experienced a transformation of their relationships to their fellow citizens, and to friends and relatives dispersed throughout different countries. In this sense, imagined and physical distances within their personal networks of mobilities were in a process of transformation.

As noted in the first half of this book, 'place-making' is informed by particular juxtapositions of physical movement and long-distance communication. While I first looked at the issue in relation to earlier histories of dispersion (such as migration, exile, exodus or business expeditions), later in the text I noted that relationships with the wider world informed zones of accessibility for my informants, reflected in the articulations of a mobile home in Anahid's case, a temporally multi-layered homeland for Hranoush, homely and unhomely homelands for Anna, and an ethnically defined inside in the accounts of Ani and Mariam. However, in the second half of the book, my ethnographic focus shifted away from accounting for the 'diffusion' of place, or in other words its making as a series of locations as per the everyday understandings of place and belonging of my informants from Turkey (see Clifford 1989). I detected that in Kurtuluş and Kınalıada, both of which were referred to as physically and/or ethnically enclosed islands by my informants for different reasons, one's own place in the world (*yer*) took into account personal and family histories of displacement rather than of Armenians as a whole. This has perhaps also been why the capacities of place to shrink and expand are expressed differently in Istanbul, where my informants took into consideration not all Armenians who once lived and continued living in ancestral homelands or in the diaspora – as Armenians in Armenia were much more prone to doing – but rather only direct personal and family histories of displacement within Turkey and the subsequent dispersion of relatives and friends who maintained contact and communication over long distances. For instance, in the latest historical episodes of shifting insides and outsides in Istanbul, '*dünyadan kopuyoruz*' (in Turkish: we are breaking off from the world) and '*dünyadan gitgide uzaklaşıyoruz*' (in Turkish: we are moving away from the world) were the two most common expressions I heard from the people around me in general and the people whom I researched in particular. For instance, many Armenians on Kınalıada firmly believed that the island was increasingly being abandoned by Armenians from the diaspora. They expressed that the last time they experienced such a historical moment of abandonment was following the 1999 Marmara earthquake that hit Istanbul and its surroundings, when many Armenians from abroad left the city immediately after and did not come back for some years.

For Armenians in Istanbul a vast array of state policies resulted in this situation: suppression of the Kurdish political movement and the other groups in the opposition against the government, including academics, journalists and intellectuals; rumours of fraud during elections; restrictions on the consumption of alcohol; limitations on formerly liberal abortion rights; internet bans; decrease in foreign investments; and rapid devaluation of the Turkish lira against world currencies, which created significant increases in the cost of travelling abroad. The world that Turkey found itself distancing from was thus defined both through the physical distances one was capable of travelling herself and as a set of liberal and democratic values in which citizens were recognized as free and equal. In other words, over the course of these past years, it became even more difficult for Armenians to live in this 'new Turkey' (as Erdoğan, in his political rallies, mostly refers to the reshaping and restructuring of the country over the past fifteen years), where they simultaneously wanted to connect with friends and families abroad and to be equal and free citizens of Turkey. However, as discussed in the sections on the zonal constitution of Turkishness, Turkey was already a political context where they had found themselves in a situation where they could not be simultaneously Armenian and Turkish-through-citizenship. Moreover, as portrayed in the last chapter of this book, Armenians were not very vocal in expressing dissent in public loudly; one needed to know when, where and how to talk in Istanbul. This situation was in stark contrast to what I observed in Armenia, where not only my informants and friends but also everyone I met including the cashier at a supermarket, the marshrutka driver or the ticket officer at a museum were publicly very critical of the government and Prime Minister/President Sargsyan. In many ways what was unexpected in Armenia perhaps came as a direct outcome of years of circulation and accumulation of open sentiments about such dissatisfaction with politics.

During the 'Armenian velvet revolution', as it is widely referred to, I was in Yerevan as a Hrant Dink Foundation Fellow at the Institute of Archaeology and

Ethnography of the Armenian National Academy of Sciences. As part of my fellowship, I was asked to organize two public seminars and a conference based on my research that is now spread across the pages of this book. In order to reconnect with my past research in Armenia, I decided to revisit some of the former sites of fieldwork, land-crossings between Armenia and Georgia where I once observed cross-border mobility. As a start, I planned a day trip to some of the border villages on the Armenian side of the border, just to have a look and remember. I decided to go by private taxi, but there was a split between my friends in Yerevan as to which smart phone application to use to call the taxi. I had two options: the Russian-owned Yandex Taxi and the Armenian-owned GG. The discussion between my friends followed an expected trajectory (at least on my part), as the GG supporters claimed that it was important for an Armenian company to make money instead of the Russians and that it was wise to keep in mind that it was perhaps better not to let Russians learn about my global imprint and history of travelling. According to them, Russians were 'watching everything closely'. The Yandex Taxi camp, which was much smaller in comparison to the first camp, claimed that Russians were better businesspeople and more professional. They trained their taxi drivers better and they had many more cars. At the end I took into consideration only the price asked, and because of the momentary surplus of taxi drivers, Yandex offered me a slightly better deal – and this was how I met Tiko.

For the three-and-a-half months I stayed in Yerevan in 2018, Tiko would become not only my main provider of transport but also a dear friend. He was almost ten years younger than me, about twenty-five, and married with a newly born daughter. As a teenager, he had wanted to be a pilot, but once he realized that he could not pass the tests for that, he decided to be a taxi driver instead. He was of the post-socialist generation of Armenia, but nevertheless firmly believed that those were better times in terms of making a living. He was from a provincial town in the south of the country but had no prospects of going back. When I visited his place of origin and his family home, and met his relatives, he told me that almost all of his friends had left for Russia. For him, moving to Russia was certainly on the agenda, but he had decided to wait until his daughter reached school age. He found Moscow too dirty and polluted to raise a toddler.

Tiko drove crazily in the city, but he followed all the rules in the countryside. He had extensive knowledge about the speed cameras all across Armenia. Similar to many other drivers I met over the course of my research, he was always very vocal in expressing criticisms against the government. Over the course of his driving career, he had closely observed corruption in person. Every time the police asked for bribes, it was yet another opportunity to talk about the inefficiency of Armenian democracy. When Sargsyan announced on 23 April, just a day before Genocide Memorial Day, that he was leaving office, Tiko was as happy as the rest of the celebrating crowd in the streets of Yerevan. By the time I met him, just a couple of days following the resignation, Tiko's telephone was full of photographs taken in Republic Square, the centre of demonstrations in Yerevan, celebrating the moment of political change with flags and family. On the day we met at the end of April, we were off to Javakheti, an Armenian-dominated province in southern

Georgia, on the immediate other side of the border. It was impossible not to notice the huge Armenian flag that covered the entire bonnet of the car. He told me that he decorated to celebrate and to see how the Georgian authorities would react to it.

I saw no reason for the flag to draw any attention as we were off to a region with a 95 per cent Armenian population. However, at the Bavra border crossing that connected Gyumri to the villages of Javakheti, the Georgian police forced Tiko to remove the flag. When he asked whether it was really necessary, the policeman responded that it was for our safety as in Georgia nobody could guarantee what would happen to us and a car with a huge Armenian flag. Tiko was perfectly aware that the policeman was being rather arbitrary, but he nevertheless removed the flag with a smile. When I asked him why he was smiling, he responded that he had expected this attitude from the Georgian police. He added in English that these were 'the kinds of things that should also change in Armenia'. For him, this was a 'small country situation', referring to an inferiority complex that came as a direct result of the changing place of Georgia in world politics.

All through our journeys in Georgia, where we visited not only Javakheti but also Batumi and Tbilisi, Tiko repeatedly made attempts to talk to the Georgian police in Russian. He had a certain joy in stopping the car, asking for directions that we already knew, seeing whether the police would respond in Russian and reporting the entire conversation back to me. At the end, he came to the conclusion that the younger generation of Georgians did not know as much Russian as the older generation. As he expressed many times, it was 'such a pity to distance from a leading world power'.

After our return to Armenia from Javakheti, people were still in the streets. They were anxious to see whether a pro-Sargsyan candidate would be elected as the new prime minister of Armenia. However, on 8 May, the parliament elected Nikol Pashinyan, the opposition MP who was leading the popular protest since its inception in mid-April. With his camouflage pants, cap and backpack, Pashinyan looked very much different than Sargsyan with his tailored suit, bodyguards and escort cars. It was no wonder that, in the following days, there were photos of new ministers taking the metro, walking or cycling to the parliament circulating via social media. It was in this political context in which the new government looked more down-to-earth than its predecessor that Tiko – in addition to many other friends in Armenia – expressed that he was observing 'change' everywhere. He noted that even the attitudes of the police were changing; they were not seeking bribes anymore and they were willing to help drivers as much as they could. He believed that in a small country like Armenia, if one single person changed, the entire society changed.

I would see him for the last time – at least for now – on the day I packed my suitcases and left Yerevan for Istanbul in mid-May 2018. He came to pick me up from my apartment in central Yerevan relatively sooner than I expected so that we could chat a little more before I departed. On the way to Yerevan's Zvartnots Airport, Tiko was telling me that he expected 'many things to be given back to Armenian people'. I asked him what he meant, and he responded that it was time that the moguls – widely referred to as the *oligarkh*s in Armenia – learned how to share their wealth with ordinary people. He added that nationalization of the formerly privatized state institutions should follow. As I was opening the trunk of the car to get my suitcases, he kept talking: 'The airport you see now belongs to a European businessman. When you come back to Armenia in the future, you will see that this will also change. The state will take the airport back. We will travel for cheaper and Armenia will be a bigger country than it is now'.

In writing the very last paragraph of this book, I find it important to bridge Tiko's sentiments about Georgia, which he found to have been reduced to a small country, and post-revolution Armenia, where he believed there was a prospect of becoming a bigger country. In line with the narratives of 'travelling' and 'dwelling' presented in this book, distances between people and places were in a constant process of reconfiguration in Tiko's world. There were historical moments of shrinking and expanding 'insides'. However, for him, what made Georgia a small country did not merely lie in its transformation from a member state of the Soviet Union to a post-socialist state in tension with Russia. In his view, what mattered most was the attitude of younger generations in turning away from what was once the lingua franca of the region, Russian, to the extent that they could no longer communicate with their neighbours. Similarly, the possibility of Armenia becoming a bigger country in the future lays in its transformation to a country with better connections to the rest of the world. While in the case of Georgia language increasingly became a barrier in reaching out to a wider world, in the case of Armenia the barriers were of more physical substance. Tiko believed that improvement of means of travelling would immediately open up his country, which he found as key in becoming a 'bigger country'. While Covid-19 and the Forty-Four Day War between Armenia and Azerbaijan in 2020 – two subject matters that I have been researching and writing about during the printing of the present book – have impeded the prospects of such transformation, I still hope his wish will come true sooner than he expects.

NOTES

Chapter 1

1. Both of these treaties annulled former border treaties signed between the Ottoman and Russian Empires, which also implied a 'new start' for the parties involved. It would not be misleading to suggest that both treaties were foundational in the making of modern Turkey. They brought recognition to the Turkish Grand National Assembly located in Ankara as the government of Turkey (as opposed to the Ottoman government in Istanbul occupied by the Allied Powers) two years before the Turkish Republic was founded in 1923.
2. The only other border crossing between the Soviet Union and Turkey, the Margara/Alican crossing, was also located in Armenia. However, it was never permanently in operation (Gültekin 2007).
3. Although I object to the term 'historical peninsula' as it de-historicizes other historically significant parts of the city, it demonstrates how the making of marginality and centrality are intertwined spatial arrangements in contemporary Istanbul. Su (forthcoming) playfully introduces the term 'Old City Peninsula' to stress the juxtaposition of a geographical term with a capital-driven claim on historicity (see also the next chapters).
4. In this understanding of the terms, 'locality' should go beyond defining the physical component of 'place'. This premise also lays the foundation of how I define 'locality' in the following pages – and how in the previous pages I defined 'mobilities' between two localities. On the one hand, following Tsing (2000) here, 'locality' is not merely a physical meeting point for people, goods or capital. It is where people, goods and capital change and are remade. This is how, on the other hand, my particular understanding of the term is in line with the idea of 'territory' presented by Deleuze and Guattari (1987), a term with unstable qualities, both in physical and in discursive substance.
5. Culture is inherently a site of travel and a zone of contact for anthropologists, too (see Rabinow 1986: 242). See the 'Getting There' section of the Introduction for a similar discussion on how 'travelling to the fieldwork site' should be understood as an essential component of anthropological research.
6. The new regulation did not specifically target Armenian nationals. In fact, before 2000, Armenians were exempt from visas for entering Turkey (Gültekin 2003). In 2000, Turkey was required to de-liberalize its visa policy to prevent irregular migration into the country as part of a potential EU deal granting visa-free travel for Turkish citizens in the Schengen zone (Tolay 2012; Soyaltın 2013; Açıkgöz 2015). Therefore, the gradual change in Turkey's visa regulations has to be understood in relation to the wider scope of Turkish foreign relations (Kirişçi 2005; Tolay 2012).
7. Although Helms applies 'long-distance specialists' in the historical contexts of preindustrial societies, I find the term relevant to my ethnographic material as it stresses a feeling of pride in going on an expedition.

Chapter 2

1. It should also be noted that Armenians often themselves reflected upon the frequency of these narratives through jokes; for instance, once in a gathering among anthropologists from Armenia, a friend satirically told me that 'everyone has Armenian roots, even Barack Obama' (in Armenian: *bolory unen Haykakan dzakum, ankam Barack Obama*).
2. As noted in the previous chapter, the only other border crossing in the South Caucasus was also located in Armenia, but it was never permanently open.
3. In the time period in which Ani first moved to Turkey, the regulation limiting the number of days within 180 days for visits on tourist visas to Turkey was not in effect (for more information, see the previous chapter). When she attempted to visit Armenia with the plan of coming back to Turkey, she simply did not know that she had overstayed her visa.
4. I find ethnicity similar to what John Comaroff (1992) defined as a 'process of classification' (and relating things and people to one another in a way resembling totemism) (54). In this sense the term does not presume any primordial substance or impose any necessity of consensus on group definition by members (see next chapter). To the contrary, its constant reformulation should shed light onto the ways one makes sense of her place in relation to the wider world.
5. Although Clifford's observations on the diasporization of natives are specifically based on Native American, First Nations and aboriginal experiences in the settler states of the United States, Canada and Australia, respectively, fundamental elements are shared between Turkey and these countries in relation to genocidal processes, population engineering, brutal policies of resettlement and legalization of discrimination.

Chapter 3

1. See Chapter 1, footnote 3.
2. Baronian notes that this was already the case in the 1880s.
3. We will see in Chapter 5 that the situation also resulted in the concentration of non-Muslim populations in other particular neighbourhoods.
4. However, see also Adelson (2000) on how Turks in Germany 'are rarely seen as intervening meaningfully in the narrative of postwar German history' (96).
5. The term has several other nuanced meanings, as we will see in the following pages.
6. Law No: 5580 of 2007, based on a former 1985 regulation.
7. See Article 51/d/5 of the Regulation on Private Education Institutions dated 20.02.2012.
8. I need to stress that here in this specific sentence and section I specifically engage with the term 'community' in the context of migrant Armenians. In Chapter 6, I provide a similar discussion in relation to Armenians from Istanbul.
9. The term *garip*, in both Turkish and Arabic, emphasizes 'moving away from home' and a process of 'estrangement' or exile from one's community. The term has its roots in *garb*, which means 'west' in Arabic. In this sense, the term is based on the loss of orientation that comes with the setting of the sun and the turning of light into darkness (see Sayad 2000: 166–7 for how the term is used in Arabic; see Zirh 2012: 1760 for how the term is used in Turkish; see also Su forthcoming).

10 This is in line with what Zirh (2017) argued on Alevis in/from Turkey. As opposed to majority Sunni Muslim Turks, for whom some administrative regions such as the Black Sea and the Aegean could function in defining a collective identity, Alevis tend to refer specifically to a town or village in elaborating where they are from (159). Zirh writes that this distinction between Sunnis and Alevis points to the tension between state-imposed cartographies and the public's imagination of space (ibid.) (see Chapter 5 for more on this tension). In the post-genocide context of Turkey, Armenians also refer to specific towns, villages and provinces as places of origin but never to entire administrative regions.

11 Although the nation-state ideology and its indoctrination in the early decades of the Republic aimed at defining the category of the 'Turk' as an umbrella term to refer to all citizens of Turkey, the outcome was remarkably different for non-Muslim populations of Greeks, Jews and Armenians. I explore this situation of the making of 'foreigners' from Turkish citizens in detail in Chapter 5.

Chapter 4

1 Macdonald writes that she adapted this term from what Alpers (1991) and Kirshenblatt-Gimblett (1998) formerly called 'the museum effect' (see also Macdonald 2006).

2 I believe that 'heritage effect' is applicable to analyses of recognized heritage sites, but also to more contested sites of heritage and even individuals' very own personal 'sites of memories' (as elaborated by Nora 1989).

3 A second Jewish museum was in the process of opening in Izmir, again in Turkey, at the time of writing.

4 The museum was relocated to a much smaller site within the nearby Neve Shalom Synagogue in 2016.

5 Dost-Niyego and Aytürk (2016) note that, for the broader public in Turkey, the Holocaust is irrelevant in the Turkish context, a nonissue (259). This 'irrelevance' of the Holocaust is widely understood as a result of Turkey's neutrality during the Second World War, but it is also directly related to how official Turkish historiography silenced its own crimes as thousands of Turkish Jews perished in death camps as they were denied entry into the country (260). A 'rescue myth' has been used to fill the gaps in this silenced history, in which the country has been presented as a refuge for European Jews fleeing prosecution at the hands of Nazis (Bali 1999; Guttstadt 2012; Bahar 2015).

6 Marcy Brink-Danan (2012) notes that Jews from Turkey also criticized the museum for omitting other issues, such as dwindling demographics, anti-Semitism, terrorism, relationships between diaspora communities and Israel, and the Istanbul synagogue attacks of the past (51).

7 In a newspaper interview, the curator implied that the museum was only concerned with Jews in Turkey and added that, when compared to other Jewish museums in the world, the Istanbul collection was unique. There is a section dedicated to Turkish Jewish diplomats that stresses the high official positions Jews acquired in Turkey, for example (3 April 2013, *Sabah*).

8 Anna directly refers here to the stigmatization of the concept of 'genocide' as a taboo subject in Turkey, and her remark could not have been timelier in relation to the recent scholarly turn that has invited us to rethink the impact of Turkish-German

political relationships, both on the extermination of Armenians in the Ottoman Empire and for Jews in Nazi-occupied Europe in the first half of the twentieth century. In relation to endnote 28, a new body of scholarship has not only criticized Turkey's role and responsibility during the Holocaust (Bali 1999; Guttstadt 2012; Bahar 2015; Dost-Niyego and Aytürk 2016) but has also attempted to reveal Turkish-German cooperation, mutual admiration and ideological exchange (see Ihrig 2014, 2016).

9   It was only after the relocation of the museum to its new site that these 'grey pages' along with the pink pages' of Jewish history in Turkey were incorporated into the exhibition (25 February 2016, *bianet*).

10 Suciyan (2015) notes that this situation is also reflected in the absence of legal consequences for racist crimes – other than those targeting Turks – until this day (see also endnote 268 in Suciyan).

Chapter 5

1   Murat Belge (1994) notes that until 1964 Greeks were the majority in Kurtuluş and Armenians were a minority. However, the existence of Surp Vartanants Armenian Church, first built in 1861, and the adjacent Armenian primary school that opened in 1912 clearly indicates that the number of Armenians was large enough to form a congregation or a neighbourhood community.

2   Greek community resources indicate that there are about 500 Greeks residing in the neighbourhood (tatavla.org), while it is estimated that about 20,000 Armenians live in the greater borough of Şişli, where Kurtuluş is located (Buchwalter 2002: 23, cited in Özdoğan, Üstel, Karakaşlı and Kentel 2009: 350).

3   We can also think about these name changes of places within the wider context of language reform that was at the core of the nation-building process in Turkey. Sadoğlu (2003) and Okutan (2004) both note that nationalist discourses on 'language purification' (in Turkish: *dilde sadeleşme*) catalysed a discussion on what to do with 'foreign elements' in vocabulary and grammar during the period of transformation from a multi-ethnic empire to a nation-state. For the secular Kemalist elites, language purification initially implied replacing words of Arabic and Persian origin with Turkic ones, a process that also resulted in the alphabet change from Arabic to Latin script in 1928. However, as Turkishness was in the making, the state came up with new policies that were not always in harmony with each other. Literary critic Murat Belge (1982) notes that there were at least two camps among linguists (and two periods of language reform) in the first three decades of the post-Ottoman period. In the first decade, between 1923 and 1935, the primary objective was to replace all 'foreign' words – not only words originating from Arabic or Persian, but also words from Greek and Armenian as well as words adapted during the Ottoman Westernization period from French, Italian and English. It is important to note here that the definition of 'foreign' (in Turkish: *yabancı*) also included the languages of Greek and Armenian citizens of the new republic. The name of Tatavla and most street names in the neighbourhood were all changed in this period. In these very early days of the nation-state, the policy of purification was borrowed from the late Ottoman policies, which best demonstrated itself in the Turkification of place names as early as the First World War (Sadoğlu 2003). In the second decade that followed, however, the language reform took a new direction with a new ideological lens on language and national history. In

the interwar period, Turkish realpolitik increasingly moved away from irredentism (in Turkish: *fütühat*) that had concentrated on establishing Turkish power in former Ottoman territories towards managing national unity in the country. For this reason, Turkish history and language had to be imagined beyond the time period and state boundaries of the Ottoman Empire (Belge 1982). This is why, within the framework of the Turkish History Thesis (1931–9), historians established links between Turks and pre-Ottoman Anatolian (and Mesopotamian) populations such as the Hittites and Sumerians, with an urge to blend all the non-Turkic autochthonous populations of Turkey in national unity. In the post-1935 period reformists did not feel the need to replace 'foreign' elements in the language as they believed every other language originated from proto-Turkish.

4   The newspaper specifically uses the word *Yunan*, not *Rum*, thus referring to Greek newspapers published in Greece, not in Istanbul.

5   There are various ways to account for the particular imaginations of non-Muslims as 'dirty' (as opposed to 'clean'), and that is beyond the scope of this book. Briefly, though, the first explanation that comes to mind takes Islamic food and body purification as its centre. However, Astourian (1999) calls our attention to the political roots of prejudices against non-Muslims in Turkey. He argues that the Ottoman Westernization project and introduction of equal citizenship rights in the mid-nineteenth century undermined the feelings of superiority among Muslims against non-Muslims, as the once *dhimmi* (i.e., protected but restricted) subjects of the sultan were made equal to Muslims. In the case of Armenians, he also suggests considering the geographical concentration of Armenians in eastern Anatolia within the pan-Turkist imagery as another political source of these prejudices. He notes that Armenians were seen as a barrier of people against the unification of Turkic peoples, between Turks in Anatolia and Turkic people around the Caspian Sea (Astourian 1999: 28–34). In terms of the spatial organization of the city, historically the Ottoman cities were divided into neighbourhoods based on religious differences (Duben and Behar 1995 [1991]: 41, cited in Saybaşılı 2008: 163). Saybaşılı (2008) specifically notes that neighbourhoods in Ottoman cities represented collective identities in which 'purity' was an essential component (163).

6   Krikor Zohrab died during the Genocide in 1915 in eastern Turkey. Zabel Yeseyan managed to flee the Genocide, but allegedly could not escape prosecution under Stalin in the Soviet era.

7   'Indivisible' is repeated sixteen times, 'indivisibility' five times and 'indivisible integrity' eight times in the 1982 Turkish constitution.

Chapter 6

1   There are more than two modes of sea travel between mainland Istanbul and the islands. There are also the *motor*, smaller boats run by cooperatives, and *deniz taksi*, or sea taxis.

2   The first boat started to operate en route to the islands on a regular basis in 1846, and until they were finally and completely nationalized in 1954 they were run by various private companies.

3   In the summer of 2021, the ratio between the prices of vapur and seabus tickets was still more or less the same; the former cost 10 Turkish lira while the latter

cost 19 Turkish lira for *Istanbul Kart* holders, namely the city's urban commuter transportation card.

4   In Turkey, perhaps like any other country in the world, census data are collected through compulsory registration of residency in places of dwelling. In the case of the Prince Islands Archipelago it is possible to argue that many summertime residents – those with Muslim and non-Muslim backgrounds alike – register instead in their places of 'permanent residency', which is more than usually understood as the dwellings where winter and most autumn and spring months are spent in mainland Istanbul. As the population of the islands changes depending on the seasons, official data are far from reflecting the full extent of the demographics on Kınalıada and its neighbouring islands.

5   My informants only used the word 'community' (in Turkish: *cemaat*) to refer to the body of historical Armenian organizations (the Church, schools, orphanages, hospitals, etc.), i.e., 'community' was not used to refer to Armenians from Turkey. The terms *bizimkiler* (ours or our people) or *bizim haylar* (our Armenians) would substitute. In contrast, Armenians frequently refer to Jews and Greeks as a *cemaat*. I argue that this contrasting and selective use of 'community' enabled my informants to deny or acknowledge their links to other Armenians (from Armenia or the diaspora) when necessary and also enabled them to articulate their own diversity while positioning Jews or Greeks – or others – as monolithic communities.

6   Contrary to this, Greeks are admired for other reasons; they are usually praised for their insistence on speaking their own language and preserving their culture, and for their openness to the wider world, despite their dramatically diminishing population. They are believed to be less business-oriented than Jews and adept at enjoying life no matter what.

Chapter 7

1   I find a noteworthy similarity between how Alen made sense of his wealth in relation to the Genocide and what Örs (2018) observed vis-à-vis post-exodus Greeks in Istanbul. One of her informants, a community leader, noted that there was 'a lot of space to conduct business' for Greeks in Istanbul. Her particular encounter suggests a connection between migration and accumulation of capital by the remaining people. However, as she wrote, this sentiment was also 'another way of looking at the grim emptiness of urban space' left behind by Greeks in Istanbul (209).

2   It should be added here that this historical moment of emergence of the island as a nodal point in the 1990s corresponds to a time period in which Turkey decided to open up to the world through a series of liberalization projects initiated by the late Prime Minister and President Turgut Özal. As many informants noted, Turkey became accessible once again to Armenians from all around the world with the end of the politically oppressive previous decade shaped by the military coup of 1980. Most informants added that most of their Armenian friends from abroad stopped coming to the island after the devastating earthquake of August 1999, the epicentre of which was only some 70 kilometres away from the island but heavily felt in Istanbul in general. However, the end of the 1990s also marked a time period in which most of these teenagers, both in Turkey and in abroad, reached their mid-twenties and started to get married and have their own families, a situation that should have resulted in their decreasing frequency in visiting the island.

BIBLIOGRAPHY

Books and articles:

Abbeele, G. van den. 1992. *Travel as Metaphor: From Montaigne to Rousseau*. Minneapolis (MN) and London: University of Minnesota Press
Abrahamian, L. 2006. *Armenian Identity in a Changing World*. Costa Mesa (CA): Mazda Publishers
Abu-Lughod, J. L. 1989. *Before European Hegemony: The World System AD 1250–1350*. New York (NY): Oxford University Press
Abu-Lughod, L. 1991. 'Writing against Culture' in *Recapturing Anthropology: Working in the Present*, edited by Richard G. Fox. Santa Fe (NM): School of American Research Press, pp. 137–62
Açıkgöz, M. 2015. 'Turkey's Visa Policy: A Migration-Mobility Nexus'. *Turkish Policy Quarterly* 14(2): 97–107
Adelson, L. A. 2000. 'Touching Tales of Turks, Germans and Jews: Cultural Alterity, Historical Narrative, and Literary Riddles for the 1990s'. *New German Critique* 80: 93–124
Agamben, G. 2001 [1993]. *The Coming Community*. Minneapolis (MN) and London: University of Minnesota Press
Ahmad, F. 1991. *The Making of Modern Turkey*. London and New York (NY): Routledge
Ahmed, S. 1999. 'Home and Away: Narratives of Migration and Estrangement'. *International Journal of Cultural Studies* 2(3): 329–47
Ahmed, S. 2004. *The Cultural Politics of Emotion*. London and New York (NY): Routledge
Akçam, T. 2006. *A Shameful Act: The Armenian Genocide and the Question of Turkish Responsibility*. New York (NY): Metropolitan Books
Akçam, T. and Ümit Kurt. 2012. *Kanunların Ruhu: Emval-i Metruke Kanunlarında Soykırımın İzini Sürmek*. Istanbul: İletişim
Akpınar, I. 2016. 'Urbanization Represented in the Historical Peninsula: Turkification of Istanbul in the 1950s' in *Mid-Century Modernism in Turkey: Architecture across Cultures in the 1950s and 1960s*, edited by Meltem Ö. Gürel. London and New York (NY): Routledge, pp. 56–84
Aktar, A. 2002. *Varlık Vergisi ve Türkleştirme Politikaları*. Istanbul: İletişim
Akyüz, L. 2017. *Ethnicity, Gender and the Border Economy: Living in the Turkey-Georgia Borderlands*. London: Routledge
Alpers, S. 1991. 'The Museum as a Way of Seeing' in *Exhibiting Cultures: The Poetics and Politics of Museum Display*, edited by Ivan Karp and Steven Lavine. Washington (DC): Smithsonian Institution Press, pp. 25–32
Al-Rustom, H. 2015. 'Rethinking the "Post-Ottoman": Anatolian Armenians as an Ethnographic Perspective' in *A Companion to the Anthropology of the Middle East*, edited by Soraya Altorki. Hoboken (NJ): Blackwell, pp. 452–79
Altınay, A. G. 2014. 'Unraveling Layers of Silencing: Where Are the Converted Armenians?' in *The Grandchildren: The Hidden Legacy of 'Lost' Armenians in Turkey*,

edited by Ayşe Gül Altınay and Fethiye Çetin. New Brunswick (NJ): Transaction Publishers, pp. 197–216
Altınay, A. G., and Fethiye Çetin. 2014. 'Foreword to the Turkish Edition' in *The Grandchildren: The Hidden Legacy of 'Lost' Armenians in Turkey*, edited by Ayşe Gül Altınay and Fethiye Çetin. New Brunswick (NJ): Transaction Publishers, pp. xi–xvi
Amygdalou, K. 2014. *A Tale of Two Cities in Search of a New Identity: The Politics of Heritage and Modernisation in Early 20th-Century Izmir and Thessaloniki*. PhD Dissertation in Architecture: University College London
Anderson, B. 1983. *Imagined Communities: Reflections on the Origin and Spread of Nationalism*. London: Verso
Appadurai, A. 1988. 'Putting Hierarchy in Its Place'. *Cultural Anthropology* 3: 36–49
Aras, R. 2014. *The Formation of Kurdishness in Turkey: Political Violence, Fear and Pain*. Abingdon and New York (NY): Routledge
Arutiunian, V. 2006. 'On the Potential of Interethnic Integration in the Megalopolis of Moscow'. *Sociological Research* 45(6): 26–50
Aslanian, S. 2011. *From the Indian Ocean to the Mediterranean: The Global Trade Networks of Armenian Merchants from New Julfa*. Berkeley (CA) and London: University of California Press
Astourian, S. 1999. 'Modern Turkish Identity and the Armenian Genocide, from Prejudice to Racist Nationalism' in *Remembrance and Denial: The Case of the Armenian Genocide*, edited by Richard Hovannisian. Detroit (MI): Wayne University Press, pp. 23–50
Augé, M. 1995. *Non-Places: Introduction to an Anthropology of Supermodernity*. London and New York (NY): Verso
Axel, B. K. 2001. *The Nation's Tortured Body: Violence, Representation, and the Formation of a Sikh 'Diaspora'*. Durham (NC): Duke University Press
Bahar, I. 2015. *Turkey and the Rescue of European Jews*. New York (NY): Routledge
Bakhtin, M. 1981. *The Dialogic Imagination*. Austin (TX): University of Texas Press
Bali, R. 1999. *Cumhuriyet Yıllarında Türkiye Yahudileri: Bir Türkleşme Serüveni (1923–1945)*. Istanbul: İletişim
Bali, R. 2012. *6-7 Eylül Olayları: Tanıklıklar-Hatıralar*. Istanbul: Libra Yayıncılık ve Kitapçılık
Barkey, K. 2008. *Empire of Difference: The Ottomans in Comparative Perspective*. New York (NY): Cambridge University Press
Barkey, K., and George Gavrilis. 2016. 'The Ottoman Millet System: Non-Territorial Autonomy and Its Contemporary Legacy'. *Ethnopolitics* 15(1): 24–42
Baronyan, H. 2014 [1880]. *İstanbul Mahallelerinde Bir Gezinti*. Istanbul: Can Yayınları
Barsegian, I. 2000. 'When Text Becomes Field: Fieldwork in "Transitional" Societies' in *Fieldwork Dramas: Anthropologists in the Postsocialist States*, edited by Hermine G. De Soto and Nora Dudwick. Madison (WI): University of Wisconsin Press, pp. 119–29
Barth, F. 1959. *Political Leadership among Swat Pathans*. London: Athlone Press
Bartu, A. 1999. 'Who Owns the Old Quarters? Rewriting Histories in Global Era' in *Istanbul: Between the Global and the Local*, edited by Çağlar Keyder. Lanham (MD): Rowman & Littlefield Publishers, Inc., pp. 31–46
Bataille, Georges. 1962. *Death and Sensuality. A Study of Eroticism and Taboo*. New York (NY): Walker and Company
Bauman, Z. 1993. *Postmodern Ethics*. London: Routledge
Belge, M. 1982. 'Türkçe Sorunu'. *Yazko Edebiyat* 3(19): 88–102
Belge, M. 1994. *İstanbul Gezi Rehberi*. Istanbul: Tarih Vakfı Yurt Yayınları

Belge, M. 1995. 'Yeni Birlik Biçimleri ve Azınlıklar'. *Birikim* 71-72: 13-16
Bennani-Chraïbi, M. 1994. *Soumis et Rebelles: Les Jeunes au Maroc*. Paris: Editions Le Fennec
Benninghaus, R. 2007. 'Turks and Hemshinli: Manipulating Ethnic Origins of Identity' in *The Hemshin: History, Society and Identity in the Highlands of Northeast Turkey*, edited by Hovann H. Simonian. London and New York (NY): Routledge, pp. 353-88
Biehl, K. 2015. 'Spatializing Diversities, Diversifying Spaces: Housing Experiences and Home Space Perceptions in a Migrant Hub of Istanbul'. *Ethnic and Racial Studies* 38(4): 596-607
Biner, Z. 2010. 'Acts of Defacement, Memory of Loss: Ghostly Effects of the "Armenian Crisis" in Mardin, Southeastern Turkey'. *History & Memory* 22(2): 69-96
Björklund, U. 2003. 'Armenians of Athens and Istanbul: The Armenian Diaspora and the "Transnational Nation"'. *Global Networks* 3(3): 337-54
Bjørnlund, M. 2009. 'A Fate Worse Than Dying: Sexual Violence during the Armenian Genocide' in *Brutality and Desire: War and Sexuality in Europe's Twentieth Century*, edited by Dagmar Herzog. New York (NY): Palgrave Macmillan, pp. 16-58
Bloch, A. 2011. 'Intimate Circuits: Modernity, Migration and Marriage among Post-Soviet Women in Turkey'. *Global Networks* 11(4): 502-21
Bloch, A. 2014. 'Citizenship, Belonging, and Moldovan Migrants in Post-Soviet Russia'. *Ethnos* 79(4): 445-72
Bloch, A. 2017. *Sex, Love, and Migration: Postsocialism, Modernity, and Intimacy from Istanbul to the Arctic*. Ithaca (NY) and London: Cornell University Press
Bode, B. 1989. *No Bells to Toll: Destruction and Creation in the Andes*. New York (NY): Scribners
Bodenhorn, B., and Gabriele vom Bruck. 2006. 'Entangled in Histories': An Introduction to the Anthropology of Names and Naming' in *The Anthropology of Names and Naming*, edited by Gabriele vom Bruck and Barbara Bodenhorn. New York (NY): Cambridge University Press, pp. 1-30
Bora, T. 1998. *Türk Sağının Üç Hali: Milliyetçilik, Muhafazakarlık, İslamcılık*. Istanbul: Birikim Yayınları
Bourdieu, P. 1977. *Outline of a Theory of Practice*. Cambridge and New York (NY): Cambridge University Press
Bowman, G. 1993. 'Nationalizing and Denationalizing the Sacred: Shrines and Shifting Identities in the Israeli-Occupied Territories'. *Man* 28(3): 431-60
Boyarin, D., and Jonathan Boyarin. 1993. 'Diaspora: Generation and the Ground of Jewish Identity'. *Critical Inquiry* 19(4): 693-725
Brah, A. 1996. *Cartographies of Diaspora: Contesting Identities*. London and New York (NY): Routledge
Braidotti, R. 1994. *Nomadic Subjects*. New York (NY): Columbia University Press
Braudel, F. 1972. *The Mediterranean and the Mediterranean World in the Age of Philip II*. New York (NY): Harper & Row
Brink-Danan, M. 2012. *Jewish Life in Twenty-First-Century Turkey: The Other Side of Tolerance*. Bloomington (IN) and Indianapolis (IN): Indiana University Press
Brubaker, R. 2004. *Ethnicity without Groups*. Cambridge (MA): Harvard University Press
Buchwalter, B. 2002. 'Portrait de La Communauté Arménienne d'Istanbul' in *Les Relations Turco-Arméniennes: Quelles Perspectives?* edited by George Dumezil. Istanbul: Institut Français d'études Anatoliennes, pp. 19-45
Bulliet, R. 1978. 'First Names and Political Change in Modern Turkey'. *International Journal of Middle East Studies* 9: 489-95

Butler, J. 1990. *Gender Trouble: Gender and the Subversion of Identity*. New York: Routledge
Cagaptay, S. 2005. *Islam, Secularism and Nationalism in Modern Turkey: Who Is a Turk?* New York (NY) and London: Routledge
Çelik, Z. 1986. *The Remaking of Istanbul: Portrait of an Ottoman City in the Nineteenth Century*. Seattle (WA): University of Washington Press
Çetin, F. 2002. 'Yerli Yabancılar' in *Ulusal, Ulusalustu ve Uluslararası Hukukta Azınlık Hakları*, edited by İbrahim Kaboğlu. Istanbul: İstanbul Barosu İnsan Hakları Merkezi, pp. 70–81
Chambers, I. 1994. *Migrancy, Culture, Identity*. London and New York (NY): Routledge
Chari, S., and Katherine Verdery. 2009. 'Thinking between the Posts: Postcolonialism, Postsocialism, and Ethnography after the Cold War'. *Comparative Studies in Society and History* 51(1): 6–34
Cheng, S. 2010. *On the Move for Love: Migrant Entertainers and the U.S. Military in South Korea*. Philadelphia (PA): University of Pennsylvania Press
Clifford, J. 1986a. 'On Ethnographic Allegory' in *Writing Culture: The Poetics and Politics of Ethnography*, edited by James Clifford and George Marcus. Berkeley (CA): University of California Press, pp. 98–121
Clifford, J. 1986b. 'Partial Truths' in *Writing Culture: The Poetics and Politics of Ethnography*, edited by James Clifford and George Marcus. Berkeley (CA): University of California Press, pp. 1–26
Clifford, J. 1989. 'Notes on Travel and Theory'. *Inscriptions* 5: 177–88
Clifford, J. 1992. 'Travelling Cultures' in *Cultural Studies*, edited by Lawrence Grossberg, Cary Nelson and Paula Treichler. New York (NY): Routledge, pp. 96–116
Clifford, J. 1997. *Routes: Travel and Translation in Late Twentieth Century*. Cambridge (MA): Harvard University Press
Clifford, J. 2013. *Returns: Becoming Indigenous in the Twenty-First Century*. Cambridge (MA) and London: Harvard University Press
Cohen, S. 2002 [1972]. *Folk Devils and Moral Panics: The Creation of the Mods and Rockers*. New York (NY): Routledge
Comaroff, J. 1992. 'Of Totemism and Ethnicity' in *Ethnography and the Historical Imagination*, edited by John Comaroff and Jean Comaroff. Boulder (CO): Westview Press, pp. 49–67
Creswell, T. 1996. *In Place/Out of Place: Geography, Ideology, and Transgression*. Minneapolis (MN) and London: University of Minnesota Press
Creswell, T. 1999. 'Embodiment, Power and the Politics of Mobility: The Case of Female Tramps and Hobos'. *Transaction of the British Institute of Geographers* 24(2): 175–92
Dadrian, V. 2005 [1995]. *The History of the Armenian Genocide: Ethnic Conflict from the Balkans to Anatolia to the Caucasus*. Providence (RI) and Oxford: Berghahn Books
Danielson, M., and Ruşen Keleş. 1985. *The Politics of Rapid Urbanization: Government and Growth in Modern Turkey*. New York (NY): Holmes and Meier
Danış, D. and Ayşe Parla. 2009. 'Nafile Soydaşlık: Irak ve Bulgaristan Türkleri Örneğinde Göçmen, Dernek ve Devlet'. *Toplum ve Bilim* 114: 131–58
Darieva, T. 2006. 'Bringing Soil back to the Homeland: Reconfigurations of Representation of Loss in Armenia'. *Comparativ* 16(3): 87–101
De Certeau, M. 1984. *The Practice of Everyday Life*. Berkeley (CA) and London: University of California Press
De Waal, T. 2013 [2003]. *The Black Garden: Armenia and Azerbaijan through Peace and War*. New York (NY) and London: New York University Press

Delaney, C. 1991. *The Seed and the Soil: Gender and Society in Turkish Village Society*. Berkeley (CA), Los Angeles (CA) and London: University of California Press

Deleuze, G. 2004. *Desert Islands and Other Texts 1953–1974*. Cambridge (MA): MIT Press

Deleuze, G., and Félix Guattari. 1987. *A Thousand Plateaus: Capitalism and Schizophrenia*. Minneapolis (MN): University of Minnesota Press

Demir, I. 2012. 'Battling with Memleket in London: The Kurdish Diaspora's Engagement with Turkey'. *Journal of Ethnic and Migration Studies* 38(5): 815–31

Derrida, J. 1974. *Of Grammatology*. Baltimore (MD) and London: The Johns Hopkins University Press

Derrida, J. 1982. *Margins of Philosophy*. Chicago (IL): University of Chicago Press

Derrida, J. 1992. 'Force of Law' in *Deconstruction and the Possibility of Justice*, edited by Drucilla Cornell, Michael Rosenfeld and David Gray Carlson. New York (NY): Routledge, pp. 3–67

Dink, H. 2000. 'Türkiyeli Ermenilerin Nüfus Hali'. *Tarih ve Toplum* 34(202): 31–15

Dost-Niyego, P., and İlker Aytürk. 2016. 'Holocaust Education in Turkey: Past, Present and Future'. *Contemporary Review of the Middle East* 3(3): 250–63

Douglas, M. 1966. *Purity and Danger: An Analysis of Concepts of Pollution and Taboo*. London: Routledge & Kegan Paul

Duben, A., and Cem Behar. 1995 [1991]. *İstanbul Haneleri: Evlenme, Aile, Doğurganlık 1880–1940*. Istanbul: İletişim

Dudwick, N. 1997. 'Political Transformations in Post-Communist Armenia: Images and Realities' in *Conflict, Cleavage, and the Change in Central Asia and the Caucasus*, edited by Karen Dawisha and Bruce Parrot. Cambridge: Cambridge University Press, pp. 69–109

Dudwick, N. 2002. 'No Guests at Our Table: Social Fragmentation in Georgia' in *When Things Fall Apart: Qualitative Studies of Poverty in the Former Soviet Union*, edited by Nora Dudwick, Elizabeth Gomart, Alexandre Marc and Kathleen Kuehnast. Washington (DC): World Bank, pp. 213–58

Durkheim, E. 1995 [1912]. *The Elementary Forms of Religious Life*. New York (NY): The Free Press

Duru, N. D. 2013. *Coexistence and Conviviality in Multi-Faith, Multi-Ethnic Burgazadası, the Princes' Islands of Istanbul*. PhD Dissertation in Social Anthropology: University of Sussex

Eder, M., and Özlem Öz. 2010. 'From Cross-Border Exchange Networks to Transnational Trading Practice? The Case of Shuttle Traders in Laleli, Istanbul' in *Transnational Communities: Shaping Global Governance*, edited by Marie-Laure Djelic and Sigrid Quack. New York (NY): Cambridge University Press, pp. 82–104

Ekmekcioglu, L. 2013. 'A Climate for Abduction, a Climate for Redemption: The Politics of Inclusion during and after the Armenian Genocide'. *Comparative Studies in Society and History* 55(3): 522–53

Ekmekçioğlu, L. 2016. *Recovering Armenia: The Limits of Belonging in Post-Genocide Turkey*. Stanford (CA): Stanford University Press

Eldem, E. 2009. 'Istanbul: From Imperial to Peripheralized Capital' in *The Ottoman City between East and West: Aleppo, Izmir and Istanbul*, edited by Edhem Eldem, Daniel Goffman and Bruce Masters. New York (NY): Cambridge University Press, pp. 135–206

Elliot, A. 2012. *Reckoning with the Outside: Emigration and the Imagination of Life in Central Morocco*. PhD Dissertation in Anthropology: University College London

Elliot, A. 2016. 'Gender' in *Keywords of Mobility: Critical Engagements*, edited by Noel B. Salazar and Kiran Jayaram. New York (NY) and Oxford: Berghahn Books, pp. 73–92

Enloe, C. 1989. *Bananas, Beaches and Bases: Making Feminist Sense of International Politics*. London: Pandora Press

Erdenen, O. 2014. *İstanbul Adaları*. Istanbul: Adalı Yayınları

Etkind, A. 2011. *Internal Colonization: Russia's Imperial Experience*. Cambridge: Polity Press

Fabian, J. 1983. *Time and the Other: How Anthropology Makes Its Object*. New York (NY): Columbia University Press

Fortier, A. M. 2000. *Migrant Belongings: Memory, Space, Identity*. Oxford: Berg

Foucault, M. 1972. *The Archaeology of Knowledge*. New York (NY): Harper and Row

Foucault, M. 1977. *Discipline and Punish: The Birth of the Prison*. London: Penguin

Foucault, M. 1980. *Power/Knowledge: Selected Interviews and Other Writings 1972–1977*, edited by Colin Gordon. New York (NY): Pantheon Books

Freud, S. 1955 [1919]. 'The Uncanny' in *The Standard Edition of Complete Works of Sigmund Freud, Vol. 17*, edited by James Strachey, Anna Freud, Alix Strachey and Alan Tyson. London: Hogarth Press and the Institute of Pyscho-Analysis, pp. 219–56

Freud, S. 2001 [1913]. *Totem and Taboo: Some Points of Agreement between the Mental Lives of Savages and Neurotics*. London and New York (NY): Routledge

Firsov, E. 2006. 'Российские Армяне и их исследователи'. *Этнографический Обозрение* 1: 72–91

Gaibazzi, P. 2015. *Bush Bound: Young Men and Rural Permanence in Migrant West Africa*. New York (NY): Berghahn

Galkina, T. 2006. 'Contemporary Migration and Traditional Diasporas in Russia: The Case of the Armenians in Moscow'. *Migracijske i Etničke Teme* 22(1–2): 181–93

Geertz, C. 1972. 'Deep Play: Notes on the Balinese Cockfight'. *Daedalus* 101(1): 1–37

Gilbert, M. R. 1998. '"Race," Space, and Power: The Survival Strategies of Working Poor Women'. *Annals of the Association of American Geographers* 88(4): 595–621

Glick-Schiller, N., and Ayşe Çağlar. 2008. 'Beyond Methodological Ethnicity and towards the City Scale: An Alternative Approach to Local and Transnational Pathways of Migrant Incorporation' in *Rethinking Transnationalism: The Meso-link of Organisations*, edited by Ludger Pries. London: Routledge, pp. 40–61

Glick-Schiller, N., Tsypylma Darieva and Sandra Gruner-Domic. 2011. 'Defining Cosmopolitan Sociability in a Transnational Age: An Introduction'. *Ethnic and Racial Studies* 34(3): 399–418

Glick-Schiller, N., and Noel Salazar. 2013. 'Regimes of Mobility across the Globe'. *Journal of Ethnic and Migration Studies* 39(2): 183–200

Gordillo, G. 2014. *Rubble: The Afterlife of Destruction*. Durham (NC) and London: Duke University Press

Goshgarian, R. 2005. 'Breaking the Stalemate: Turkish-Armenian Relationships in the 21st Century'. *Turkish Policy Quarterly* 4(4). Available at: https://www.esiweb.org/pdf/esi_turkey_tpq_id_46.pdf

Goshgarian, R. 2018. 'A Stroll through the Quarters of Constantinople: Sketches of the City as Seen through the Eyes of the Great Satirist Hagop Baronian' in *Istanbul – Kushta – Constantinople: Narratives of Identity in the Ottoman Capital, 1830–1930*, edited by Christian Herzog and Richard Wittmann. London: Routledge, pp. 213–30

Green, S. 2005. *Notes from the Balkans: Locating Marginality and Ambiguity on the Greek-Albanian Border*. Princeton (NJ): Princeton University Press

Green, S. 2011. 'What Is a Tidemark?' *Anthropology News* 52(2): 15

Green, S. 2012. 'A Sense of Border' in *A Companion to Border Studies*, edited by Thomas W. Wilson and Hastings Donnan. Hoboken (NJ): Wiley-Blackwell, pp. 573–92

Grigoryan, I. 2018. *Armenian Labor Migrants in Istanbul: Reality Check*. Report for the Migration Research Center at Koc University (MIREKOC). Available at: https://mirekoc.ku.edu.tr/wp-content/uploads/2018/10/Report_Armenian-Labor-Migrants-in-Istanbul.pdf

Grossman, V. 2013 [1998]. *An Armenian Sketchbook*. London: MacLehose Press

Gülçür, L., and Pınar İlkkaracan. 2000. 'The "Natasha Experience": Migrant Sex Workers from the Former Soviet Union and Eastern Europe in Turkey'. *Women Studies International Forum* 25(4): 411–21

Gültekin, B. 2003. *The Stakes of Opening the Armenian-Turkish Border; the Cross-Border Contacts between Armenia and Turkey*. Report for the Turkish-Armenian Business Development Council (TABDC). Available at: http://www.tabdc.org/wp-content/uploads/THE-STAKES-OF-THE-OPENING-OF-TURKISH-ARMENIAN-BORDER.pdf

Gültekin, B. 2007. *Evaluating the Impact of the Opening of the Border on the Normalization of Turkish-Armenian Relations*. Conference Paper: Yerevan. Available at: http://citeseerx.ist.psu.edu/viewdoc/download?doi=10.1.1.559.4175&rep=rep1&type=pdf

Gupta, A. 1995. 'Blurred Boundaries: The Discourse of Corruption, the Culture of Politics and the Imagined State'. *American Ethnologist* 22(3): 375–402

Gupta, A., and James Ferguson. 1997. 'Beyond "Culture": Space, Identity, and the Politics of Difference'. *Cultural Anthropology* 7(1): 6–23

Gürbilek, N. 2020. *İkinci Hayat: Kaçmak, Kovulmak, Dönmek Üzerine Denemeler*. Istanbul: Metis

Guttstadt, C. 2012. *Türkiye, Yahudiler ve Holokost*. Istanbul: İletişim

Güven, D. 2006. *Cumhuriyet Dönemi Azınlık Politikaları Bağlamında 6-7 Eylül Olayları*. Istanbul: Tarih Vakfı Yurt Yayınları

Haakanson, Jr. S. 2001. 'Can There Be Such a Thing as a Native Anthropologist?' in *Looking Both Ways: Heritage and Identity of the Alutiiq People*, edited by Aron Crowell, Amy Stefan and Gordon Pullar. Fairbanks (AK): University of Alaska Press, p. 79

Hall, S. 1994. 'Cultural Identity and Diaspora' in *Colonial Discourse and Post-Colonial Theory: A Reader*, edited by Patrick Williams and Laura Chrisman. London: Harvester Wheatsheaf, pp. 227–37

Hall, S. 1996. 'When Was the "Post-Colonial"? Thinking at the Limit' in *The Post-Colonial Question: Common Skies, Divided Horizons*, edited by Iain Chambers and Lidia Curti. London: Routledge, pp. 242–60

Hanafi, S. 2003. 'Rethinking the Palestinians Abroad as a Diaspora: The Relationships between the Palestinian Territories and the Diaspora'. *International Social Science Review* 4(1–2): 157–82

Hanson, S. 2010. 'Gender and Mobility: New Approaches for Informing Sustainability'. *Gender, Place & Culture: A Journal of Feminist Geography* 17(1): 5–23

Hardt, M., and Antonio Negri. 2000. *Empire*. Cambridge (MA) and London: Harvard University Press

Heller, D. 2004. 'Let It Flow: Economy, Spirituality and Gender in the Sindhi Network' in *Diaspora, Identity and Religion: New Directions in Theory and Research*, edited by Waltraud Kokot, Khachig Tölölyan and Carolin Alfonso. London and New York (NY): Routledge, pp. 189–204

Helms, M. 1988. *Ulysses' Sail: An Ethnographic Odyssey of Power, Knowledge and Geographical Distance*. Princeton (NJ) and Guildford: Princeton University Press

Heper, H. 1987. 'Introduction' in *Democracy and Local Government: Istanbul in the 1980s*, edited by Metin Heper. Beverley (North Humberside): The Eothen Press

Herzfeld, M. 1997. *Cultural Intimacy: Social Poetics in the Nation-State*. New York (NY): Routledge
Heyat, F. 2002. 'Women and the Culture of Entrepreneurship in Soviet and Post-Soviet Azerbaijan' in *Markets and Moralities: Ethnographies of Postsocialism*, edited by Ruth Mandel and Caroline Humphrey. Oxford and New York (NY): Berg, pp. 19–32
Hochschild, A. R. 2000. 'Global Care Chains and Emotional Surplus Values' in *On the Edge: Living with Global Capitalism*, edited by Will Hutton and Anthony Giddens. London: Jonathan Cape, pp. 130–46.
Hoelscher, S. 2008. 'Angels of Memory: Photography and Haunting in Guatemala City'. *GeoJournal* 73: 95–217
Hoffman, K. E. 2009. 'Culture as Text: Hazards and Possibilities of Geertz's Literary/Literacy Metaphor'. *The Journal of North African Studies* 14(3/4): 417–30
Holbraad, M. 2010. 'The Whole beyond Holism' in *Experiments in Holism: Theory and Practice in Contemporary Anthropology*, edited by Ton Otto and Nils Bubandt. Chichester and Malden (MA): Wiley-Blackwell, pp. 67–86
hooks, b. 1992. *Black Looks: Race and Representation*. Boston (MA): South End Press
Hovannisian, R. 2007. 'The Armenian Genocide: Wartime Radicalization or Premediated Continuum?' in *The Armenian Genocide: Ethical and Cultural Legacies*, edited by Richard Hovannisian. New Brunswick (NJ): Transaction Publishers, pp. 3–18
Hovannisian, R. 2009. *Armenian Pontus: The Trebizond: Black Sea Communities*. Costa Mesa (CA): Mazda Publishers
Hoving, I. 2001. *In Praise of New Travelers: Reading Caribbean Women's Writing*. Stanford (CA): Stanford University Press
Humphrey, C. 2002. *The Unmaking of Soviet Life: Everyday Economies after Socialism*. Ithaca (NY): Cornell University Press
Humphrey, C., and Ruth Mandel. 2002. 'The Market in Everyday Life: Ethnographies of Postsocialism' in *Markets and Moralities: Ethnographies of Postsocialism*, edited by Ruth Mandel and Caroline Humphrey. Oxford: Berg, pp. 1–18
İçduygu, A., and Damla B. Aksel. 2013. 'Turkish Migration Policies: A Critical Historical Retrospective'. *Perceptions* 18(3): 167–90
İçduygu, A., and B. Ali Soner. 2006. 'Turkish Minority Rights Regime: Between Difference and Equality'. *Middle Eastern Studies* 42(3): 447–68
Ihrig, S. 2014. *Atatürk in the Nazi Imagination*. Cambridge (MA) and London: The Belknap Press of the Harvard University Press
Ihrig, S. 2016. *Justifying Genocide: Germany and the Armenians from Bismarck to Hitler*. Cambridge (MA) and London: Harvard University Press
Inalcik, H. 1954. 'Ottoman Methods of Conquest'. *Studia Islamica* 2: 103–29
Inan, F., and Diana Yayloyan. 2018. *New Economic Corridors in the South Caucasus and the Chinese One Belt One Road*. Report for the Economic Policy Research Foundation of Turkey (TEPAV). Available at: http://www.tepav.org.tr/upload/files/1523615843-0.New_Economic_Corridors_in_the_South_Caucasus_and_the_Chinese_One_Belt_One_Road.pdf
Ingold, T. 2000. *The Perception of the Environment: Essays on Livelihood, Dwelling and Skill*. London and New York (NY): Routledge
Ingold, T. 2011. *Being Alive: Essays on Movement, Knowledge and Description*. Abingdon: Routledge
Irmak, H. 2003. *Tatavla'dan Kurtuluş'a*. Istanbul: Aras Yayıncılık
Ishkanian, A. 2002. 'Mobile Motherhood: Armenian Women's Labor Migration in the Post-Soviet Period'. *Diaspora: A Journal of Transnational Studies* 11(3): 383–415

Işın, E. 2002. *Being Political: Genealogies of Citizenship*. Minneapolis (MN): University of Minnesota Press

Johnson, C. 1922. *Constantinople To-Day, or the Pathfinder Survey of Constantinople: A Study in Oriental Social Life*. New York (NY): MacMillan

Jongerden, J. 2009. 'Crafting Space, Making People: The Spatial Design of Nation in Modern Turkey'. *European Journal of Turkish Studies* 10 (online journal). Available at: https://ejts.revues.org/4014

Kaneff, D. 2002. 'The Shame and Pride of Market Activity: Morality, Identity and Trading in Postsocialist Rural Bulgaria' in *Markets and Moralities: Ethnographies of Postsocialism*, edited by Ruth Mandel and Caroline Humphrey. Oxford and New York (NY): Berg, pp. 33–52

Kaplan, C. 1987. 'Deterritorialization: The Rewriting of Home and Exile in Western Feminist Discourse'. *Cultural Critique* 6: 187–98

Kaplan, C. 1996. *Questions of Travel: Postmodern Discourses of Displacement*. Durham (NC): Duke University Press

Kaplan, S. 2006. *The Pedagogical State: Education and the Politics of National Culture in post-1980 Turkey*. Stanford (CA): Stanford University Press

Kasbarian, S. 2009. 'The Myth and the Reality of "Return" – Diaspora in the "Homeland"'. *Diaspora: A Journal of Transnational Studies* 18(3): 358–81

Kasbarian, S. 2021. 'A Defining Moment for the Armenian Diaspora? Some Preliminary Reflections'. *EVN Report*. Available at: https://old.evnreport.com/magazine-issues/a-defining-moment-for-the-armenian-diaspora-some-preliminary-reflections

Kaya, N. 2014. *Hopa Hemsinlis: History, Language and Identity*. MA Thesis in Cultural Studies: Sabancı University

Kayaboğazı, Ş. 1942. *İstanbul ve Dolayı Coğrafyası: Tabii, Beşeri, İktisadi*. İstanbul: Tecelli Matbaası

Kaymak, Ö. 2016. *İstanbul'da Rum, Yahudi ve Ermeni Cemaatlerinin Sosyo-Mekansal İnşası*. PhD Dissertation in Political Science and Public Administration: Istanbul University

Kazanjian, D. 2018. 'Diasporic *Flânerie*: From Armenian *Ruinenlust* to Armenia's Walkspaces' in *An Armenian Mediterranean: Words and Worlds in Motion*, edited by Kathyrn Babayan and Michel Pifer. Cham: Palgrave Macmillan, pp. 221–46

Kévorkian, R. 2011. *The Armenian Genocide: A Complete History*. London and New York (NY): I.B. Tauris

Kévorkian, R., and Paul B. Paboudjian. 2012. *1915 Öncesinde Osmanlı İmparatorluğu'nda Ermeniler*. Istanbul: Aras

Keyder, Ç. 1999. 'The Setting' in *Istanbul: Between the Global and the Local*, edited by Çağlar Keyder. Lanham (MD): Rowman and Littlefield, pp. 3–30

Keyder, Ç. 2008. 'A Brief History of Modern Istanbul' in *The Cambridge History of Turkey, Volume 4: Turkey in the Modern World*, edited by Reşat Kasaba. Cambridge: Cambridge University Press, pp. 504–23

Keyman, F., and Tuba Kancı. 2011. 'A Tale of Ambiguity: Citizenship, Nationalism and Democracy in Turkey'. *Nations and Nationalism* 17(2): 318–36

Khan, N. 2016. 'Immobility' in *Keywords of Mobility: Critical Engagements*, edited by Noel B. Salazar and Kiran Jayaram. New York (NY) and Oxford: Berghahn Books, pp. 93–112

Kharatyan, L., İsmail Keskin, Avetis Keshishyan, Salim Aykut Öztürk, Nane Khachatryan, Nihal Albayrak and Karen Hakobyan. 2013. *Moush, Sweet Moush: Mapping Memories from Armenia and Turkey*. Bonn: DVV International

Kiliçdağı, O. 2010. 'The Armenian Community of Constantinople in the Late Ottoman Empire' in *Armenian Constantinople*, edited by Richard Hovannisian and Simon Payaslian. Costa Mesa (CA): Mazda Publishers, pp. 231–41

Kirişçi, K. 2000. 'Disaggregating Turkish Citizenship and Immigration Policies'. *Middle Eastern Studies* 36(3): 1–22

Kirişçi, K. 2005. 'A Friendlier Schengen Visa System as a Tool of "Soft Power": The Experience of Turkey'. *European Journal of Migration and Law* 7: 343–67

Kirshenblatt-Gimblett, B. 1998. *Destination Culture: Tourism, Museums, Heritage*. Berkeley (CA) and London: University of California Press

Kısakürek, N. F. 1969 [1939]. *Şiirlerim*. Istanbul: Fatih Yayınları

Klein, N. 2007. *The Shock Doctrine: The Rise of Disaster Capitalism*. New York: Metropolitan Books

Komins, B. 2002. 'Cosmopolitanism Depopulated: The Cultures of Integration, Concealment and Evacuation in Istanbul'. *Comparative Literature Studies* 39: 360–85

Koobak, R., and Raili Marling. 2014. 'The Decolonial Challenge: Framing Post-Socialist Central and Eastern Europe within Transnational Feminist Studies'. *European Journal of Women's Studies* 21(4): 330–43

Körükmez, L. 2012. *Ulus-ötesi Göç Ağları ve Sosyal Alanların Oluşumu: Ermenistan'dan Türkiye'ye İşgücü Göçü Üzerine Sosyolojik Bir Araştırma*. PhD Dissertation in Sociology: Ege University

Kristeva, J. 1991. *Strangers to Ourselves*. New York (NY): Columbia University Press

Kurt, Ü. 2016a. 'Cultural Erasure: The Absorption and Forced Conversion of Armenian Women and Children, 1915–1916'. *Études Arméniennes Contemporaines* 7: 71–86

Kurt, Ü. 2016b. 'The Plunder of Wealth through Abandoned Properties Laws in the Armenian Genocide'. *Genocide Studies International* 10(1): 37–51

Lambek, M. 2007. 'Foreword' in *Struggling with History: Islam and Cosmopolitanism in the Western Indian Ocean*, edited by Edward Simpson and Kai Kresse. New York (NY): Columbia University Press, pp. xiv–xix

Leivestad, H. H. 2016. 'Motility' in *Keywords of Mobility: Critical Engagements*, edited by Noel B. Salazar and Kiran Jayaram. New York (NY) and Oxford: Berghahn Books, pp. 133–51

Levi-Strauss, C. 1955. 'The Structural Study of Myth'. *The Journal of American Folklore* 68(270): 428–44

Levi-Strauss, C. 1969. *Elementary Structures of Kinship*. Boston (MA): Beacon Press

Lewis, B. 1968. *The Emergence of Modern Turkey*. London and New York (NY): Oxford University Press

Libaridian, G. 2007. *Modern Armenia: People, Nation, State*. New Brunswick (NJ): Transaction Publishers

Libaridian, G. 2014. 'Introduction' in *The Grandchildren: The Hidden Legacy of 'Lost' Armenians in Turkey*, edited by Ayşe Gül Altınay and Fethiye Çetin. New Brunswick (NJ): Transaction Publishers, pp. xxix–xxxiv

Light, M. 2010. 'Policing Migration in Soviet and Post-Soviet Moscow'. *Post-Soviet Affairs* 26(4): 275–313

Lowenthal, D. 1985. *The Past Is a Foreign Country*. Cambridge: Cambridge University Press

Lury, C. 1997. 'The Objects of Travel' in *Touring Cultures*, edited by John Urry and Chris Rojek. London: Routledge, pp. 75–95

Macdonald, S. 2006. 'Undesirable Heritage: Fascist Material Culture and Historical Consciousness in Nuremberg'. *International Journal of Heritage Studies* 12(1): 9–28

Macdonald, S. 2009. *Difficult Heritage: Negotiating the Nazi Past in Nuremberg and Beyond*. Abingdon and New York (NY): Routledge
Mahler, S. J., and Patricia R. Pessar. 2006. 'Gender Matters: Ethnographers Bring Gender from the Periphery toward the Core of Migration Studies'. *International Migration Review* 40(1): 27–63
Mandel, M. 2003. *In the Aftermath of Genocide: Armenians and Jews in Twentieth-Century France*. Durham (NC) and London: Duke University Press
Mandel, R. 1996. 'A Place of Their Own: Contesting Spaces and Defining Places in Berlin's Migrant Community' in *Making Muslim Space in North America and Europe*, edited by Barbara Daly Metcalf. Berkeley (CA), Los Angeles (CA) and London: University of California Press, pp. 147–66
Mandel, R. 2008. *Cosmopolitan Anxieties: Turkish Challenges to Citizenship and Belonging in Germany*. Durham (NC) and London: Duke University Press
Marcus, G. 2010. 'Holism and Expectations of Critique in Post-1980s Anthropology: Notes and Queries in Three Acts and an Epilogue' in *Experiments in Holism: Theory and Practice in Contemporary Anthropology*, edited by Ton Otto and Nils Bubandt. Chichester and Malden (MA): Wiley-Blackwell, pp. 67–86
Marcus, G., and Michael M. J. Fischer. 1986. *Anthropology as Cultural Critique: An Experimental Moment in the Human Societies*. Chicago (IL): University of Chicago Press
Mardin, Ş. 2002. 'Playing Games with Names' in *Fragments of Culture: The Everyday of Modern Turkey*, edited by Deniz Kandiyoti and Ayse Saktanber. London: I.B. Tauris, pp. 115–27
Markowitz, F. 1993. *A Community in Spite of Itself: Soviet Jewish Émigrés in New York*. Washington (DC) and London: Smithsonian Institution Press
Marmara, R. 2001. *Pangaltı (Pancaldi): 19. yüzyılın Levanten semti = Quartier levantin du 19e siècle*. Istanbul: Şişli Belediyesi
Marsden, M. 2015. 'From Kabul to Kiev: Afghan Trading Networks across the Former Soviet Union'. *Modern Asian Studies* 49(4): 1010–48
Marsden, M. 2017. 'Actually Existing Silk Roads'. *Journal of Eurasian Studies* 18(1): 22–30
Massey, D. 1984. *Spatial Divisions of Labour*. London: Macmillan
Massey, D. 2005. *For Space*. London: SAGE
Mignolo, W. 2000. *Local Histories/Global Designs: Coloniality, Subaltern Knowledges and Border Thinking*. Princeton (NJ): Princeton University Press
Mignolo, W., and Madina V. Tlostanova. 2012. *Learning to Unlearn: Decolonial Reflections from Eurasia and the Americas*. Colombus (OH): Ohio State University Press
Miller, D., and Lorna Touryan Miller. 1993. *Survivors: An Oral History of the Armenian Genocide*. Berkeley (CA): University of California Press
Mills, A. 2010. *Streets of Memory: Landscape, Tolerance, and National Identity in Istanbul*. Athens (GA): University of Georgia Press
Morokvasic, M. 1984. 'Birds of Passage Are Also Women'. *International Migration Review* 18(4): 886–907
Morris, J., and Abel Polese. 2014. *The Informal Post-Socialist Economy: Embedded Practices and Livelihoods*. London: Routledge
Muradyan, A. 2015. *An Island within an Island: Educational Needs Assessment of Armenian Migrants in Turkey*. Istanbul: Yuva Association
Narayan, K. 1993. 'How Native Is a "Native" Anthropologist?' *American Ethnologist* 95(3): 671–86
Navaro-Yashin, Y. 2002. *Faces of the State: Secularism and Public Life in Turkey*. Princeton (NJ): Princeton University Press

Navaro-Yashin, Y. 2012. *The Make-Believe Space: Affective Geography in a Postwar Polity*. Durham (NC): Duke University Press

Neyzi, L. 2002. 'Remembering to Forget: Sabbateanism, National Identity, and Subjectivity in Turkey'. *Comparative Studies in Society and History* 44(1): 137–58

Nichanian, M. 2009. *The Historiographic Perversion*. New York (NY): Columbia University Press

Nichanian, M., and David Kazanjian. 2003. 'Between Genocide and Catastrophe' in *Loss: Politics of Mourning*, edited by David L. Eng and David Kazanjian. Berkeley (CA) and London: University of California Press, pp. 125–47

Nora, P. 1989. 'Between Memory and History: Les Lieux de Mémoire'. *Representations* 26 (Special Issue: Memory and Counter-Memory): 7–24

Nyers, P. 2003. 'Abject Cosmopolitanism: The Politics of Protection in the Anti-Deportation Movement'. *Third World Quarterly* 24(6): 1069–93

Ohnuki-Tierney, E. 1984. '"Native" Anthropologists'. *American Ethnologist* 11(3): 584–6

Öktem, K. 2008. 'The Nation's Imprint: Demographic Engineering and the Change of Toponymes in Republican Turkey'. *European Journal of Turkish Studies* 7 (online journal). Available at: https://journals.openedition.org/ejts/2243

Okutan, Ç. 2004. *Tek Parti Döneminde Azınlık Politikaları*. Istanbul: Istanbul Bilgi Üniversitesi Yayınları

Öncü, A. 1999. 'Istanbulites and Others: The Cultural Cosmology of Being Middle Class in the Era of Globalism' in *Istanbul: Between the Global and the Local*, edited by Çağlar Keyder. Lanham (MD): Rowman and Littlefield, pp. 95–120

Örs, İ. R. 2018. *Diaspora of the City: Stories of Cosmopolitanism from Istanbul and Athens*. New York (NY): Palgrave Macmillan

Ortner, S. 1984. 'Theory in Anthropology since the Sixties'. *Comparative Studies in Society and History* 26(1): 126–66

Ortner, S. 1997. 'Introduction: The Fate of "Culture": Geertz and beyond'. *Representations* 59: 1–13

Osella, F., and Caroline Osella. 2007. 'I Am Gulf: The Production of Cosmopolitanism in Kozhikode, Kerala, India' in *Struggling with History: Islam and Cosmopolitanism in the Western Indian Ocean*, edited by Edward Simpson and Kai Kresse. New York (NY): Columbia University Press, p. 323

Osella, F., and Caroline Osella. 2009. 'Muslim Entrepreneurs in Public Life between India and the Gulf: Making Good and Doing Good'. *Journal of the Royal Anthropological Institute* 15: 5202–21

Özdoğan, G., Füsun Üstel, Karin Karakaşlı and Ferhat Kentel. 2009. *Türkiye'de Ermeniler: Cemaat-Birey-Yurttaş*. Istanbul: Istanbul Bilgi Üniversitesi Yayınları

Özgül, C. 2014. 'Legally Armenian: Tolerance, Conversion, and Name Change in Turkish Courts'. *Comparative Studies in Society and History* 56(3): 622–49

Ozinian, A. 2009. *Identifying the State of Armenian Migrants in Turkey*. Report for Eurasia Partnership Foundation (EPF). Available at: https://epfarmenia.am/sites/default/files/inline-files/Full_report_on_state_of_Armenian_irregular_migrants_in_Turkey_0.pdf

Özkan, B. 2012. *From Abode of Islam to the Turkish Vatan: The Making of National Homeland in Turkey*. New Haven (CT) and London: Yale University Press

Paksoy, M. 2017. *Encountering the Armenian Community: Experiences of Armenian Domestic Workers in Istanbul*. MA Thesis in Media and Cultural Studies: Middle East Technical University

Pamuk, O. 2006. *Istanbul: Memories of a City*. New York (NY): Vintage International

Pamuk, O. 2010. *Manzaradan Parçalar: Hayat, Sokaklar, Edebiyat*. Istanbul: İletişim

Panossian, R. 2006. *The Armenians: From Kings and Priests to Merchants and Commissars*. London: Hurst & Co.

Papazian, H. 2020. *Contesting Armenianness: Plurality, Segregation and Multilateral Boundary Making among Armenians in Contemporary Turkey*. PhD Dissertation in Anthropology: University of Oxford

Parla, A. 2009. 'Remembering across the Border: Postsocialist Nostalgia among Turkish Immigrants from Bulgaria'. *American Ethnologist* 36(4): 750–67

Parmentier, R. 1987. *The Sacred Remains: Myths, History, and Polity in Belau*. Chicago (IL): University of Chicago Press

Parmentier, R. 2007. 'It's about Time: On the Semiotics of Temporality'. *Language and Communication* 27(3): 272–7

Pattie, S. 1997. *Faith in History: Armenians Rebuilding Community*. Washington (DC) and London: Smithsonian Institution Press

Pattie, S. 2004. 'From the Centers to the Periphery: "Repatriation" to an Armenian Homeland in the Twentieth Century' in *Homecomings: Unsettling Paths of Return*, edited by Fran Markowitz and Anders F. Stefansson. Lanham (MD): Lexington Books, pp. 109–24

Pattie, S. 2005. 'New Homeland for Old Diaspora' in *Homelands and Disporas: Holy Lands and Other Spaces*, edited by André Levy and Alex Weingrod. Stanford (CA): University of Stanford Press, pp. 49–67

Pelkmans, M. 2006. *Defending the Border: Identity, Religion, and Modernity in the Republic of Georgia*. Ithaca (NY): Cornell University Press

Pervititch, J. 1927. *Plan cadastral d'assurances. Péra. Sıra-Seviler [Sıraselviler]*. Available at: https://archives.saltresearch.org/handle/123456789/114978

Pessar, P. R., and Sarah J. Mahler. 2003. 'Transnational Migration: Bringing Gender'. *International Migration Review* 37(3): 812–46

Platz, S. 2000. 'The Shape of National Time: Daily Life, History, and Identity during Armenia's Transition to Independence, 1991–1994' in *Altering States: Ethnographies of Transition in Eastern Europe and the Former Soviet Union*, edited by Daphne Berdahl, Matti Bunzl and Marika Lampland. Ann Arbor (MI): The University of Michigan Press, pp. 114–38

Pratt, M. L. 1992. *Imperial Eyes: Travel Writing and Transculturation*. London: Routledge

Rabinow, P. 1986. 'Representations Are Social Facts: Modernity and Post-Modernity in Anthropology' in *Writing Culture: The Poetics and Politics of Ethnography*, edited by James Clifford and George Marcus. Berkeley (CA): University of California Press, pp. 234–61

Rapaport, L. 1997. *Jews in Germany after the Holocaust: Memory, Identity, and Jewish-German Relations*. Cambridge: Cambridge University Press

Rapport, N., and Ronald Stade. 2007. 'A Cosmopolitan Turn or Return?' *Social Anthropology* 15(2): 223–35

Reed, A. 2004. *Papua New Guinea's Last Place: Experiences of Constraint in a Postcolonial Prison*. New York (NY) and Oxford: Berghahn Books

Reeves, M. 2014. *Border Work: Culture and Society after Socialism*. Ithaca (NY): Cornell University Press

Rich, A. 1984. *Blood, Bread and Poetry*. London: The Women's Press

Rodrigue, A. 2013. 'Reflections on Millets and Minorities: Ottoman Legacies' in *Turkey between Nationalism and Globalisation*, edited by Riva Kastoryano. New York (NY): Routledge, pp. 36–46

Rogers, D. 2010. 'Postsocialisms Unbound: Connections, Critiques, Comparisons'. *Slavic Review* 69(1): 1–15

Rogoff, I. 2000. *Terra Infirma: Geography's Visual Culture*. London and New York (NY): Routledge
Roseberry, W. 1989. *Anthropologies: Essays in Culture, History, and Political Economy*. New Brunswick (NJ) and London: Rutgers University Press
Rouse, R. 1991. 'Mexican Migration and the Social Space of Postmodernism'. *Diaspora: A Journal of Transnational Studies* 1(1): 8–23
Saçlıoğlu, M. Z. 2013. 'Winter' in *Istanbul*, edited by Heather Reyes. Dorchester: Oxygen Books, pp. 93–7
Sadoğlu, H. 2003. *Türkiye'de Ulusçuluk ve Dil Politikaları*. Istanbul: Istanbul Bilgi Üniversitesi Yayınları
Safran, W. 1991. 'Diaporas in Modern Societies: Myths of Homeland and Return'. *Diaspora* 1(1): 83–9
Sahlins, M. 1985. *Islands of History*. Chicago (IL): University of Chicago Press
Said, E. 1989. 'Representing the Colonized: Anthropology's Interlocutors'. *Critical Inquiry* 15(2): 205–25
Salazar, N. B. 2011. 'The Power of Imagination in Transnational Mobilities'. *Identities* 18(6): 576–98
Salazar, N. B., and Alan Smart. 2011. 'Anthropological Takes on (Im)Mobility'. *Identities: Global Studies in Culture and Power* 18(6): i–ix
Salzman, P. C. 2004. *Pastoralists: Equality, Hierarchy and the State*. Oxford: Westview Press
Sarafian, A. 2001. 'The Absorption of Armenian Women and Children into Muslim Households as Structural Component of the Armenian Genocide' in *Genocide and Religion in the Twentieth-Century*, edited by Omer Bartov and Mack Phylis. Oxford: Berghahn Books, pp. 209–21
Sayad, A. 2000. 'El Ghorba: Original Sin and Collective Lie'. *Ethnography* 1(2): 147–71
Saybaşılı, N. 2008. *Borders and 'Ghosts': Migratory Hauntings in Contemporary Visual Culture*. PhD Dissertation in Visual Cultures: Goldsmiths College
Saybaşılı, N. 2011. *Sınırlar ve Hayaletler: Görsel Kültürde Göç Hareketleri*. Istanbul: Metis
Scheper-Hughes, N. 1992. *Death without Weeping: The Violence of Everyday Life in Brazil*. Berkeley (CA) and Los Angeles (CA): University of California Press
Schott, J., and Talin Kalatas. 2014. 'The Earthquake of Spitak, Armenia, and Its Socio-economic Implications' in *Natural Disasters and Sustainable Development*, edited by Hans Meliczek and Christoph Kätsch. Göttingen: Cuvillier, pp. 77–89
Seferis, G. 1995. *Collected Poems*. Translated and Edited by Edmund Keeley and Philip Sherrard. Princeton (NJ): Princeton University Press
Şeker, N. 2007. 'Demographic Engineering in the Late Ottoman Empire and the Armenians'. *Middle Eastern Studies* 43(3): 461–74
Seremetakis, N. 1991. *The Last Word: Women, Death, and Divination in Inner Mani*. Chicago (IL) and London: University of Chicago Press
Shagoyan, G. 2010. 'Anthropological Notes on a City That Survived an Earthquake (Summary)'. *Laboratorium: Russian Review of Social Research* 1: 160–81 and 348
Shagoyan, G. 2011. 'The Second City as the First City: The Development of Gyumri from an Anthropological Perspective' in *Urban Spaces after Socialism: Ethnographies of Public Places in Eurasian Cities*, edited by Tsypylma Darieva, Wolfgang Kaschuba and Melanie Krebs. Frankfurt and New York (NY): Campus Verlag, pp. 57–80
Shirinian, T. 2016. *Survival of a Perverse Nation: Sexuality and Kinship in Post-Soviet Armenia*. PhD Dissertation in Cultural Anthropology: Duke University
Shirinian, T. 2018. 'The Nation-Family: Intimate Encounters and Genealogical Perversion in Armenia'. *American Ethnologist* 45(1): 48–59

Shohat, E. 1991. 'Gender and Culture of Empire: Toward a Feminist Ethnography of the Cinema'. *Quarterly Review of Film and Video* 13(1–3): 45–84

Shohat, E. 2006. *Taboo Memories, Diasporic Voices*. Durham (NC) and London: Duke University Press

Siekierski, K. 2016. 'Studying Armenians in Post-Socialist Europe: Problems and Perspectives' in *Armenians in Post-Socialist Europe*, edited by Konrad Siekierski and Stefan Troebst. Cologne, Weimar and Vienna: Böhlau Verlag, pp. 13–25

Simpson, E. 2013. *The Political Biography of an Earthquake: Aftermath and Amnesia in Gujarat, India*. London: Hurst

Sökefeld, M. 2006. 'Mobilizing in Transnational Space: A Social Movement Approach to the Formation of Diaspora'. *Global Networks: A Journal of Transnational Affairs* 6(3): 265–84

Soyaltın, D. 2013. 'Good News, Bad News or No News: Management of Irregular Migration in Turkey'. *ResearchTurkey* 2(3): 33–45

Soytemel, E. 2014. '"Belonging" in the Gentrified Golden Horn/Haliç Neighborhoods of Istanbul'. *Urban Geography* 36(1): 64–89

Smith, A. 1986. *The Ethnic Origins of Nations*. Oxford: Blackwell

Smith, A. 2009. *Ethno-Symbolism and Nationalism: A Cultural Approach*. London and New York (NY): Routledge

Spencer, R. 1961. 'The Social Context of Modern Turkish Names'. *Southwestern Journal of Anthropology* 17: 205–18

Spivak, G. C. 1988. 'Can the Subaltern Speak?' in *Marxism and Interpretation of Culture*, edited by Cary Nelson and Lawrence Grossberg. Urbana (IL): University of Illinois Press, pp. 271–313

Steiner, F. B. 1967 [1957]. *Taboo*. London: Pelican Books

Stewart, C. 2012. *Dreaming and Historical Consciousness in Island Greece*. Cambridge (MA): Harvard University Press

Stewart, C. 2017. 'Uncanny History: Temporal Topography in the Post-Ottoman World'. *Social Analysis* 61(1): 129–42

Strathern, M. 1985. 'Dislodging a World View: Challenge and Counter-Challenge in the Relationship between Feminism and Anthropology'. *Australian Feminist Studies* 1(1): 1–25

Strathern, M. 1991. *Partial Connections*. Savage (MD): Rowman and Littlefield

Strittmatter, K. 2013. 'User's Guide to Istanbul' in *Istanbul*, edited by Heather Reyes. Dorchester: Oxygen Press, pp. 85–6

Su, J. [Forthcoming]. '"*Asılmak Tehlikeli ve Yasaktır*": Unintelligible Mobility and Uncertain Manhood in Istanbul's Old City' in *Ordinary/Extraordinary: Ethnographies of Risk, Limits and Exposure*, edited by Beata Switek, Hannah Swee and Allen Abramson. London: Palgrave Macmillan

Suciyan, T. 2015. *The Armenians in Modern Turkey: Post-Genocide Society, Politics and History*. London and New York (NY): I.B. Tauris

Suny, R. G. 1993a. *Looking toward Ararat: Armenia in Modern History*. Bloomington (IN) and Indianapolis (IN): Indiana University Press

Suny, R. G. 1993b. *The Revenge of the Past: Nationalism, Revolution, and the Collapse of the Soviet Union*. Stanford (CA): Stanford University Press

Tambar, K. 2013. 'Historical Critique and Political Voice after the Ottoman Empire'. *History of the Present* 3(2): 119–39

Taşçı, N. 2010. *Armenian Migrants in Turkey: History of a Journey*. MA Thesis in Modern Turkish History: Boğaziçi University

Tashjian, V. 2009. 'Gender, Nationalism, Exclusion: The Reintegration Process of Female Survivors of the Armenian Genocide'. *Nations and Nationalism* 15(1): 60–80

Taussig, M. 1999. *Defacement: Public Secrecy and the Labor of the Negative*. Stanford (CA): Stanford University Press

Tilley, C. 1994. *A Phenomenology of Landscape: Places, Paths and Monuments*. Oxford: Berg

Tlostanova, M. V. 2018. *What Does It Mean to Be Post-Soviet? Decolonial Art from the Ruins of the Soviet Empire*. Durham (NC) and London: Duke University Press

Tolay, J. 2012. 'Turkey's "Critical Europeanization": Evidence from Turkey's Immigration Policies' in *Turkey, Migration and the EU*, edited by Seçil Paçacı Elitok and Thomas Straubhaar. Hamburg: Hamburg University Press, pp. 39–61

Tölölyan, K. 2000. 'Elites and Institutions in the Armenian Transnation'. *Diaspora: A Journal of Transnational Studies* 9(1): 107–36

Tölölyan, K. 2010. 'Beyond the Homeland: From Exilic Nationalism to Diasporic Transnationalism' in *The Call of the Homeland: Diaspora Nationalisms, Past and Present*, edited by Allon Gal, Athena S. Leoussi and Anthony D. Smith. London and Boston (MA): Brill, pp. 27–46

Tsing, A. 1993. *In the Realm of the Diamond Queen: Marginality in an Out-of-the-way Place*. Princeton (NJ): Princeton University Press

Tsing, A. 2000. 'The Global Situation'. *Cultural Anthropology* 15(3): 327–60

Türker, N. 2015. *Vatanım Yok, Memleketim Var: İstanbul Rumları: Mekan-Bellek-Ritüel*. Istanbul: İletişim

Türker, O. 1998. *Osmanlı İstanbul'undan bir Köşe: Tatavla*. Istanbul: Sel Yayıncılık

UNDP. 1990. UNDP Human Development Report. New York (NY) and Oxford: Oxford University Press. Available at: http://hdr.undp.org/sites/default/files/reports/219/hdr_1990_en_complete_nostats.pdf

UNDP. 1996. UNDP Human Development Report. New York (NY) and Oxford: Oxford University Press. Available at: http://hdr.undp.org/sites/default/files/reports/257/hdr_1996_en_complete_nostats.pdf

Urry, J. 2000. *Sociology beyond Societies: Mobilities for the Twenty-First Century*. London and New York (NY): Routledge

Verluise, P. 1995. *Armenia in Crisis: The 1988 Earthquake*. Detroit (MI): Wayne State University Press

Vertovec, S. 2007. 'Super-diversity and Its Implications'. *Ethnic and Racial Studies* 29(6): 1024–54

von Bieberstein, A. 2017. 'Treasure/Fetish/Gift: Hunting for "Armenian Gold" in Post-Genocide Turkish Kurdistan'. *Subjectivity* 10: 170–89

Wallerstein, I. 1974. 'The Rise and Future Demise of World Capitalist System: Concepts for Comparative Analysis'. *Comparative Studies in Society and History* 16(4): 387–415

Wanner, C. 2005. 'Money, Morality and the New Forms of Exchange in Postsocialist Ukraine'. *Ethnos* 70(4): 515–37

Westin, C., and Sadia Hassanen. 2013. *People on the Move: Experiences of Forced Migration*. Trenton (NJ): Red Sea Press

White, H. 1981. 'The Value of Narrativity in the Representation of Reality' in *On Narrative*, edited by W. J. T. Mitchell. Chicago (IL): University of Chicago Press, pp. 1–24

Wishnitzer, A. 2015. *Reading Clocks, Alla Turca: Time and Society in Late Ottoman Empire*. Chicago (IL) and London: The University of Chicago Press

Wolf, E. 1982. *Europe and the People without History*. Berkeley (CA): University of California Press

Wolff, J. 1993. 'On the Road Again: Metaphors of Travel in Cultural Criticism'. *Cultural Studies* 7(2): 224–39

Yenal, D. 2000. *Weaving a Market: The Informal Economy and Gender in a Transnational Trade Network between Turkey and the Former Soviet Union*. PhD Dissertation in Sociology: Binghamton University

Yükseker, D. 2004. 'Trust and Gender in a Transnational Market: The Public Culture of Laleli, Istanbul'. *Public Culture* 16(1): 47–65

Yükseker, D. 2007. 'Shuttling Goods, Weaving Consumer Tastes: Informal Trade between Turkey and Russia'. *International Journal of Urban and Regional Research* 31(1): 60–72

Zirh, B. C. 2012. 'Following the Dead beyond the "Nation": A Map for Transnational Alevi Funerary Routes from Europe to Turkey'. *Ethnic and Racial Studies* 35(10): 1758–74

Zirh, B. C. 2017. 'Kırmanćiya Belekê: Understanding Alevi Geography in between Spaces of Longing and Belonging' in *Alevis in Europe: Voices of Migration, Culture and Identity*, edited by Tözün Issa. London: Routledge, pp. 157–71

Zürcher, E. J. 2004. *Turkey: A Modern History*. London: I.B. Tauris

Zürcher, E. J. 2005. 'Giriş: Demografi Mühendisliği ve Modern Türkiye'nin Doğuşu' in *İmparatorluktan Cumhuriyete Türkiye'de Etnik Çatışma*, edited by Erik Jan Zürcher. Istanbul: İletişim, pp. 9–17

Zürcher, E. J. 2010. *The Young Turk Legacy and Nation Building: From the Ottoman Empire to Atatürk's Turkey*. London: I.B. Tauris

News articles (including unauthored pieces and interviews)

'Ateşyan'dan Tartışılacak Sözler'. 25 February 2012. *Agos*. Available at: http://www.agos.com.tr/tr/yazi/10690/atesyandan-tartisilacak-sozler

'Azınlık Okullarının Dertleri Birkaç Günde Çözülebilir'. 6 February 2015. *Agos*. Available at: http://www.agos.com.tr/tr/yazi/10511/azinlik-okullarinin-dertleri-birkac-gunde-cozulebilir

'Batum Kumarhaneleri: Karadeniz'in Las Vegas'ı'. 1 October 2012. *BBC Türkçe*. Available at: http://www.bbc.com/turkce/haberler/2012/10/121001_batum_casinos.shtml

'Dini İslam, Cenazesi Kilisede'. 17 December 2014. *Radikal*. Available at: http://www.radikal.com.tr/turkiye/dini-islam-cenazesi-kilisede-1253206/

Emin, M. 31 March 2008. 'Kurtuluş İstanbul'un Harlemi mi?' *Akşam*. Available at: http://v3.arkitera.com/h26685-kurtulus-istanbulun-harlemi-mi.html

'Exhibition at the Pictures: Orhan Pamuk's Museum of Innocence on Screen'. 23 January 2016. *The Guardian*. Available at: https://www.theguardian.com/books/2016/jan/23/exhibition-at-the-pictures-orhan-pamuks-museum-of-innocence-on-screen

'Genelkurmay: Gökçen Türk Kadını Sembolü'. 23 February 2004. *Bianet*. Available at: http://bianet.org/bianet/siyaset/30301-genelkurmay-gokcen-turk-kadini-sembolu

Hür, A. 'Tez zamanda yer isimleri değiştirile!' 31 March 2009. *Radikal*. Available at: http://www.haksozhaber.net/tez-zamanda-yer-isimleri-degistirile-9312yy.htm

'İstanbul'un En Gizli Müzesi'. 3 April 2013. *Sabah*. Available at: https://www.sabah.com.tr/turizm/2013/04/03/istanbulun-en-gizli-muzesi

'Istanbul Winds Battle over the City'. 15 October 2009. *Hürriyet Daily News*. Available at: http://web.hurriyetdailynews.com/istanbul-winds-battle-over-the-city.aspx?pageID=438&n=istanbul-winds-2009-10-15

'Kışlık Vapur Tarifesi Adalıları Bıktırdı'. 15–31 October 2007. *Adalı* (47)

'Kumkapı'da Her Çarşamba Küçük Bir Ermenistan Kuruluyor'. 5 August 2006. *Hürriyet*. Available at: http://www.hurriyet.com.tr/kumkapi-da-her-carsamba-kucuk-bir-ermenistan-kuruluyor-4873037

'MEB'den Azınlık Okulları için Beklenen Düzenleme'. 21 March 2012. *Agos*. Available at: http://www.agos.com.tr/tr/yazi/936/meb-den-azinlik-okullari-icin-beklenen-duzenleme

'Misafir Öğrenci'nin Geleceği Yok'. 12 March 2012. *Radikal*. Available at: http://www.radikal.com.tr/turkiye/misafir-ogrencinin-gelecegi-yok-1081468/

'Nisan'da Türkiye'yi Kaç Kişi Ziyaret Etti?' 27 May 2016. *TRT Haber*. Available at: http://www.trthaber.com/haber/yasam/nisanda-turkiyeyi-kac-kisi-ziyaret-etti-253022.html

'Nüfusunda İslam Yazıyor Cenazesi Kiliseden Kalktı'. 17 December 2014. *Sabah*. Available at: http://www.sabah.com.tr/yasam/2014/12/17/nufusunda-islam-yaziyor-cenazesi-kiliseden-kalkti

'Ölümün Ardından Kilise-Cami Gerginliği'. 17 December 2014. *Agos*. Available at: http://www.agos.com.tr/tr/yazi/9958/olumun-ardindan-kilise-cami-gerginligi

Scott, J. 1986. 'Gender: A Useful Category of Historical Analysis'. *American Historical Review* 91: 1053–75.

Suciyan, T. 2018. 'Kendi Evinde Diaspora'da Olmak' (Interview). *Express* 167: 38–42

'Turkish Author Opens Museum Based on Novel'. 29 April 2012. *The New York Times*. Available at: http://www.nytimes.com/2012/04/30/books/orhan-pamuk-opens-museum-based-on-his-novel-in-istanbul.html

'Türkiyeli Yahudileri Tanımak İster misiniz? Buyurun Müzeye'. 25 February 2016. *Bianet*. Available at: http://bianet.org/bianet/toplum/172450-turkiyeli-yahudileri-tanimak-ister-misiniz-buyrun-muzeye

'Türkiye'ye 2015'te 36 Milyon'dan Fazla Turist Geldi'. 28 January 2016. *Hürriyet*. Available at: http://www.hurriyet.com.tr/turkiyeye-2015te-36-milyondan-fazla-turist-geldi-40046480

INDEX

adalı. See islander
Anthropology
   epistemology of 5, 170
   and ethnography 13–14, 20, 38
   and mobility 34
   representation in 13–14
Anxiety 65, 89, 158
azınlık. See minority

Belonging
   Armenian 96–104, 148–9, 160, 172
   Jewish 107–8
   on Kınalıada 148, 160, 164
   in Kurtuluş 117
   in Muş 101–4
   as relationality and positionality 50, 96, 117, 160, 165
   and Turkishness 151, 172
   and unity 164
birlik. See unity
Boats 12, 16, 21, 140–9
Borders 9, 12, 71, 103
   and borderness 70, 93, 102
   of ethnic communities 8, 71, 108
   (*see also* ethno-ethnocization)
   between states 7, 10, 31–4, 41–5, 61
   and transgression 10, 70, 165

cemaat. See community
Centre. *See* margins
Community 9, 12, 13
   Armenian 70, 74, 78, 162, 172
   boundaries 15, 71, 100, 104–5, 108, 156
   cemaat 7, 185 n.5
   on Kınalıada 146–8, 162
   making of 71, 84, 87–92, 153
Cultural Intimacy. *See* intimacy
Culture
   in ethnography 8–10, 21, 38–9, 89
   as a marker 82–3, 108, 124, 126, 129, 168

Depopulation. *See also* repopulation 8, 61, 78, 80, 111, 152
Deportees 61–3, 68–72
Diaspora
   Armenian 22, 37, 58, 70–2, 78, 88, 96, 102, 156, 162, 176
   definition 39, 50, 71, 88, 102, 185 n.5
Dirt 117, 184 n.5
Displacement 16–18, 22, 34, 49, 50, 68, 77, 104

Earthquakes 17, 57–8, 61, 93–4, 103, 185 n.2
Ethnicity
   and ethno-ethnocization 8, 11, 70–1, 87–9
   in social sciences 11, 83, 87–9, 181 n.4
   in Turkish national construct 4, 5, 108, 124–31, 154–7

Fear of the unknown 83–5, 172
Foreigners 8–9, 12, 19–20, 91, 95, 111, 161, 163–6
   See also native
   yabancı 19, 21, 172

Genocide
   and autobiographical knowledge 56
   definition 8, 17, 21–5
   silencing of 13, 22, 98–9, 103–4, 146, 156
Greeks 19, 62, 76–8, 84, 86, 91, 107, 112, 123–6, 133, 146, 151, 155, 160, 162, 172, 182 n.11, 183 n.1, 183 n.2, 183 n.3, 185 n.5, 185 n.6, 185 n.1

Heritage 7, 11, 78, 79, 94–6, 98–9, 103, 107, 182 n.2
Homeland 17, 39, 56, 58, 71, 74, 82, 90, 98, 101, 162
   and home 16, 101–4, 108
   memleket 90–2, 101
Hrant Dink 2, 86, 119–20, 122, 171

Immobility. *See* mobility
Islander(s) 16, 140, 141, 152, 153, 159, 160
Islands
   metaphor of 8, 59, 71
   natives of 16, 159, 160, 165
Intimacy
   collective 5, 71, 101, 134, 148, 161, 166
   personal 69, 89

Jews 19, 76–8, 86, 97, 100–1, 105–8, 124–6, 136, 146–8, 154–6, 161–3, 172, 182 n.11, 182 n.3, 182 n.5, 182 n.6, 182 n.7, 182 n.8, 183 n.9, 185 n.5, 185 n.6

Karabakh Movement 57–8
Kurds 62, 76–7, 80, 86, 132–3, 165

Local. *See* native
Locality 5, 13, 37, 41, 50–1, 180 n.4
   See also place

Minority 7–9, 12–13, 126, 144
memleket. *See* homeland
Migration. *See* mobility
Minority 7–13, 19, 111, 153, 160, 166, 183 n.1
   azınlık 7
Mobility 7, 9, 18, 34, 39, 49, 67, 85, 90, 100, 141, 148, 172
   and gender 35, 41, 47–53, 51, 68, 86
   and immobility 7, 10, 18, 30, 34, 47, 48, 50, 52, 56, 96, 72, 172
   migration 3, 10, 11, 12, 16–17, 33–5, 37, 41, 46, 48–51, 72, 76–8, 81, 83, 85, 90–1, 111, 117, 126, 127, 132–3, 156, 172
   and other forms of movement 9, 34, 35, 37, 41, 48, 49, 50, 67, 86, 101, 103, 141
   regimes of 21, 30, 32, 50, 56, 96, 102
Movement. *See* mobility
Myth 47, 59–60, 71, 88

Naming Practices 1–3, 9, 22–4, 62–3, 111–24, 127–31, 136, 149, 157, 183 n.3

Native 10
   in anthropology 18–21, 71, 181 n.5
   everyday theory of 71
   yerli 16, 152, 159–61, 165–6, 172

Place
   definitions of 12, 15, 17, 21, 22, 34, 37, 38, 41, 48–53, 90, 91–2, 99, 101, 104, 165, 180 n.4
   and locality 5, 13, 37, 41, 48, 50, 51, 180 n.4
   making of 6, 7, 10, 12, 15, 17, 21, 38, 42, 48, 50, 57, 60, 67, 69–71, 75, 80, 84, 87, 95, 98, 99, 100, 103, 107, 108, 111–24, 136, 147–8, 160, 164–6, 173
   yer 139, 145–8, 158–60, 165, 165
Pogroms of 1955 77, 107, 112, 123, 131, 159–60

Repopulation 8, 78, 80, 97, 106, 111, 152
Ruins 95–6, 99–104, 104

Shuttle-traders 68–9, 87

Temporal Pollution 21, 95, 101–2, 104
Travel(ling)
   and dwelling 9–10, 17–8, 20, 34, 42, 169–72
   in literature 15, 49–51
   and women 47–53

Unity
   birlik 2, 6, 11, 128, 133, 136, 147, 171
   in building names 2, 11, 128, 133
   in collective imagination 6, 55, 133, 134, 135, 147–8, 151, 164
   in nation-state politics 128–9, 134, 136, 164, 171, 183 n.3

vapur. *See* boats

yabancı. *See* foreigner
yer. *See* place
yerli. *See* native

www.ingramcontent.com/pod-product-compliance
Lightning Source LLC
Chambersburg PA
CBHW062228300426
44115CB00012BA/2265